Turning Japanese?

Turning Japanese?

BRITAIN WITH A PERMANENT PARTY OF GOVERNMENT

Edited by

*Helen Margetts
& Gareth Smyth*

Lawrence & Wishart
LONDON

Lawrence & Wishart Limited
144a Old South Lambeth Road
London sw8 1xx

First published 1994 by Lawrence and Wishart in
association with the LSE Public Policy Group and
with financial assistance from the Joseph Rowntree
Charitable Trust

Cover by Jan Brown Design
Set in Baskerville by Ewan Smith
Printed and bound in Great Britain by
Redwood Books, Trowbridge

Contents

Acknowledgements

This book arose from a symposium held at the London School of Economics and Political Science in June 1992, organised by the LSE Public Policy Group and Common Voice. We would like to acknowledge inspiration of David Marquand of the University of Sheffield and Joe Kogaly of the *Financial Times* in first drawing our attention to the parallels between British and Japanese politics.

In preparing the manuscript Ruth Borthwick remained persistent. Financial assistance for publication was provided by the Joseph Rowntree Charitable Trust, without which the project would have been impossible. We would also like to thank Josie Dixon, Patrick Dunleavy, Amanda Francis and Klaus Goetz for their support and advice and Miranda Basey from the Japanese Embassy for Japanese election data.

Introduction

When, in 1992, the Conservatives won their fourth consecutive general election victory few 18 year old voters could remember any other kind of government. The mere fact that one party has governed for so long changes the way British politics works. All aspects of public life are affected: the structure of the dominant party; the civil service and their relationship to the government; the options available to the opposition. The British system is usually compared with European countries, Australia, New Zealand or the United States, but if British politics has changed, the accepted comparisons may no longer be useful. We should turn our comparative gaze to countries with concrete experience of one party dominance. Although Japanese economic success means the bookshops of Heathrow airport abound with books on Japanese managerial technique, the wide differences in culture have discouraged commentators from exploring comparisons with Japanese politics.

The Japanese were ruled for 38 years by a single party, the Liberal Democratic Party (LDP). Towards the end of its rule, the LDP recorded staggering levels of unpopularity. By the time of the general election of 1993 which brought LDP rule to an end, at least temporarily, the prime minister's approval rating had fallen to 7 per cent. In the same year Britain found itself facing the future with its most unpopular prime minister since polling began, but with the Conservative Party widely regarded as the most likely victor in the next general election, there may be something to learn from the Japanese experience.

In both Britain and Japan, politics takes place on the terrain created by a sustained period of dominant party rule: understanding the nature of that terrain is crucial to understanding politics. One demanding set of criteria for defining a 'dominant party' in democratic conditions is provided by Brendan O'Leary in Chapter 1:

— it must be a party which regularly wins a majority of legislative seats
— it must be able to stay in government on a regular basis
— it must govern continuously for a long time

it must be ideologically dominant

There can be no absolute definition, rather it is a question of degree. In *Electoral Foundations*, our contributors explore the contemporary basis of Conservative success. Between 1945 and 1979 the multi-party nature of British politics was seldom in doubt. As Brendan O'Leary shows, Labour and Conservative governments alternated in power and governed for equivalent amounts of time in this period. But the 1980s present a very different picture, with the Conservatives consistently winning a majority share of the vote. Some commentators at Labour's headquarters have suggested that the increase in Labour's share of the vote from a low point of 28 per cent in 1983 to 34 per cent in 1992 represents respectable progress towards Labour regaining its place as a viable alternative to the Conservatives. They predict that 'one more heave' at the next election will produce Labour victory. Others view the Conservative's fourth successive election victory despite a period of deep recession as evidence of Tory hegemony stretching into the foreseeable future. They argue that unique social conditions after 1945 produced a consensus around the welfare state and other social democratic ideals which is unlikely to be repeated. John Curtice and Bob Waller assess these debates on the basis of hard evidence. In the third section of the book, Patrick Dunleavy suggests that the roots of the Conservatives' 'natural party of government' mantle lie far deeper in British political history than most observers recognize.

William Horsley and Katsuya Hirose in *Government and Opposition in Japan*, show how, during the sustained period of LDP rule in Japan, political debates came to be centred around factions within the ruling party rather than including all the political parties. The factions formed the focal points of 'money politics' whereby a system of bribes and pay-offs became intertwined with political processes. We have not seen this happen in Britain. But increasingly journalists and academics have come to analyse policy debate in terms of conflict and compromise between different 'tendencies' inside the Conservative Party, as described by Philip Norton. At times, divisions between the tendencies of the Conservative Party seem greater than those between the Tories and the opposition parties.

Has the lack of competition in British politics been accompanied by a diminishing level of ideology in political debate? In Japan the activities and personalities of faction leaders characterise election campaigns, rather than particular ideologies or policy programmes. Certainly during the 1992 British general election campaign, the differences between the parties were more about management than doctrine. Patrick Dunleavy argues that the current Conservative party's lack of ideological coherence and the centralisation of power within the executive have created a debilitating vacuum at the centre of the British political system; 'Strength without Purpose' is its motto. In Japan, one-party rule and centralization of power within the bureaucracy for a time seemed to aid economic growth, long-term policy making and renewed public sector infrastructures, but we have yet to see any similar results in Britain.

Concern over the 'neutrality' of the civil service increases the longer one party is in charge. Katsuya Hirose describes the symbiotic relationship between the LDP and the civil service in Japan, in which the historically powerful bureaucracy used the LDP's political position to strengthen its own role, just as the LDP used the bureaucracy to sustain and stabilise their government. In Britain the political neutrality of the civil service has always rested on the assumption that governments would change with reasonable regularity. But by now many civil servants have never known a Labour government. Peter Hennessy argues that 'Bluehall' is not yet a reality, but there are signs that even civil servants themselves perceive likely problems should they be asked to work with a Labour government: before the 1992 election one department arranged seminars for younger civil servants to talk to older colleagues who had worked for the last Labour administration.

There are some parallels between the history of the Japanese Socialist Party (JSP) and the British Labour Party, the largest opposition parties in their repective countries. Internal disputes, ideological inflexibility, association with ultra-leftism, radical defence policies and strong links with trade unions have been perceived as problems for both parties. While many of these have affected left or centre-left parties all over the world, they are exacerbated by the frustrations of long-term opposition helping to produce a culture of opposition within both parties. As Ryoishi Nishida and Gareth Smyth show, this has at times given an 'other worldliness' to both parties, with policy debate cushioned in a cosy, self-contained world.

In different ways, the media in Britain and Japan have played a role in sustaining one-party rule. But in both countries the media have also been affected by the lack of competitive party politics. David McKie looks at the part the pro-Conservative tabloid press, notably the *Sun*, played in articulating opposition to the government after the 1992 election. At times since 1992 the tabloids have seemed to assume the role of principal opposition, justifying their stance by the lack of effective opposition from the established political parties. This, McKie argues, may be an example of a wider tendency for the opposition to come from within the ruling party, or at least from its friends rather than its political opponents. By partial contrast, William Horsley shows how the media in Japan were drawn into being an integral and key part of Japan's conservative, LDP-dominated Establishment.

The last section of the book considers the options for the future. In Japan dominance ended when factions broke away from the LDP and formed rival parties, causing the LDP to lose the 1993 election. The opposition played little role in the government's downfall, as Ryoishi Nishida describes. Could a similar situation happen in Britain? Since the 1992 election, the security of the Conservative government has been continuously threatened as much by its own back-benchers as by the opposition parties.

Alternatively, perhaps a mood change will sweep over the electorate, attracted by a fresh alternative to a tired and tattered government, a factor contributing to Bill Clinton's 1992 victory in the USA. Will Hutton argues that great opportunities now exist for the opposition in Britain to popularise the politics of regulated markets, provided it can finally jettison the fixation with socialism-as-ownership-of-the-means-of-production embodied in Clause 4 of the Labour Party constitution. To some extent his plea is answered by the New Agenda group of Labour MPs who, in Chapter 14, advocate that Labour restate its basic values. But Labour has yet to translate these potential new messages into electoral success.

Another way in which the main opposition parties might further their chances of success is through establishing electoral pacts, a strategy which Vernon Bogdanor recommends. Proponents of electoral reform argue that more fundamental change is necessary if we are to see competitive and representative politics again. They argue that the first-past-the-post electoral system is an important factor contributing to Conservative electoral success. In Japan the LDP benefitted from an electoral system, unique to Japan, where voters are given one vote to choose between candidates in multi-member constituencies. However, the relationship between electoral systems and dominant party systems is not a simple one, as Brendan O'Duffy and Brendan O'Leary demonstrate. Their evidence from countries with various types of electoral system suggests that non-proportional systems like first past the post are positively associated with one-party dominance in majority governments. However, a different type of dominant party can occur under proportional systems.

The questions addressed in this book have only just begun to be seriously debated. In Japan the by-product of the era of one-party government, economic success, obscured the malign effects from most voters until spiralling political corruption erupted into the public arena. Political observers in Britain must be alert to the possibility of similar processes beginning here. George Orwell once said of his novel 1984: 'I do not believe that the kind of society which I described necessarily will arrive, I believe ... that something resembling it could arrive.' Similarly, this book is not suggesting that Britain will necessarily 'Turn

Japanese'. Rather, we seek to use the comparison with Japan to learn about the possible consequences of prolonged one-party rule for democratic politics in Britain.

Helen Margetts
Gareth Smyth
March 1994

ONE

Electoral Foundations

Britain's Japanese Question: 'Is There a Dominant Party?'

Brendan O'Leary

Britain's Japanese question arose from the Conservatives' fourth successive general election victory in April 1992. It suggested to many that competitive party politics, the hallmark of vibrant liberal democracy, had given way to a dominant party system, the post-war badge of Japanese democracy. The heyday of British social democracy, the era which lasted from the end of the Second World War until the termination of James Callaghan's government, had seen very effective party competition for votes and seats. True, the Conservative party won three parliamentary majorities in a row, in 1951, 1955 and 1959, but in 1955 and 1959 their margin of victory over Labour in the popular vote was relatively small (3.3 per cent and 5.6 per cent respectively), while in 1951 it actually won less votes than Labour. That the Labour party could have won each of these three elections in the 1950s was entirely 'thinkable', even if Jeremiahs suggested otherwise. In this post-war period 17 years of Labour governments (1945–51, 1964–70, 1974–79) matched 17 years of Conservative governments (1951–64, 1970–74). Proportional tenure of governmental office existed across the two main parties, if not proportional representation of all parties in parliament. Moreover, between 1945 and October 1974 the average gap between the share of the votes won by the Conservative party and the Labour party was less than four per cent.

In contrast in the four general elections since 1979 the Conservative party's margin of victory over Labour has averaged over 10 per cent of the vote. The Conservatives' share of the vote has remained very stable across the last four elections, and in 1992 they won a fourth outright single-party majority government, unprecedented in the epoch of universal suffrage. In the 1980s it was 'unthinkable' for all but the most wishful that the Labour party would win an overall majority, while in 1992 the 'thinkability' of a Labour victory, amongst both the party's

3

supporters and opponents, was inflated by imperfect polling. In April 1992 the Conservatives' past longevity in office conveyed an air of future invincibility. They looked set to emulate the pre-eminence of the Liberal Democratic Party in Japan. That is one reason to ask 'Is Britain Turning Japanese?' Has the British political system, once the exemplary model of competitive party politics, once a quality export demanded by its former colonies and other allegedly benighted lands, become spoiled by a dominant party? And if it has, what are the implications for its democracy?

Political scientists are often like politicians: we rarely open our mouths without subtracting from the sum of human knowledge. However, we know what we mean by a dominant party in democratic conditions. First, it must be a party which is dominant in number: it must regularly win more legislative seats in parliamentary or congressional elections than its opponents. The Conservatives have been in this position for the last four elections. Secondly, this party must enjoy a dominant bargaining position. It must be able to stay in government on a regular basis. If it must share power with smaller parties, as the Italian Christian Democrats did for half a century, it is nevertheless the key agent in the political system, with privileged access to the principal executive and legislative posts. Thirdly, as the citation of the Christian Democrats suggests, a dominant party must be chronologically pre-eminent. It must govern continuously for a long time, although analysts might differ over whether three or four general election victories, and whether a decade or a decade and a half are the crucial benchmarks of dominance. Finally, a dominant party must be ideologically dominant: it must be capable of using government to shape public policy so that the nature of the state and society over which it presides is fundamentally changed. This feature of a dominant party was singled out as definitive by the first political scientist to name the phenomenon:

> A party is dominant when it is identified with an epoch; when its doctrines, ideas, methods, its style so to speak, coincide with those of the epoch. ... A dominant party is that which public opinion believes to be dominant ... Even the enemies of the dominant party, even citizens who refuse to give it their vote, acknowledge its superior status and its influence; they deplore it but admit it.[1]

Indeed we might go one stage further, and declare that a dominant party must be capable of so establishing the rules of the game that it transforms its political opponents, in the manner, for example, in which the Swedish Social Democrats successfully managed to make all its opponents into *de facto* social democratic parties in the 1970s.

Everyone will have their own views about the extent to which the Conservative and Unionist party's recent electoral successes meet the four criteria for a dominant party. Proponents would point to the victories of the Conservatives in elections, in monopolising the cabinet, their longevity in office, and their double success in defining free market ideology as the orthodoxy in public policy and in re-shaping the Labour Party and the Liberal Democrats. Sceptics would point to the precariousness of the Conservatives' electoral successes and their failure to alter the British public's stubborn adherence to welfarist values. However, if we accept the contestable premise that the Conservatives have become a dominant party, certain obvious questions follow:

— why has the UK developed a dominant party?
— is the dominance of the Conservative party an artefact of the electoral system?
— what are the consequences of a dominant party system?
— how can the dominant party system come to an end?

The *why* question poses many imponderables. Is the Conservative pre-eminence, as New Rightist intellectuals insist, the logical outcome of the structural crisis of British social democracy in the late 1970s, the local resultant of the wider collapse of socialism? Another version of this argument suggests that the Conservatives' eminence is the consequence of a transformed class structure and the electoral corollary of a more individualist and less generous society. Numerous political scientists, historians and sociologists have shared these assumptions, whether or not they are sympathetic to the cause of Labour. The obvious alternative perspective is that the Conservative pre-eminence is merely apparent, superficial, the contingent consequence of three election victories that might so easily have been defeats. Had the Conservatives not been so skilful, and not so luckily endowed with the Falklands, North Sea Oil, and the effective leadership of Margaret Thatcher, and had their opponents had not been so divided and inadequately led, then things might have been so very different. However, this voluntarist and contingent perspective, the staple fare of 'high politics' and effervescent journalism, is less persuasive on the morrow of an election won by a political party led by a man called John Major. His victory brings to mind the famous adage of Charles de Gaulle, 'Since politicians never believe what they say, they are surprised when others believe them'. The election in 1992 suggested that the domination of the Conservatives, and their credibility, are more deeply rooted than Major's leadership gifts or Neil Kinnock's alleged deficiencies.

The next question is whether Conservative dominance is an artefact of the electoral system. Plurality rule, or first past the post, is associated with dominant party systems, at a national level, as with the Congress party in post-independence India, but especially at a regional level – as with the Democratic party in the deep south of the USA from the

1880s until the 1960s, and with the Ulster Unionist Party in Northern Ireland between 1921 and 1972[2]. However, there is no axiomatic relationship between plurality rule and a dominant party: plurality rule can co-exist with competitive party politics and alternations in government; and non-plurality systems do not preclude a dominant party. One clear case of a nation-wide dominant party outside the UK, of course, was that of Japan between 1955 and 1993; and the hegemony of the LDP was facilitated by a peculiar non-proportional electoral system – the single non-transferable vote in multi-member constituencies. However many of the best-known cases of a dominant party in a democratic system have developed despite the existence of proportional representation. The ascendancy of the Swedish Social Democrats between 1932 and 1976, of the Italian Christian Democrats from 1948 until the present, and of the Israeli Labour Party from 1948 until 1977, developed under party list systems of proportional representation. In the Republic of Ireland, Fianna Fail has twice enjoyed sixteen year periods of office under the single transferable vote system of proportional representation (1932–48 and 1957–73), although it has never won three successive periods of power as a majority government. These observations suggest that the explanatory power of the electoral system in facilitating the dominance of the Conservatives is not straightforward, a point which I elaborate in a later chapter with my colleague Brendan O'Duffy.

The third major question is whether we should be disturbed by the consequences of a dominant party, and the lack of alternation in government. What are the consequences of a dominant party system? One possibility is that once dominance is established the governing party becomes 'de-ideologised'. We might therefore expect or look forward to the withering away of New Right ideology, something which appears evident in the disappointment of rightist think-tanks with the Major government, and the rediscovery of traditionalist conservative virtues by weathervane intellectuals like John Gray and David Willetts. The prediction of the ideological deprogramming of the dominant party follows from Duverger's pioneering analysis, which suggested that for the dominant party 'the continued exercise of responsibility for government diminishes demagogy and the need for innovation ... Domination takes the zest from political life, simultaneously bringing stability'.[3] If this analysis is right we might expect the Conservatives to become conservative in all senses, gradually de-radicalised, abandoning the full-blooded market-programme of the New Right while trying to cement their position as the natural party of government.

Another possibility is that one-party dominance engenders wider and more extensive corruption. If there is one dominant party there is only one party which is worth joining if one seeks worthwhile patronage, only one whose political elites are worth buying (before or after they become ministers), and only one whose coffers are worth swelling. The 'factionalisation' of the dominant party and the opening of the factions to external corruption, was obvious in other dominant right-wing parties, like the LDP in Japan and the Christian Democrats in Italy. Can we expect the same here? The vista of wider and more deep-rooted corruption, although famously absent from most accounts of twentieth century British government, may be encouraged given that party dominance now co-exists with a continuous transformation of public administration – in which Weberian norms are not being abandoned in favour of the 'new public management'[4] and in which quasi-governmental agencies are continually replacing government by elected officials. Effective political competition may be just as necessary as effective market competition to ensure the honourable delivery of effective goods and services, a point that is often lost in the Conservative press, with the honourable exception of the *Economist* magazine.

These speculations raise others. Does one-party dominance further weaken the alleged autonomy and neutrality of other public institutions – the civil service, the judiciary, the police, the public broadcasting media, the agencies of quasi-government and the health and educational subsystems? Does one-party dominance produce sporadic riots and anomic discontent amongst those excluded from influence within the system? Does one-party dominance simultaneously encourage both extremist opposition of the type proudly advertised by Arthur Scargill, and utterly tame and overly cautious opposition as Bryan Gould suggested had become true of the Labour Party before he left it for New Zealand?

Finally, there are the questions of how and why dominance comes to an end. Dominant parties can wear themselves out in office, lose their vigour, harden their arteries with too much of the food of success, and become so arrogant and corrupt as to make themselves contemptible. This outcome is not uncommon, and we have seen something like it occur in the case of the Italian Christian Democrats. Duverger suggested that every system of domination bears within itself the seeds of its own destruction. Perhaps he was right. Intra-party strife and internecine rivalry to succeed John Major to the premiership may well undermine the Conservatives. As the saying goes 'A government is the only known vehicle that leaks from the top'.

Since a dominant party must rely on, and continually aim to preserve the fragmentation of the opposition, its opponents know it is mortal. A dominant party can forge the conditions for its own collapse by compelling the opposition to renew themselves, to redefine the salient cleavages and issues in political society, and even to forge electoral alliances. Albert Camus wrote in *The Rebel* 'The future is the only kind of property that the masters willingly concede to their slaves'. If the opposition under dominant party systems are analogous to slaves we know they must work co-operatively to accomplish their collective emancipation.

Notes

1. Duverger, M., *Political Parties: Their Organization and Activity in the Modern State*, Methuen, London 1954, p 308–9.

2. O'Leary, B. and McGarry, J., *The Politics of Antagonism: Understanding Northern Ireland*, Athlone Press, London 1993.

3. *Op. cit.*, Duverger 1954 p 312.

4. Hood, C. 'A Public Management for All Seasons', *Public Administration* 69(1), pp 3–19, 1991.

2

Why Do the Conservatives
Keep on Winning?

John Curtice

Lightning, it is said, never strikes twice in the same place. So if a party wins power four times in a row, as the Conservative Party has done since 1979, it is difficult to argue it has simply benefited from good fortune. It would seem to have some inbuilt advantages over its opponents.

Claims that the British electorate has become inherently more pro-Conservative have not been short on the ground. This chapter reviews a number of these arguments, using evidence from the substantial academic literature on electoral behaviour, to see whether the results of the last four elections are a reliable guide to what might happen in the foreseeable future. Do the Conservatives now enjoy such long-term structural advantages over their opponents that defeat seems inconceivable in the near future? Or is there need for a little caution about assuming that the past is the best guide to the future?

Social Change

Probably the most important of the claims that have been made is that social changes during the 1970s and 1980s have produced an electorate which believes its material interests are more likely to be served by a Conservative than a Labour government. This thesis comes in a number of different, and in some respects contradictory, forms.

It has long been argued that the main, and indeed only, social division in British politics is social class.[1] But in the early 1970s the claim began to emerge that social class was declining as an influence on voting behaviour.[2] The premise of this argument, which is known as the 'class de-alignment' thesis, is that social class has declined as an influence in people's social lives. Increased social mobility, widening education opportunities, greater geographical mobility and growing

9

affluence have together, it is argued, served to reduce the impact that the kind of job someone has (and the kind of job their parents have) on how they get on in life or the kinds of lifestyles that they lead.[3] In particular, people from working class backgrounds have found it easier to get into middle class jobs, and even if they did not, increasing affluence meant that they could enjoy the material comforts of a 'middle class' lifestyle.

This decline in the importance of social class in everyday life has also had its impact, according to the thesis, on how people vote.[4] If social class no longer matters so much outside the polling booth, then it will also not matter so much when the voter marks his or her ballot. Traditional class based appeals no longer have any resonance and voters turn instead to parties such as the Liberal Democrats who do not make class part of their appeal. Meanwhile Labour particularly suffers because in contrast to the Conservatives it was founded as a class party and the advancement of the working class is central to its raison d'etre.[5]

This thesis has however come under considerable challenge in recent years. In part some sociologists have questioned the claim that social class has declined as an influence in people's lives.[6] In particular, Goldthorpe has argued that although the chances of someone from a working class background ending up in a middle class job increased in the post-war period, so also did the chances of someone from a middle class background doing so. The difference between their respective chances had not changed. And if what matters to people is the difference between how well they do in life and how well other people do, and not just simply their absolute level of well-being, then recent patterns of social mobility give no reason to believe that class has become less important.

This logic of looking at differences between the classes also lies at the heart of Heath *et al*'s claim that social class has not evidently declined as an influence on voting behaviour.[7] True, the proportion of the working class that votes Labour has declined – down from 69 per cent in 1966 to as little as 42 per cent in 1983. But they note Labour's middle class vote has declined as well. The difference between how middle class people vote and how working class people vote has not consistently declined over time in the way that the class de-alignment thesis would predict. Instead it has simply fluctuated up and down from one election to another.

This argument continues to provoke considerable controversy.[8] But in any event irrespective of whether the class de-alignment thesis is correct, it is by no means clear that it can account for the Conservatives' success in the last four general elections. For one clear social trend that is widely acknowledged to have occurred in the post-war period has been a change in the size of the social classes.[9] In the 1950s Britain was a predominantly blue-collar society, but now it is a majority white-collar one. Reinforced by other social trends such as the growth of owner-occupation, the pool of 'natural' Conservative supporters has been growing and the Labour one slowly drying up.

Given these trends a decline in class voting would be good news for Labour, not bad. For it would imply that the party was improving its appeal amongst the growing middle class and had become less reliant on the declining working class. In truth, one of Labour's problems in recent years has been the continued importance of class as an influence on voting, not its absence.

But just how substantial an advantage are the changes in the sizes of the various social groups to the Conservatives? We should for example bear in mind that, as Robert Waller's figures in his chapter show, nearly a half of middle class people do not vote Conservative. A one per cent growth in the size of the middle class results in far less than a one per cent increase in Conservative support. Further, as Heath et al.[10] point out, not all the social trends of the last thirty years have been to the Conservatives' advantage. For example, those who attend church are in general more likely to vote Conservative – and church attendance has fallen. The adult ethnic minority population, another pro-Labour group, has also gradually grown in size.

To get a measure of the overall effect of all the major social trends on party support Heath et al calculated what the 1987 general election result would have been if the size of each social group had been the same as in 1964. They found that Labour's support would have been as much as four points higher while the Conservatives would have been nearly three points lower. While this is clearly not an insubstantial disadvantage for Labour, it is not sufficient to account for the Conservatves' sequence of victories. The Conservatives won the 1987 election with a lead over Labour of 12 per cent, so even without the disadvantageous social trends Labour would still have been five points behind. Similarly in 1992 they would still have been one point behind.

Some recent social trends have of course been the consequence of government action rather than economic change. Two in particular which have attracted much attention have been the policies of selling council houses to tenants at a discount and increasing share ownership by selling off nationalised industries at a price substantially below what proved to be their market value. These have been widely seen as masterstrokes for the Conservatives.[11] They enlarged the number of people (especially working class people) with a substantial capital stake and thus an interest in the free market, people who would as a consequence be more likely to vote Conservative.

It is certainly the case that those who bought their council houses are more likely to vote Conservative than those who did not. For example, 35 per cent of those who had bought their council house voted Conservative in 1987 while only 21 per cent of those who remained council tenants did so. Equally those who bought shares for the first time in one of the privatised industries were more likely to vote Conservative than those who did not. But this on its own does not prove that their conversion into share owners or owner occupiers also helped to convert them to the Conservative cause. That would only be true if those who bought their council houses were politically and socially the same as those who remained council tenants before they changed their status, and equally that the new share owners were identical to those who remained non-share owners.

But this was not the case. The average householder who bought a council house was sociologically and economically distinct from his or her neighbours.[12] He or she was far more likely to be in employment, enjoyed a higher income and was less likely to be in a working class occupation. Equally purchasers of privatised shares were more likely to be middle class owner occupiers than those who did not buy shares. So, not surprisingly we find that those who bought their council houses or bought privatised shares were also more likely to vote Conservative before they had changed their status. Indeed those who bought their council houses were just as likely to have voted Conservative in 1979 (36 per cent) before they became owner occupiers as they were in 1987. Selling council houses or privatised shares has done little or nothing so far at least to enlarge the base of Conservative support.

So it is clear then that we should not exaggerate the electoral impact of recent social trends. They have been a disadvantage for Labour but not a disaster. After all, being the party which represented the minority social class did not stop the Conservatives winning elections on three occasions in a row in the 1950s. So equally we should not rush to the conclusion that because Labour are now the party of the minority they are inevitably doomed to electoral failure.

Changing Attitudes

Margaret Thatcher came to office determined not only to make a radical change in government policy, but also to produce a sea-change in social attitudes. She wished to convert people to her own faith in the virtues of the free market, hard work and self-reliance. Perhaps here lies a possible clue to the Conservatives' success. Has Britain adopted Conservative values? Some commentators, and from the left as much as the right, have certainly argued that it has.[13]

It is undoubtedly true that Mrs. Thatcher's first election victory in 1979 was accompanied by a shift to the right on some issues. Support for both nationalisation and welfare spending fell between 1974 and

1979, although on other issues the evidence of any change is more scanty.[14] Sarlvik and Crewe calculated that these shifts were worth as much as 4.4 per cent to the Conservatives at the 1979 election, as much as a half of the actual increase in their vote with compared with October 1974. So Mrs. Thatcher's first election victory was certainly heralded by a shift to the right. But this shift was a reaction to the failures of the 1974–79 Labour government rather than an endorsement of anything Mrs. Thatcher had done. Did Mrs Thatcher succeed in sustaining and building on the change once she had secured the reins of office? The question has been researched using both data from the opinion polls, the British Social Attitudes Survey and the British Election Study.[15] And all of the sources agree. There is not any evidence that the electorate shifted to the right in the 1980s. If anything, there has been something of a shift to the left.

The move to the right between 1974 and 1979 can be seen in the virtual halving in the proportion of those in favour of further nationalisation and a decline in the level of support for welfare benefits (see Table 2.1 overleaf). But between 1979 and 1987 there were signs of a drift back to the left. Support for privatisation fell away somewhat while the reaction against welfare benefits had more than reversed itself by 1987. Attitudes towards trade unions and giving workers more say at work also moved sharply away from the nostrums of Thatcherism. Further, this shift to the left seems to have continued between 1987 and 1992 and extended even to the issue of nationalisation.

Indeed, on the face of it the electorate is even more left-wing now than it was in 1974. We need though to be cautious about this. Many of the questions in Table 2.1 ask people whether or not they think things should be changed from the status quo. And of course thanks to the policies of Conservative governments since 1979 the status quo is now very different from twenty years ago. More and more companies were privatised, welfare benefits were cut back, and the laws on trade unions progressively tightened. So some people might well give a more left-wing answer to the questions in the table now not because their own attitudes have changed but because the status quo has changed. Further, on the two items in this table which are most strongly correlated with voting behaviour – nationalisation and income redistribution – the electorate is manifestly not more left-wing than 20 years ago.

But despite all these caveats, it is difficult to argue that the Conservatives have retuned the ideological heartstrings of the British electorate to a more right-wing pitch. Rather, the figures suggest that an ideological gap may be opening up between the party and the electorate. Of course, whether or not there is such a gap depends also on voters' perceptions of where the parties stand. If their perception of where the Conservatives stand has shifted to the left in tandem with the leftward drift in the

Table 2.1 Changing attitudes (percentage)

Agreeing government should:	(Oct) 1974	1979	1987	1992
Redistribute income & wealth to ordinary working people	54	52	50	48
Spend more money to get rid of poverty	84	80	86	93
Nationalise more companies	30	16	16	24
Privatise more companies	20	38	31	23
Not introduce stricter laws to regulate trade unions	–	16	33	40
Give workers more say in running places where they work	58	55	76	79
Put more money into the NHS	84	87	90	93
Per cent agreeing that:				
Welfare benefits have not gone too far	22	17	34	46

Source: British Election Studies.[16]

electorate, then the shift to the left would be of little import. And indeed, the 1992 British Election Study suggests that on privatisation the elector-ate did feel that the Conservatives were further to the left in 1992 than five years previously.[17] But even so, if voters voted for the party which they felt was closest to them on the issues which mattered to them most, only 31 per cent would have voted Conservative in 1992 compared with the 43 per cent who actually did so.

This gap between the apparent ideological preferences of the elector-ate and they way they vote was of course the cause of some considerable comment in 1992. Clear majorities of the electorate said that they preferred tax rises to public spending cuts. For example, according to Gallup at the time of the 1992 election just ten per cent favoured public spending cuts and lower taxes while 63 per cent favoured higher taxes and better services.[18] Yet despite this the one party which opposed higher taxes won the election. Claims that voters were not saying how they really felt about increased taxation were legion: Robert Harris suggested in the *Sunday Times* that 'We are a Nation of Liars'.[19]

But in fact the existence of a gap between the ideological preferences of the electorate and the way in which they voted was nothing new. It underpinned Mrs. Thatcher's electoral landslides in 1983 and 1987 when, if the electorate had voted for the party which they felt was closest to them on what they felt was the most important issue of the day, no more than 35 per cent would have voted Conservative. The mistake that many commentators have made is to assume that voters simply vote on the basis of issues. In fact, not only did the Conservatives fail to change the ideological culture of Britain, but their electoral success has never rested on their being closer to the wishes of the average voter. The foundations of the Conservatives' success rest on less secure foundations than we might have imagined.

Emotional Loyalties

Such scepticism about how far issues influence the way in which people vote is not uncommon among psephologists. Many have argued that what most influences voters are emotions and loyalties. Voters, they argue establish an emotional attachment to a party rather like football fans develop a love for a particular club. Just as a son is introduced to following a football club by his father so this attachment to a party, or 'party identification', is most commonly learnt as a child sitting on a parent's knee.[20] And just as a loyal fan still supports his team when it falls to the bottom of the league, so also the strong party identifier keeps on voting for his or her party even when disappointed with its current performance.

Table 2.2 Trends in party identification (percentage)

	Con	Lab	Lib	Other	None
1964	39	42	12	1	7
1966	36	45	10	1	9
1970	40	43	8	1	8
1974 Feb	35	40	13	2	10
1974 Oct	34	40	14	2	10
1979	38	36	12	1	13
1983	36	31	17	2	14
1987	37	30	16	2	14
1992	43	31	12	3	11

Source: British Election Studies.[21] 'Liberal etc.'; Liberal, 1964–79; Liberal, SDP or Alliance, 1983–87, Liberal Democrat, 1992.

At first glance this view of voting behaviour is hardly one that seems well qualified to explain why the balance of party competition has apparently changed. It portrays voters as largely loyal and unchanging. But in practice there are a number of ways in which the balance of party identification can change. Young voters might be more Conservative than those who die. And supporters of the theory of party identification have always acknowledged that a voter's identification needs to be reinforced in adulthood (through for example talking to people of a similar persuasion, and by going out and voting for one's party) or else it may wither away.

As Table 2.2 shows there has been a dramatic change in the distribution of party identifiers. In the 1960s and 1970s rather more people described themselves as Labour than Conservative. But between 1974 and 1983 the number of Labour identifiers dropped and it has shown no sign of recovering since. In contrast the number of Conservative identifiers reached an all-time high in 1992.

So one of the reasons why the Conservatives apparently keep on winning is that the pool of voters with an emotional attachment to Labour has declined significantly. But that of course begs the question why that may have happened. Unfortunately very little research has been undertaken into this question. One explanation however can be ruled out; the fall in Labour support has not simply been caused by generational change, that is by younger voters entering the electorate being more pro-Conservative than older voters who left.[22] Voters who had Labour sympathies in the 1960s had lost them by the 1980s.

Exactly why this was the case must remain speculation. But any explanations based on social trends seems implausible; the speed and scale of the fall in Labour identification was too rapid. More likely it would seem that the fall in party identification is evidence that Labour's political difficulties in the late 1970s and the early 1980s (such as the 'winter of discontent', the departure of the 'Gang of Four' to found the SDP and the divisions about nuclear weapons) not only had a serious and immediate impact on the party's level of electoral support but also eroded the wellspring of empathy upon which the party can draw.

The Electoral System

Looking at survey evidence for signs of a dramatic pro-Conservative shift amongst individual voters is ultimately bound to be a fruitless exercise simply because there has not been any long-term pro-Conservative trend among voters over the last twenty or thirty years. Looking at the serried ranks of Conservative MPs at Westminster it is all too easy to forget that the Conservatives won each of the last three general elections with just 43 per cent of the vote, six points lower than they secured in their three election victories in the 1950s. We need always to remember that who 'wins' or 'loses' an election is determined not simply by how many votes each party wins, but also by how those votes are translated into seats. This is particularly the case in Britain with our continued use of the first-past-the-post electoral system.

Indeed the way the electoral system has operated has been indispensable to the Conservatives' ability to keep on winning elections. Since 1979 Labour's vote has been consistently lower than at any time between 1945 and 1974. Meanwhile, the vote for the main third party option reached a post-war high in 1983 and even in 1992 was higher than at any election between 1945 and 1970. But while the electoral system reflected the extent of the Conservatives' lead over Labour, it did not reflect the strength of the Alliance or the Liberal Democrats.

It has long been argued that first-past-the-post discriminates against small third parties. In truth there is no guarantee that it does any such thing. For example, in 1992 Plaid Cymru with just 0.3 per cent of the UK vote won twice as many seats as it would have received under a purely proportional system.[23] Rather the system discriminates against not only small but even medium-sized parties whose vote is geographically evenly spread.

It is this which has been the Achilles' heel of the third party challenge in Britain and enabled the Conservatives to retain power. Even in 1983 when the Alliance won 26 per cent of the vote, just two per cent behind the Labour party, it won just 23 seats to Labour's 209. Even if the Alliance's challenge in 1983 had been considerably more successful and it had won as much as 35 per cent of the vote, 11 per cent ahead of Labour and just four per cent behind the Conservatives, it would still have won just 82 seats while the Conservatives would still have had a safe overall majority.[24]

This state of affairs has led some to argue that the reason why the Conservatives continue to win is the failure of the opposition parties to form an electoral pact. What should happen, it is argued, is that the better placed of the two opposition parties should stand down in each constituency in order to present a united front against the Conservatives. A difficulty is that not all Alliance/Liberal Democrat voters would back a Labour candidate against the Conservatives if they could not vote Liberal Democrat. In truth, the evidence is that this is far from being the case. According to the British Election Study in 1992, as many as 45 per cent of Liberal Democrats said that the Conservatives were their second preference while only 38 per cent backed Labour. Alliance voters were equally Conservative inclined in 1983 with a 43–36 preference for the Conservatives, while in 1987 the pro-Conservative tide was even greater at 52–33.

But if the operation of the electoral system has been essential to the Conservatives' ability to keep on winning, can we necessarily assume that it will continue to deliver them victory in future? The 1992 election result certainly gives one reason to pause for thought. With the electoral system largely crowding out the Liberal Democrats we would expect the size of the Conservatives' overall majority to vary according to the size of their lead in votes over Labour. The Conservatives secured a 7.5

per cent voting lead over Labour in 1992, larger than in any of their three election victories in the 1950s or on the occasion of Edward Heath's victory in 1970. But their overall majority was just 21, smaller than in 1955, 1959 or 1970. Indeed, thanks to the loss of two by-elections in the first session of the new parliament and divisions amongst his backbenchers, John Major had to reach an early understanding with the Ulster Unionists to shore up his parliamentary majority, bringing back recollections of the kinds of deals that the last minority Labour government had to make in the late 1970s.

Two developments hold the potential to undermine the Conservatives' position. The first is that although still much more evenly distributed than either the Conservative or the Labour vote, the Liberal Democrat vote has become somewhat more geographically concentrated. In 1992 the party managed to win more seats than the Liberals did in February 1974 despite securing a smaller share of the vote. But potentially even more important is the fact that the Liberal Democrats are now relatively stronger than they were in 1983 in many of the seats – and particularly those in the South West of England – where they lie second to the Conservatives.[25] A repeat of their 1983 performance would now give them a harvest of almost 40 seats rather than just 23, the extra seats coming entirely at the expense of the Conservatives.

The second development is the geographical concentration of Conservative support in the South and rural areas. It is frequently noted that Labour's task in winning an election has been made more difficult by its heavy loss of support over the last thirty years in rural and southern England. But the implications for the Conservatives of their equally heavy loss of support in the North and in the inner cities is less widely appreciated. It has reduced the size of the reward the Conservatives receive in seats for any given lead over Labour they secure in votes.[26] For example if in 1983 the electoral system had operated like it used to in the 1950s the Conservatives' overall majority would have been over 300 rather than the 144 they actually secured, and Labour's parliamentary ranks would have been down to 1935 proportions.

With a landslide victory, as in 1983, all this seems academic. But it does mean the Conservatives cannot be sure that they can keep on winning an overall majority if their lead over Labour is relatively small. With the electoral system working against them in a number of other ways as well (in particular a more efficient distribution of the Labour vote and a continued decline in the size of Labour seats),[27] then as in 1992 even a 7.5 per cent lead could almost be insufficient; indeed as much as a 6.5 per cent lead would not have been.[28] And as Robert Waller notes it looks likely that the current review of parliamentary constituency boundaries will do little to make life significantly easier for the Conservatives.

So while the electoral system has been crucial to the Conservatives' ability to keep on winning in the past, it is by no means clear that winning just over 40 per cent of the vote will always be sufficient to deliver them an overall majority. Labour may not be able to win an election in such circumstances but the Conservatives could certainly lose.

Conclusion

Our search for inherent advantages for the Conservatives over the last four elections has uncovered some important clues. The way in which the electoral system operated was crucial to each of the party's election victories; in terms of its share of the vote none of the performances since 1979 has been particularly impressive. Social trends in the form of a larger middle class and a smaller working class have undoubtedly been to the Conservatives' advantage. And there has been a significant decline in the number of voters with a loyal attachment to the Labour Party.

But the notion that each of the Conservatives' four victories was somehow inevitable and that there has been an irreversible shift of political advantage in their favour is misguided. The electorate is not and never has been clearly ideologically Thatcherite. Selling council houses and privatised shares seems to have had no discernible political impact, while the growth of the middle class is not a sufficient explanation for why Labour has kept on losing. The fall in the number of Labour identifiers was probably caused by the party's political difficulties in the 1980s and this is in principle reversible by political action. Further, there are signs that the electoral system may not continue to be as favourable to the Conservatives as it has been in the past.

Each of the Conservatives' victories probably did have an element of luck (or perhaps judgement) attached to it, in that on each occasion the party was able to benefit from important short-term conditions. As Sanders has argued,[29] each election has been graced by sufficiently favourable economic trends to promote a 'feel-good' factor. Political image as well also probably played its part with Labour dogged for much of the 1980s by the perception that they were extreme and disunited. But whether the Conservatives' luck can continue to hold out must remain an open question.

Notes

1. See Alford, R., *Party and Society: Anglo-American Democracies*, Rand McNally, Chicago 1963 and Pulzer, P., *Political Representation and Elections in Britain*, Allen and Unwin, London 1975, 3rd edition.

2. Butler, D. and Stokes, D., *Political Change in Britain*, Macmillan, London 1974, 2nd edition.

3. See, for example, Franklin, M., *The Decline of Class Voting in Britain*, Clarendon Press, Oxford 1985, and Rose, R., *Class Does Not Equal Party*, University of Strathclyde Papers in Public Policy, No. 74, 1980.

4. Ivor Crewe, 'The Electorate: Partisan De-alignment Ten Years On', in Berrington, H. (ed), *Change in British Politics*, Frank Cass, London 1984.

5. Robertson, D., *Class and the British Electorate*, Basil Blackwell, Oxford 1984.

6. See Goldthorpe, J. (in collaboration with Llewellyn, C. and Payne, C.) *Social Mobility and Class Structure in Britain*, Clarendon, Oxford 1987, 2nd. edition; and Marshall G., Newby, H., Rose, D. and Vogler, C., *Social Class in Modern Britain*, Hutchinson, London 1988.

7. Heath, A., Jowell, R. and Curtice, J., *How Britain Votes*, Pergamon, Oxford 1985; Heath, A., Jowell, R. and Curtice, J. 'Trendless Fluctuation: A Reply to Crewe', *Political Studies*, XXXV, 1987, pp 256–77; Evans, G., Heath, A. and Payne, C., 'Modelling Trends in the Class/Party Relationship 1964–87', *Electoral Studies*, X, 1991, pp 99–117.

8. See especially Crewe, I., 'On the death and resurrection of class voting: some comments on How Britain Votes', *Political Studies*, XXXIV, 1986, pp 620–38; and Crewe, I., 'Changing Votes and Unchanging Voters', *Electoral Studies*, XI, 1992, pp 335–45.

9. Heath, A. and McDonald, S. 'Social Change and the Future of the Left', *Political Quarterly*, LVIII, 1987, pp 364–77.

10. Heath, A., Jowell, R., Curtice, J., Evans, G., Field, J., and Witherspoon, S., *Understanding Political Change: The British Voter 1964–87*, Pergamon, Oxford 1991.

11. See for example, Andrew Gamble 'Crawling from the wreckage', *Marxism Today*, July 1987, pp 12–17.

12. Heath, A., Jowell, R., Curtice, J., Evans, G., Field, J., and Witherspoon, S., *Understanding Political Change: The British Voter 1964–87*, Pergamon, Oxford 1991.

13. See, for example, Stuart Hall, *The Hard Road to Renewal: Thatcherism and the Crisis of the Left*, Verso, London 1988.

14. Ivor Crewe, 'The Labour Party and the Electorate', in Dennis Kavanagh (ed), *The Politics of the Labour Party*, Allen and Unwin, London 1982; Sarlvik, B. and Crewe, I., *Decade of De-alignment*, Cambridge University Press, 1983.

15. Ivor Crewe, 'Has the Electorate become Thatcherite', in Robert Skidelsky (ed), *Thatcherism*, Blackwell, Oxford 1988; Ivor Crewe, 'The Thatcher Legacy', in Anthony King (ed), *Britain at the Polls 1992*, Chatham House, Chatham NJ, 1992; John Curtice, 'Political Partisanship', in Jowell R., Witherspoon, S. and Brook, L. *British Social Attitudes; the 1986 report*, Gower, Aldershot 1986; Heath, A., Jowell, R., Curtice, J., Evans, G., Field, J., and Witherspoon, S., *Understanding Political Change: The British Voter 1964–87*, Pergamon, Oxford 1991; Heath, A. and McMahon, D., 'Changes in Values', in Jowell, R., Brook, L., Prior, G., and Taylor, B. (eds), *British Social Attitudes; the 9th report*, Gower, Aldershot 1992.

16. See also Heath, A., Jowell, R., Curtice, J., Evans, G., Field, J., and Witherspoon, S., *Understanding Political Change: The British Voter 1964–87*, Pergamon, Oxford 1991.

17. Heath, A. and Jowell, R., 'Labour's Policy Review', in Heath, A., Jowell, R. and Curtice, J., with Taylor, B. (eds), *Labour's Last Chance? The 1992 Edition and Beyond*, Aldershot, Dartmouth, 1994.

18. Sanders, D., 'Why the Conservative Party Won – Again', in Anthony King (ed), *Britain at the Polls 1992*, Chatham House, Chatham, NJ, 1992.

19. *Sunday Times*, 12 April, 1992.

20. Butler, D. and Stokes, D., *Political Change in Britain*, Macmillan, London 1974, 2nd edition.

21. See also Heath, A., Jowell, R., Curtice, J., Evans, G., Field, J., and Witherspoon, S., *Understanding Political Change: The British Voter 1964–87*, Pergamon, Oxford 1991.

22. John Curtice, 'L'approche generationnelle peut-elle expliquer les recents changements politiques en Grande Bretagne?', in Crete, J. and Favre, P. (eds), *Generations et Politique*, Economica, Paris 1989.

23. Curtice, J. and Steed, M., 'Appendix 2: The Results Analysed', in David Butler and Dennis Kavanagh, *The British General Election of 1992*, Macmillan, London 1992.

24. Curtice, J. and Steed, M., 'Appendix 2: An Analysis of the Voting', in David Butler and Dennis Kavanagh, *The British General Election of 1983*, Macmillan, London 1984.

25. Curtice, J. and Steed, M., 'Appendix 2: The Results Analysed', in David Butler and Dennis Kavanagh, *The British General Election of 1992*, Macmillan, London 1992.

26. Curtice, J. and Steed, M., 'Proportionality and Exaggeration in the British Electoral System', *Electoral Studies*, V, 1986, pp 209–28.

27. Curtice, J. (1992), 'The Hidden Surprise: The British Electoral System in 1992', *Parliamentary Affairs*, VL, 466–74.

28. Curtice, J. and Steed, M., 'Appendix 2: The Results Analysed', in David Butler and Dennis Kavanagh, *The British General Election of 1992*, Macmillan, London 1992.

29. Marsh, D., Ward, H. and Sanders, D., 'Modelling government popularity in Britain, 1979–87: a disaggregated approach', in Crewe, I. and Norris, P., (eds), *British Elections and Parties Yearbook 1991*, Harvester Wheatsheaf, London, 1991; Sanders, D., 'Forecasting the 1992 British general election outcome', in Denver, D., Norris, P., Broughton, D. and Rallings, C., *British Elections and Parties Yearbook 1993*, Harvester Wheatsheaf, London, 1993.

Stable Support? Polling Evidence and Conservative Ascendancy

Robert Waller

As we have passed through the twentieth century, the Conservative Party's dominance of British (and especially English) electoral politics has seemed to get stronger. In the fourteen general elections since the war the Conservatives have won an overall majority of at least ten seats on seven occasions, Labour on only two.

The 1980s, even more than the 1950s, proved to be a true-blue decade. The unprecedented fourth Conservative general election victory in 1992 opened up the possibility of 18 year old first-time voters in 1997 who had spent their entire lives under Conservative rule. It also brought to six the number of occasions this century that a Conservative government had been re-elected for a full term after a full term; no other party has achieved this in the same period. The victorious Conservative party's share of the vote throughout Britain in 1979 was 44.9 per cent, in 1983 43.5 per cent, in 1987 43.3 per cent and in 1992 42.8 per cent, in each case at least seven per cent ahead of Labour, its nearest challenger.

Does this highly successful and steady performance betoken an invincible grip on the British electoral system through the creation of a permanent coalition of voters preferring right of centre government? It is certainly true that the Conservative achievement of 1979–92 (as in previous periods of success) could not have existed had the party relied on a narrow base of support confined to one class, age group or region.

We have a valuable tool which enables us to assess the stable or dynamic social and demographic basis of Conservative support over the period since 1979 in the series of Harris/ITN exit polls carried out on the day of each general election. These polls, free of any problems caused by a significant gap in time between interview and voting, and conducted by secret ballot among a large random sample of voters outside the polling station, have proved very accurate in reproducing the parties' share of the vote. On no occasion in any of the four Harris/ ITN analysis exit polls since 1979 has any party's vote been estimated incorrectly by as much as 2 per cent, and the average error for the three main party groupings has been 0.7 per cent. They can therefore be relied on to provide accurate data to illustrate the roots of Conservative support in their era of 'hegemony'.

The Roots of Conservative Support

Sex

As Table 3.1 shows, in each of the four general elections the Conservative party retained a lead over Labour among both men and women, but in each election that lead was larger among women – the so-called 'gender gap'.

Table 3.1 Voting by Sex 1979–92 (percentage)

	Con	Lab	Lib Dem	Con lead over Lab
Men:				
1979	43	39	13	4
1983	41	30	26	11
1987	41	33	23	8
1992	39	38	18	1
Women:				
1979	46	36	15	10
1983	44	28	26	16
1987	43	31	23	12
1992	43	34	18	9

Source: Harris/ITN analysis exit polls

Age

The Conservatives proved too to have the greatest appeal of any party to all age groups as defined in the Harris/ITN exit polls. Even among Labour's strongest cohort, the 18–29 year-olds, Labour led only in 1979 and could manage no favourable swing between 1987 and 1992. The level of Conservative support increased steadily with age, and it should be remembered that voter turnout is at its lowest among the young.

Forty eight per cent of all respondents in the 1992 exit poll, for example, were over 45 years of age. Demographic traits, including the ageing of the population, tend to strengthen the hand of the Conservative Party.

Table **3.2** Voting by age 1979–92 (percentage)

	Con	Lab	Lib Dem	Con lead over Lab
18–29 year-olds				
1979	35	41	17	-6
1983	39	32	25	7
1987	36	35	26	1
1992	40	38	17	2
30–44 year-olds				
1979	46	34	15	12
1983	39	28	30	11
1987	41	31	26	10
1992	37	37	20	0
45–64 year-olds				
1979	45	39	12	6
1983	44	26	27	18
1987	44	31	22	13
1992	42	34	20	8
65+ year-olds				
1979	43	35	16	8
1983	45	28	21	17
1987	47	31	19	16
1992	47	36	14	1

Source: Harris/ITN analysis exit polls

Class

One of the strongest of all determinants of vote is, of course, occupational class. An analysis of the socio-economic group of respondents in the Harris/ITN exit polls shows (as might be expected) that Conservative strength increases as one moves up the social scale from unskilled manual workers and those receiving only state benefits (DEs) to the professional and managerial (ABs).

Table 3.3 Voting by class 1979–92 (percentage)

	Con	Lab	Lib Dem	Con lead over Lab
AB (Professional and managerial)				
1979	61	20	15	+41
1983	55	15	27	+40
1987	54	13	30	+41
1992	53	22	21	+31
C1 (White collar)				
1979	52	29	16	+23
1983	49	20	29	+29
1987	47	24	26	+23
1992	48	28	20	+20
C2 (Skilled manual)				
1979	39	42	14	-3
1983	38	32	26	+6
1987	42	35	21	+7
1992	40	39	18	+1
DE (Unskilled manual and those receiving only state benefits)				
1979	33	51	12	-18
1983	30	45	22	-15
1987	31	46	20	-15
1992	29	52	13	-23

Source: Harris/ITN analysis exit polls

This pattern is familiar to those who believe that class has been for many decades – and is still – the most important single cleavage along which electoral choice is made (and incidentally, challenges the oft stated view that the C2s are the critically important swing group – only between 1979 and 1983 did they swing more than any other class and usually they have swung less).

There is a debate among academic psephologists as to whether voting is becoming any less class-based and whether class 'de-alignment' has taken place, but one undeniable fact is that the size of the classes is changing. The 'middle-class' ABC1 socio-economic groups have grown steadily over recent decades, and the 'working-class' C2DEs became fewer. Between 1961 and 1981, for example, the proportion of professionals and managers increased from 14 per cent to 25 per cent of the workforce while skilled manual workers declined from 24 per cent to 16 per cent. In 1981 only 45 per cent of the labour force was in the skilled, semi-skilled and unskilled manual groups compared with 58 per cent in 1961 and 62 per cent in 1951.

Although in the 1992 exit polls just under 45 per cent of the Conservative vote did still come from the C2DEs – demonstrating their continued need (and ability) to gain large numbers of voters from classes which 'should' support the Labour party – nevertheless the growth of the non-manual classes (the ABC1s) must be a significant boost for Conservative prospects, especially if class de-alignment is not taking place. As with the ageing of the population (and in consequence it becomes more female too), this development increases the difficulty of the task facing Labour, the main opposition party.

Housing Tenure

One more change which also points in the same direction lies in the important sphere of housing tenure. As the figures in Table 3.4 show, there is a vast and growing gap between the voting behaviour of owner-occupiers and council tenants.

Table 3.4 Voting by housing tenure 1979–92 (percentage)

	Con	Lab	Lib Dem	Con lead over Lab
Owner-occupier				
1979	53	29	14	+24
1983	49	21	27	+28
1987	47	25	25	+22
1992	47	30	20	+17
Council tenant				
1979	27	56	13	-29
1983	24	51	21	-27
1987	22	58	14	-36
1992	19	64	10	-45
Private rented/other				
1979	42	37	16	5
1987	37	30	29	7
1987	39	34	26	5
1992	31	49	17	-18

Source: Harris/ITN analysis exit polls

As will be seen, the Conservatives have maintained a strong lead among owner-occupiers but have done less and less well among council tenants and the privately rented/other groups. This is, however, against the background of a dramatically changing pattern of housing tenure. In 1971 50 per cent of households were owner-occupied and 30 per cent rented from a local authority or New Town. By 1981 the owner occupation rate had gone up to 56 per cent and by 1991 66 per cent were owner-occupiers and 21 per cent council tenants. What is more, owner-occupiers tend to turn out more heavily in elections: 70 per cent of respondents in the 1992 Harris/ITN exit poll owned their accommodation outright or were buying it on mortgage. It would seem that the Conservative government's policy of encouraging owner occupation and selling council houses will reap long term electoral advantages for their party.

Conservative Hegemony?

So, a picture appears to emerge of a playing field slowly but surely tilting in favour of the Conservatives, whose long standing strengths among women, the older age groups, the non-manual occupational classes and owner-occupiers become more and more decisive as these groups increase in size. Conservative supporters also tend to be concentrated in those sectors of society who turn out most heavily at general elections. Do these social, economic and demographic trends ensure continuing victories for the right, and give Labour a mountain to climb if they are ever to secure governmental office again?

Another factor to take into account is the continuing population shift from the (generally Labour voting) inner cities and metropolitan areas, to the Tory suburbs and shires which gives rise to re-distribution of seats favourable to the Conservative Party in the periodic reviews by the Parliamentary Boundary Commission. The Conservative overall majority in 1979 of 43 seats was effectively increased by 30 by boundary changes in 1983 which gave them 15 net gains at the expense of Labour. Another re-distribution is due before the next general election as the Commission is due to report by the end of 1994. The widespread acceptance of predictions of a 20 seat net gain for the Conservatives has further fuelled the view that Labour cannot win the next election, at least without some kind of pact or arrangement with the Liberal Democrats.

Everything seems to flow in the Conservatives' direction. Does their consistently strong performance since 1979 mean that they have a lock on the electoral system for the foreseeable future? Let us turn to further polling evidence, this time relating to the issues which lay behind the voting behaviour. Electors do not behave as socio-economically determined automata: they make choices based on perceptions of the vital matters of the day.

Issues Which Determine the Vote

When asked why they vote for their preferred party, by far the most common answer among the Harris/ITN exit poll respondents has been 'party policy'.

Table 3.5 Main reasons for support each party (percentages)

	1979	1983	1987	1992
Conservative				
Party Policy	62	55	56	48
Usually vote for that party	23	9	19	21
Party leader	5	17	8	10
Local candidate	4	3	3	3
Dislike another party	NA	12	9	14
Labour				
Party Policy	49	47	46	49
Usually vote that party	29	18	25	24
Party leader	12	4	6	4
Local candidate	7	10	5	5
Dislike another party	NA	18	12	13
Lib Dem				
Party Policy	52	46	48	43
Usually vote that party	11	3	8	9
Party leader	10	10	4	9
Local candidate	12	10	10	12
Dislike another party	NA	26	23	21

Source: Harris/ITN analysis exit polls

The figures given in Table 3.5 suggest that the electorate make up their minds how to vote on an 'instrumental' assessment of each party's policies rather than simply through 'kneejerk' voting for the same party every time. This indicates that a Labour party with popular and credible policies could hope to overcome the socio-economic and demographic trends I have described.

However, one polling question which is certainly not a useful predictor of voting (or even of which are the crucial policy issues) is to ask the respondent which issues are the most important when it comes to making their electoral decisions. When Harris asked this question for ITN in 1992 (23–24 March) the two 'top' issues mentioned were the NHS and unemployment. During that campaign every polling agency found that Labour was better trusted to handle the health service and unemployment issues than the Conservatives.[1] Even in their post-election survey (10–11 April) Gallup still found that when they asked about the two most urgent problems that had affected the respondents' voting choice they disclosed the following:

Table 3.6 Two most urgent problems affecting voting (percentage)

NHS	41
Unemployment	36
Education	23
Prices	11
Taxation	10

Source: Gallup. 10–11 April 1992

Yet clearly the electorate, if it was voting on policy issues, cannot have been influenced most by three strong issues for Labour; indeed if voting patterns had been determined by policies on the National Health Service, Labour would surely have won every election since the creation of the NHS! The strong suspicion remains that when people are asked on what issues they are going to vote (or have voted) they give a 'moral' or 'politically correct' answer, but that in fact they vote on other grounds – principally economic self-interest. Minds may well have been concentrated on this genuinely key issue in 1992 as the consensus came to be that Labour would actually win the election.

Table 3.7 Who do you think will win the next General Election (percentage)

		March		April
	11–17	18–23	25–30	1–6
Conservative	48	39	35	24
Labour	31	37	37	47
Hung	5	14	18	18

Source: Gallup, March–April 1992

With the benefit of hindsight, polling evidence can guide us towards an explanation of the Conservatives's fourth General Election victory in a row. Even in the darkest moments of their campaign, they kept a lead on the issues of which party would be best to handle the economy, inflation and taxation. Harris's final poll (4–6 April) for the *Daily Express* gave the Conservatives a 14 per cent lead as the party most trusted to handle taxation. While it was accepted in March–April 1992 that the economy was in poor shape, it was widely felt that things would be even worse if Labour were in government. MORI's fourth and last pre-election panel for the *Sunday Times* agreed by 52 per cent to 36 per cent that 'the country cannot afford Labour's spending plans'.

Labour's weakness on taxation was particularly clear. NOP's *Independent on Sunday* panel (2–3 April) found no fewer than 81 per cent agreed that Labour would put up taxes on those with average earnings. In the 1992 Harris/ITN exit poll 49 per cent admitted that they felt they would be worse off under Labour's tax policies and only 30 per cent thought they'd be better off. Among the C2 socio-economic group the figures were almost identical to the average – 32 per cent believed they would be better off and 48 per cent worse off. Only 14 per cent of all respondents in the NOP/BBC exit poll said they regarded income tax as one of the three most important issues – but more than twice that figure, 29 per cent, of 'switchers' to the Conservatives did.

It would seem that in 1992 the British electorate once again voted with its pocket and its purse. In Harris's final poll for the *Observer* (2–3 April) a 2 per cent Labour lead was recorded but the following answers were given when asked the result that would make the respondent best off:

— Conservative win 41%
— Labour win 29%
— Hung parliament 8%

As the electorate clearly believed the Conservatives would bring most prosperity to the country as a whole and to the respondents and their families, Labour had an impossible task on 9 April 1992. However, this does not mean that their prospects in future General Elections are hopeless. If they can convince the electorate that they will be economically better off under Labour as the Labour party in Australia did in 1991 and President Clinton and the Democrats did in the United States in 1992, they should be able to defeat the Conservatives at the next or subsequent elections.

The Major government's 'honeymoon' after April 1992 proved to be unusually short. By May 1993 voters were delivering devastating blows to the Conservatives, both at the Newbury by-election (a 12,000 Conservative majority turned into a Liberal Democrat victory of 22,000) and in county councils across England and Wales (where the Conservatives lost a third of all their councillors and retained overall control of only one county, Buckinghamshire). Labour's opinion poll lead over the Conservatives in late spring 1993 reached 15–25 per cent.

Admittedly by-election history is deviating increasingly from General Election history – the Conservatives lost seven seats in the 1987–92 parliament and regained them all while winning again in the 1992 General Election. Mid-term disasters for governments are nowadays more than commonplace, they are to be expected. Local and European elections, like by-elections, are seen as opportunities to protest at unpopular government policies and unacceptable performance, without actually changing the ruling party. Newbury and the counties in 1993 does not condemn John Major's administration to defeat in 1996 or 1997.

But this does not make governmental recovery and eventual victory anything like inevitable. If the Conservatives do not turn things round, to bring home the economic bacon, they have every chance of losing the next general election. It cannot be predicted, perhaps three years before the likely date of that event, whether they will have done or not. However, some advantages they possessed in 1992 are unlikely to be repeated.

In the Harris/ITN General Election exit poll of April 1992, voters were asked who was most to blame for the present state of the British economy.

Table 3.8 Who is most to blame for the present state of the economy? (percentage)

	All	Con	Lab	Lib-Dem
Mrs Thatcher's government	46	12	78	57
Mr Major's government	5	2	7	6
World economic condition	47	84	12	34

Source: Harris/ITN analysis exit poll 1992

Only one in twenty voters blamed John Major for the recession and over nine times as many blamed Mrs Thatcher, who had been removed from office in November 1990. Clearly there was a large element of giving Mr Major a chance of a full term – an advantage he would be unlikely to be able to repeat as the electorate's sense of his own responsibility grew. Also, his clear advantage over Neil Kinnock as favoured prime minister was nullified by Mr Kinnock's replacement shortly after the election by a new face for Labour, John Smith.

As the epoch of Conservative government stretches from 13 years towards 18 years, the cry of 'time for a change' will ever ring louder. The search for fresh policy directions will become harder and the risk will be run of familiarity breeding contempt. The Conservatives have to do only a little worse than in 1992 to lose power – for a hung parliament would be most likely to be seen as a rejection of the incumbent government and to result in a Labour minority administration (as in February 1974) or a Labour-Liberal Democrat coalition.

The Conservative overall majority in 1992 was only 21, despite a 7.5 per cent lead in votes, largely because tactical voting by opponents of the government resulted in a swing in the key marginals which was double the average for all seats. The willingness of Labour and Liberal Democrat supporters to vote for other candidates was even more apparent in the May 1993 and 1994 county council elections, and at Newbury on the same day. This results in a more efficient distribution of the opposition's votes – in the county council elections, for example, the Liberal Democrats obtained nearly 30 per cent of all seats with less than 25 per cent of the vote – an extraordinary reversal of their traditional position. If anything, the electoral system is now biased against the Conservative party.

Boundary Changes

Nor can the government pin their hopes on a favourable boundary redistribution when the Commission reports by the end of 1994. Predictions of a substantial net gain by the Conservatives are belied by detailed analysis of the changes as they have been announced county by county. The damage done to Labour will be much less than the fifteen seats (net) caused by the previous boundary changes in 1983 for two reasons. Firstly, there are no major local government reforms to take into account as there were then (those of 1974 consequent on the Redcliffe Maud report); the impact of the Banham Local Government Commission, though great, will come too late. Secondly, although the population shift from predominantly Labour inner cities to Tory suburbs and shires has continued, the resultant creation of new seats has not necessarily hurt Labour in every case.

It is the case that an extra true-blue constituency has indeed been allocated to a number of counties: Berkshire, Cambridgeshire, Cheshire, Hertfordshire, Essex, Humberside, Kent, Leicestershire, Nottinghamshire, Shropshire, Staffordshire, Suffolk and West Sussex. However, in several other counties, the picture could have been much worse for Labour.

In Gloucestershire, for example, an extra Conservative seat has been created by the splitting of Cirencester & Tewkesbury (Nicholas Ridley's old haunt), but consequent changes pare down Tory West Gloucestershire to the old Forest of Dean seat, solidly Labour except in 1931. Net gain – one to Labour. Similarly in Lincolnshire the suburbs of the county city are removed, leaving a core Lincoln seat which Labour would have won in 1992. In Hereford and Worcester, an extra rural seat is created in the heart of the county, but this results in both Worcester and Redditch losing the countryside and villages which dilute their urban vote, so making both seats realistic Labour targets. In Bedfordshire, the creation of an extra rural seat according to the same principle means that both Luton South and Luton North will now be cliffhanging marginals, and Bedford is also reduced to its urban core, giving Labour an outside chance of three seats in a county in which at present they hold none.

Hampshire, England's fastest growing county, alone gains two extra seats. Yet Labour does not suffer. One new Tory stronghold is created in the north-east of the county, and there will be two New Forest seats – hardly any cheer for the Left there. But the strongest Conservative ward in Southampton, Bassett, is moved out of the city leaving both Test and Itchen Labour seats if the new boundaries had existed in 1992. What is more, in Avon, with the same number of constituencies as before, a move of wards switches the highly marginal Bristol NW decisively over to the Labour side.

The recommendations of the Commission are not complete at the time of writing, but their eventual impact can reasonably be assessed. Most critically Greater London will certainly lose about ten seats, having been over represented for decades. However, with the Conservatives holding a majority of Greater London's current 84 seats (48 to Labour's 35) they should suffer most of the losses likely to be recommended by the Boundary Commission, such as in the boroughs of Barnet, Bexley, Bromley, Kingston and Kensington/Chelsea. Labour will lose in Newham/Tower Hamlets, Waltham Forest and Lambeth/Southwark, and also a few seats in the Metropolitan area outside London: two in Greater Manchester, one in Merseyside, one in Birmingham.

Overall, however, my current best guess is as a result of the boundary changes that the Conservatives should expect a gross gain of only about ten seats (net five) – the equivalent of only an extra 0.75 per cent swing that Labour will require to remove the Government's overall majority at the next general election and their effect on national politics should be discounted.

All Still To Play For

It is by all means possible that the Conservatives will pull off a fifth consecutive general election victory. However it would be wrong to assume that demographic and socio-economic changes in Britain make this anywhere near inevitable. It is arguable that political rather than sociological matters play the most important role in determining the outcome of elections. Perhaps the Conservative victories should be ascribed not so much to owner occupation and the growth of the middle class as to matters of policy, perception and image. In 1979 a played-out Labour government lost after the events symbolised by the Winter of Discontent. In 1983 a Falklands-confident Thatcher-led government easily disposed of Michael Foot's divided party with its 'suicide note' manifesto. In 1987 there was an economic boom. In 1992 the new Prime Minister evaded blame for recession and proved preferable to Neil Kinnock, while exploiting the fear of taxation and further economic decline under a possible Labour Government.

Next time – and the time after that – it is very hard to predict which party will appeal most and which will be the key issues, although the economy is extremely likely to figure very prominently. Voters are becoming more and more instrumental and are very volatile. This is not a stable basis on which to build an electoral hegemony which lasts several decades or even generations.

Notes

1. In the case of health Labour led by 47 per cent and 30 per cent in Harris's final ITN poll (4–6 April): the NOP/BBC exit poll found 49 per cent trusting Labour to make the right decisions on the NHS and only 37 per cent the Conservatives. Labour's lead on being trusted to handle unemployment was 16 per cent in the final Harris/ITN pre-election poll and 18 per cent in Gallup's final poll (1–6 April).

TWO

Government and Opposition in Japan

From Our Own Correspondent

William Horsley

Is Japan a True Democracy?

When the leaders of the 'Group of Seven' nations meet for their annual economic summits, they are characterised as 'the world's leading industrialised democracies'. This may be a useful shorthand, but is it true? Is Japan a democracy comparable to the others – Britain, Canada, France, Germany, Italy and the United States?

Some commentators, both Japanese and western, have answered, in effect, 'no'. They say that Japan's present form of politics was grafted after the country's wartime defeat onto a society with no tradition of popular representative government, and that the graft has still not really taken. It is said that the country is still run according to unwritten rules and self-justifying hierarchies rather than according to neutrally-applied laws. The continuous rule of one political party for nearly four decades seemed to make a mockery of the idea of pluralistic democracy. Although successive Japanese conservative rulers showed tolerance towards their political opponents, Japan shared with communist states and South Africa the dubious distinction of keeping the same party in government for over a generation. Only the fact that this was done without coercion or external *force majeure* seemed to set Japan apart.

In this scheme Japan is labelled as a mercantilist power, which has been shielded from international political responsibilities for two generations while a conservative elite ran the country, focusing the nation's energies on creating wealth. In the drive for national self-improvement basic freedoms were curtailed: power was in the hands of the state, big business and employers rather than the individual, the consumer or the employee. With the United States taking care of Japan's external security, it is argued, the nation's politics were conducted in a cocoon. Japan's is therefore a 'fair weather democracy' with no track record of surviving real domestic or international tension.

Against this, others maintain that Japan is a model of democracy, albeit a young one. The country is governed by popularly elected politicians. Voting rates are consistently high, while vote-rigging and demagoguery have been virtually unknown since the war (although inducements of various kinds are undeniably widespread). The military has no discernible influence in politics. Japan is patently a state committed to international law. It has for four decades been an unwavering ally of the United States. And having embraced its 'no-war' post-war constitution the Japanese people are strongly committed to its key provision: the renunciation of the use of force in international disputes.

Moreover, the surprise defeat of the long-ruling Liberal Democratic Party (LDP) in the elections of July 1993 and the party's banishment into opposition, has confounded the view that the mould of Japanese politics would never be broken. With the partial split of the LDP and the birth of a seven-party coalition government which excludes it, Japan has embarked on uncharted territory. The opposition Social Democratic Party (formerly the Socialists), long derided as hopeless losers, are represented in the Cabinet. The apparently unbreakable ties between the LDP and big business as well as the civil service have suddenly been loosened. Moreover, the ending of the stale system of one-party rule brought a rare surge of popular enthusiasm for politics. The new reform-minded prime minister, Morihiro Rosokawa, maintained an astonishingly high rate of popular support – close to 70 per cent – for several months after coming to power.

So the new configuration of political parties reflects a popular will for change, but it also poses sharp challenges for Japan's stilted kind of democracy. Much needs to be done to build confidence in the main political institutions, particularly the Cabinet and Parliament. The LDP's long uninterrupted rule had a stifling effect on open political debate, a vital element in lasting democratic politics. The bloated and arguably unconstitutional power assumed by leading LDP politicians, as well as senior civil servants, enabled them to flout the law, undermining judicial independence as well as political accountability. The series of political and financial scandals of the last twenty years have caught up dozens of politicians and businessmen. But while many have been found guilty in court, many more have escaped prosecution, and not one of the powerful figures has actually been sent to prison when convicted.

In a country with so little experience of the alternation of power among rival parties, the risk exists of prolonged instability. Although in the post-war period government business has mostly been conducted in an orderly way, that order did sometimes break down. In 1960, for example, the streets of central Tokyo were turned into a battle-ground when crowds of student demonstrators tried to storm the Diet in protest at the government's high-handed methods in renewing the US-Japan Security Pact. And there were fisticuffs in the House of Representatives, the Lower House, on more than one occasion in the 1980s, over such contentious measures as the introduction of a new sales tax. So the prospect cannot be dismissed of a return to an older pattern of Japanese politics, seen in the inter-war period, in which new parties and factions proliferate, and coalition governments come and go frequently. In the worst case, physical violence could play an undesirable part, as it did before the Second World War.

On the positive side, government without the LDP has an opportunity to turn Japan in a new direction in ways which would be welcome both at home and abroad. Following the LDP's 1993 defeat, the incoming government headed by a reform-minded conservative 'outsider', Norihiro Hosokawa, quickly proclaimed a shift in government support away from industrial producers and in favour of consumers. The entrenched powers of the bureaucrats are under assault as never before since the Occupation period. So is the lazy, sinecured existence of many politicians. Also, on taking office the new prime minister, Norihiro Hosokawa, gave the frankest apology ever heard from a Japanese government for what he called the 'aggressive' and 'wrong' war which Japan waged against other countries in Asia. This was in its own way an important revolution for Japan's public conscience, and an assault on one of the central bastions of reaction.

Yet it may be too soon to proclaim a profound change in Japanese political behaviour, or even an end to the domination of a like-minded elite at the top of a single conservative hierarchy. Mr Hosokawa, leader of the New Japan Party and of the 'new-look' government, is the grandson of Prince Konoye, who was Japan's prime minister for periods before and during World War Two. Hosokawa himself made his political name through the LDP, as governor of Kumamoto prefecture in the southern island of Kyushu. His first cabinet was dominated by figures known as the biggest power-brokers in the old LDP, in particular Ichiro Ozawa and Tsutomu Hata. In 1993 they saw that the LDP's corruption and exhaustion was so advanced that it would fail the coming election test. So like master string-pullers they quit the LDP and built themselves a new political platform, the Japan Renewal Party, and with their own departure they tugged the chord which they knew would bring down the creaking LDP stage.

The thrust of their move is to forge what Kenneth Courtis of Deutsche Bank Research, Asia calls a 'neo-conservative, urban based, more modernised government'. But the attempts to introduce a new electoral system and to end deep-rooted corruption – the 'political reform' issue which was the immediate cause of the LDP's election defeat – are likely to be long and painful. They are by no means assured of success.

Are British politics becoming like those of Japan? The question has a different resonance since the LDP's loss of power, as it has suddenly ceased to be a 'permanent party of government'. But the LDP remains a prototype of effective one-party dominance. Britain historically prided itself on a lively and responsive political climate, as well as an independent civil service. The possibility of the Conservative party's ouster after four consecutive terms of office is a matter of heated conjecture. In Japan, despite the birth of a non-LDP government, the distinctive characteristics associated with the long period of LDP rule remain in place.

Could it anyway be that 'conservative' forces in Japan have, ironically, won their most famous battle precisely with the defeat and reformation of the LDP? There are now, one could argue, only competing forms of conservatism for the voters of Japan to choose from, rather than any radical alternative. It is too soon to judge; but there are indeed pressures for a better pursuit of Japan's own national interests. The question arises, too: might the electoral near-collapse of the Social Democrats (formerly the Japan Socialist Party) – for long Japan's largest opposition party – presage something similar elsewhere in Europe, or perhaps in Britain?

Japan appears to have outgrown one particularly long-lived form of conservative government. But it has yet definitely to discard the formula of closed, business-oriented politics, in which policies matter less than arcane balances of factional power. It remains to be seen whether Japan will actually move from a money-power-driven framework of politics – justified in the name of providing the nation with economic security – to one that revolves around competing and accountable policies and takes the government's hands off the wheels of economic control. Seen from a British vantage-point the question is worth asking: as the Japanese have become more 'like us', are we growing more 'like them'?

How Japanese History Has Shaped its Contemporary Politics

As recently as 1945, Japan was governed according to an atavistic concept of divine imperial sovereignty which was virulently anti-western as well as anti-democratic. At the core was the transcendental idea of the *kokutai*, usually translated as the 'national polity' but better perhaps expressed as a divinely-inspired Japanese national order. Parliamentarians, trade unionists, intellectuals and others who opposed that system were derided, locked up and, in some cases, assassinated.

Basic civil rights were systematically denied in what became a police state. The foundation on which *kokutai* rested was the idea of an Emperor descended directly from the gods, a priest-king whose radiant authority was beyond rational question.

This belief was a fiction, and was privately acknowledged as such by those who wielded power in the name of the Emperor from the 1930s until the end of the Second World War. The xenophobia and international aggression that the Japanese state displayed in this period was far from typical of modern (ie post-1868) Japan. Indeed, Japan had experienced periods of great enthusiasm for western-style liberal democracy, including the experience known as 'Taisho democracy' which flourished in the 1920s.

Still, the pre-war and wartime *kokutai* displayed in an extreme form two enduring characteristics of Japanese patterns of government, which stand in strong contrast to the Anglo-Saxon concept of liberal democracy. Strong traces of the same underlying tendencies can be discerned in the post-war period.

The first is the intrusion of the state or its agencies into every field of life, even those which relate to personal behaviour or matters of conscience. Between 1940 and 1945 all Japan's political parties were abolished, and subsumed into a so-called Imperial Rule Assistance Association. This meant not only the end of politics, but also of personal and religious freedom. It was a model of totalitarianism – although it is important to note that for the great majority of the population there was little or no sense of being oppressed. The native Shinto religion became 'state Shinto'. Japanese society then was supposed to be a hierarchy in which the Emperor and the ruling authorities were at the top, with a supposed monopoly on moral as well as political power; while those furthest removed from the Imperial Throne were at the bottom. The latter included, for example, young army recruits, who during the war years were treated with systematic brutality by their own superiors. This rigid hierarchy helps to explain the inhumanity of the Japanese military machine towards those at 'the bottom of the pile', such as prisoners of war and the tens of thousands of (mostly Asian) women compelled into slavery as 'comfort women' (prostitutes) for the Imperial Armed Forces.

The suppression of civil rights during the militarist period of the mid 1930s to 1945 was one facet of Japanese fascism. But the concept of legally-enforceable civil rights had up until that time anyway never been well developed. While Shinto, the 'Way of the Gods', is a tolerant faith in so far as it celebrates life-giving forces, its simple celebration and mythology were easily applied to support the new xenophobic nationalism. The civil rights idea was also at odds with the doctrines of Japanese Confucianism, based as they are on an immutable order of seniority and male dominance. These traditions at the time proved far stronger than the enthusiasm of a small minority of the Japanese intelligentsia for any form of western-style liberalism.

In the post-war period religious and other individual freedoms have been constitutionally guaranteed. Indeed Japanese society is decidedly permissive with regard to ethical as well as sexual behaviour. Dozens of 'new religions' have sprung up which compete vigorously for adherents. Yet there is much evidence that the social and political emancipation of the individual in society has been slow to arrive. Rather, ingrained habits of social deference, played out in every field of life, still largely determine political loyalties, as much as those in the vital matter of employment. As fleshed out in countless studies of Japanese society, an 'Iron Triangle' of LDP politicians, like-minded bureaucrats and captains of industry has assumed authority for virtually all aspects of public life and social organisation.

Government and bureaucracy exercise very great discretionary power in fields which, in Britain for example, would be considered the preserve of independent bodies, or simply of market forces. The generic term 'administrative guidance' (*gyosei shido*) is used to describe the practice of bureaucratic decision-making in practically every field. Senior bureaucrats enjoy the highest social prestige, and after retirement are rewarded with lucrative posts in private business or quangos. The government's Economic Planning Agency has sought to plot the future course of the economy in five-year 'forecasts', frequently updated. The Ministry of International Trade and Industry framed detailed legislation as to direct private firms to take a world lead in high-technology products, such as video recorders and advanced computer memory chips. In the 1980s the government set up several *ad hoc* bodies to plan the re-structuring of Japan's regime of international trade, but only in response to foreign pressures.

In education hundreds of officials have constantly monitored the detailed contents of school textbooks, ordering alterations to enforce what they saw as 'political correctness', especially with regard to Japan's conduct of wars in the modern period, its relations with the rest of Asia, and touchy issues like nuclear power. Under this literal 'bureaucracy' – rule by officials – supposedly independent bodies such as the leading news organisations, business federations and Parents and Teachers Associations largely took on the character of adjuncts to the will of the officials, rather than separate forces with their own values and demands. The consensus was by no means always stable or complete. Opposition to it has often been expressed, in education by the left-wing teachers' union, in the press from time to time by unruly monthly magazines, and in industry by organised labour. Nevertheless, the consensus system proudly articulated down the years by Japan's representatives in every sphere was essential to sustaining the 'Iron Triangle' of LDP politicians, big business and a bureaucracy with sweeping powers.

A second enduring feature of Japanese political life is the separation of real power from its apparent source: in other words the dual, or multiple, structure of power. Public ceremony, or displays of authority, have always played an inordinately important role in the Japanese practice of government. Real decision-making has generally taken place elsewhere, out of the public eye.

In the militarist period, important decisions were taken by a military-mandarin-aristocratic elite, while the Emperor, Hirohito, who supposedly wielded absolute authority, was mainly an impotent figurehead. Despite the attempt of the controversial author David Bergamini (in his book *The Imperial Conspiracy*) to show that Emperor Hirohito led the pro-war faction in Japan, there is a mass of evidence showing rather that the authority of the throne was effectively used by ultra-nationalist groups to elevate the idea of the *kokutai* and take Japan along the path to war. Nevertheless, the key acts of government throughout the period 1868 to 1945 were proclaimed in the form of Imperial Rescripts. In other words, those wielding power remained behind the scenes and were not publicly accountable.

Such a dual structure was inherent to Japan's system of government after the 1889 adoption of the Meiji constitution, which proclaimed that the Emperor was 'supreme and inviolable', and the source of all sovereignty. The form of a written national constitution was new, but it mirrored similar arrangements going back to the beginnings of Japanese history, when courtiers, noble families and finally *shogun* dynasties took on the ruling authority as guardians of the imperial line and the national good.

In the post-war period another sort of 'dual structure' has operated: one in which politicians have in effect acted as figureheads, leaving policy-forming and the framing of laws to powerful bureaucrats who are not directly accountable to the public. It is standard practice for government ministers to have their department officials appear in their stead to answer policy questions in parliament, because the ministers themselves do not know enough about the subject to answer themselves.

A 'dual hierarchy' has also been at work within the political arena itself. This trait grew more marked in the last decade of the LDP's uninterrupted period of rule. Relatively weak conservative political leaders have sat nominally at the head of successive governments, but have been more or less controlled by one or more *kuromaku* ('puppeteers'), shadowy figures from the so-called LDP 'tribe'. Such was the case with Yasuhiro Nakasone (prime minister from 1982 to 1987), who was beholden to the scandal-ridden but still dominant kingmaker, the former premier Kakuei Tanaka. It was so with Noboru Takeshita (in power from 1987 to 1989), who was directed in neo-Confucian manner by his own father-in-law, LDP vice-president Shin Ranemaru. And much the same held true for both Toshiki Kaifu (1989–91) and Kiichi Miyasawa (1991–93), two LDP prime ministers without strong factional followings who were forced to heed the dictates of more powerful party bosses.

After the Second World War a number of western and Japanese writers sought to analyse what was called a 'system of irresponsibility' arising from the fallacy of imperial divinity and sovereign power. The charge of irresponsibility, or lack of proper accountability, has continued to be levelled against successive Japanese governments in the post-war period, too. The Dutch author, Karel van Wolferen, made this the major theme of his critical work, *The Enigma of Japanese Power*, which purports to show that, thanks to the multiple and confusing power structures inherent in post-war Japan, nobody is really 'in charge' there at all.

Japanese politics were completely re-moulded in 1945, along the lines of an American-inspired constitution which its patron, General Douglas MacArthur, called 'the most liberal constitution in history'. The explicit aim was to incorporate the best aspects of democracies the world over. However, some of the common patterns of behaviour observed today date back to Japan's 'middle ages', which in some ways lasted until the mid-nineteenth century. So before looking at modern practices more closely, it is worth a glance still further back into Japan's past.

The centuries of the Tokugawa *shogunate* (1603 to 1867) have left a lasting imprint on the character of Japanese society. Under the (mostly) benevolent military dictatorship of one dynastic family Japan lived in self-imposed seclusion and without warfare for about 250 years. The division of society into four distinct classes – *samurai*, farmers, artisans and merchants – was rigidly adhered to. In spite of periodic famines a vigorous mercantile culture evolved, in which Edo (present-day Tokyo) was for a time the world's largest and arguably richest city. Politics was severely proscribed. The government's agents were everywhere, seeking to detect and stifle dissent, and holding hostages to enforce their will. Regionalism flourished, with the populations of each of the *han* (clans) obliged to pledge loyalty to their own feudal lord. Lively competition among the provinces produced a highly-developed internal commerce.

Japan's shotgun modernisation in response to the arrival of Commodore Perry's Black Ships saw nineteenth-century Japan groping for the constitutional basis of a modern state. The constitution of 1889, an amalgam of Japanese traditions and the authoritarian ideas of a Prussian-led Germany, was fatally flawed. It ascribed transcendental powers to a 'divine' Emperor (Meiji), and failed to allow for broad-based popular participation, or to grant enough powers to the *Diet* (parliament) for it to play a serious and responsible role in national affairs. As the enlightened educator, Yukichi Fukuzawa, wrote graphically, the deeply-ingrained concept of feudal loyalty meant that Japanese people in the late nineteenth century had the greatest difficulty in grasping the concept of party politics, or public debate of any kind.

Traditional autocracy, practised by a generation of reformist *samurai* (warrior-mandarin) leaders who had effected the 'Restoration' of the Emperor, was in conflict with a new popular liberalism inspired by examples from the west. A myriad of political parties were founded around various former *han* leaders. Big business houses like Mitsui and Mitsubishi (also emerging out of powerful *han* commercial interests) backed rival political factions. But real power remained in the hands of the advisers to the throne, an elite civil bureaucracy and, ultimately, the army. None of these was answerable to anyone other than – in theory – the Emperor, who was only fourteen years old when 'restored' to a largely mythical central role in Japanese political life.

This fatal flaw opened the way for the disasters of the 1930s, as Japan's colonialist rivalry with the West, especially over China, coincided with the rise of a host of violent anti-parliamentary 'patriotic associations' at home. These 'double patriots', as the British historian Richard Storry called them, proclaimed their aim of ridding the Emperor of supposedly malign influences, including weak-kneed politicians and exploitative capitalists. After a period of what has been called 'government by assassination' party politics collapsed completely and Japan blundered into war against the United States, Britain and their allies.

After Japan's defeat its political destiny was dictated by the remarkably favourable conditions of the American-led occupation. Most of the Japanese political establishment still wanted to preserve at least the spirit of the old Meiji constitution. Indeed, an interim Japanese government was forced to accept an idealistic constitution, which went into force in 1947, enshrining a range of basic human rights, laying down a framework for democratic politics with a bicameral parliament, and forever renouncing war. Emperor Hirohito remained on the throne as a 'symbol of the state', stripped of all vestiges of government-related power. Sweeping land reforms freed the majority of Japanese from servitude on the land. A purge of suspected war criminals, as well as thorough-going democratic reforms of the police, the civil service and the courts, were all begun but interrupted by the start of the cold war. The Americans' top priority became making Japan a bulwark against international communism.

It took a decade after the war for the pattern of stable Liberal Democratic Party dominance to emerge. At first long-suppressed Marxist ideas found fertile ground among the population, as did a strong strain of republican feeling. A fierce struggle between left- and right-wing ideologies took place across the board – in Japanese industry, the bureaucracy and mass media. A plethora of parties competed in elections in the early post-war years, and amid deep divisions among conservatives and traditionalists the Socialist Party headed one of the resulting coalition governments (in 1947–48). A turning-point came, though, with the trade unions' threat of a general strike early in 1947 over the role and rights of organised labour. The strike was banned, and a new 'red purge' sought to weed out communists and their supporters from positions of influence.

A former diplomat who had spent the war in self-imposed retirement, Shigeru Yoshida, emerged as the dominant figure among the conservative groupings. Apart from the Socialist-led interlude, he was prime minister throughout the period 1946–54. He led the Liberal Party and became the founder of a lasting 'Yoshida doctrine' which set the tone for much of Japanese politics in the next half-century. It stood for an economically strong, militarily modest Japan lodged firmly within the western diplomatic camp.

In 1955, fearing election defeat, the conservative forces led by two parties, the Liberals and the Democrats, buried their differences and formed the Liberal Democratic Party. The LDP was born and continued as a broad coalition of business and conservative political interests, who were always ready to co-operate to keep the left-wing parties out of power. This aim was more important than ideology: the pledge made in the party's founding documents – to remove the 'peace' clause from the Japanese constitution and so recover full national sovereignty – remained a piece of 'unfinished business' throughout the next four decades of its unchallenged dominance.

The main opposition party, the Japanese Socialist Party, remained for many years the prisoner of its Marxist origins, committed to extreme policies such as workers' control of industry, and the scrapping both of defence ties with the United States and of the Japanese Self-Defence Forces. Thus Japan was furnished with what became known as a 'one-and-a half party system', in which the LDP was able to present itself as the only reliable party of government. That unbalanced set of circumstances continued until, with the worldwide collapse of communism and Japan's success in becoming the world's foremost financial power, the *raison d'etre* of Japan's original conservative alliance was lost.

How the LDP Held on to Power for so Long

There were two main factors in the sustained political success of the LDP. Firstly, it offered a real guarantee of peace and security. The main opposition argued for a deeply unpopular policy of 'unarmed neutrality', even while Chinese and Soviet communism were actively seeking to expand their worldwide alliances. The LDP embraced close ties with the United States, including its defence 'umbrella', as the best possible protection. Aspects of this policy were unpopular, especially the unequal terms of the first US-Japan Security Treaty of 1960 and Japanese support for the American war effort in Vietnam and the issue of the pace of Japan's own defence build-up remained hotly contested. Still, the basic security pledge depended on America, and it was credible.

Despite the different context there is some comparison with the defence debates in Britain. There, the refusal of the Labour party conference until 1961 to accept Britain's NATO membership, or its possession of nuclear weapons was certainly an electoral liability. The nuclear issue again dogged Labour in the 1970s and 1980s, contributing to the party's three successive defeats in 1979, 1983 and 1987. The comparison should not be taken too far: the British Labour Party enjoyed extended periods in office under Clement Attlee, Harold Wilson and James Callaghan. And after the fierce internal ideological battles and splits that followed its 1979 election defeat, the party has been able to claim once again that it stands for adequate national defence.

The Liberal Democrats in Japan combined the pragmatism of sheltering behind the US with a subtle nationalism which allowed the party to portray itself as the only true guardians of a reformed *kokutai* and of the national honour. The party's founding pledge to recover the nation's full sovereignty – including the eventual removal of all foreign troops – set down a marker for the future. The party adopted the symbol of the chrysanthemum, in a form similar to the sixteen-leaf Imperial chrysanthemum, and so appealed to the heartland of Japanese conservative voters.

Secondly, the LDP was created as the party representing the interests of business and industry – another matter of survival for Japan's status in the world. Nobusuke Kishi, who as a government minister had helped to build up Japan's so-called 'Co-Prosperity Sphere' in Asia in the war years, was typical of the pedigree of many early party managers. He was prime minister from 1957 to 1960. The *Keidanren*, the Federation of Economic Organisations, was itself midwife to the birth of the LDP, and its policy of fund-raising for the party and awarding exclusive support was crucial to the LDP's long hold on power.

In power, the LDP gradually evolved mechanisms by which it came to dominate the life of the country. The government's tight control, up to the 1960s at least, of investment funds for industry, turned the party into the conduit for life-or-death funds to private business in every sector. In return, the LDP expected lavish monetary contributions, and these were duly budgeted for in the accounts of every large firm.

As the grease in the wheels between the mandarins and the businessmen and farmers who produced the goods, the politicians of the LDP demanded they be squared at very stage. LDP committees on every industrial sector mirrored the work of similar bodies in the *Keidanren* and the Diet, preparing the way for the awarding of licences and the framing of legislation. When, in the early 1980s, Japan conceded a lowering of import tariffs on chocolate and biscuits, officials described it as an important power concession by one of the LDP's 'party barons', Shintaro Abe, because he was chairman of the LDP committee on confectionery. Yasuhiro Nakasone (in power from 1982 to 1987) was the heir to a large forestry business north of Tokyo. Noboru Takeshita (prime minister in 1987–88), comes from a powerful family of *sake*-distillers, and became a key patron of the construction industry. Such personal business interests of the nation's political leaders have been a major factor in deciding the pace of Japan's concessions in its programme of opening its domestic market to the outside world.

The LDP's power to award lucrative contracts for industrial development, as well as road and rail networks, in the backward countryside made Japan into a leading exemplar of 'pork-barrel' politics. The construction industry fed blatantly out of the party's hand, evolving an elaborate cartel (known as the *dango* or 'group accord' system) to parcel out public contracts among selected firms in disregard of any rules on open competition. The party afforded special protection, too, to the farmers, small businessmen and shopkeepers, the least efficient parts of the economy. Their special interests were looked after by a policy of blocking rice imports, limiting the building of large supermarkets, and similar exercises in regulatory control. The tax regime was consciously designed to benefit other core LDP support groups, such as doctors, to the disadvantage of the swelling ranks of middle income factory and office workers.

The long years of one-party rule led by degrees to a close identity between LDP decisions and government ones. The concept of a 'loyal opposition' has only recently been debated at all. The LDP never faced an opposition 'front bench'; the Socialist Party never even nominated spokesmen on particular subjects. The Japanese state has never set aside public funds to support the staff and research needs of the constitutional opposition, as is now the case in Britain. For most of the LDP's time in power it so dominated the Diet that the party could not only count on a majority in the full House of Representatives, but also control every policy committee in parliament.

The national power monopoly came to be abused so as to perpetuate itself through iniquities in the voting system. A drastic demographic shift from countryside to urban areas led to a grossly unfair distribution of parliamentary seats in constituencies across the country. They became skewed sharply in favour of the countryside, where the LDP's support has been highest. By the 1980s 'rural voters', broadly defined, made up only about one fifth of the population, but they alone determined the election of roughly a third of all the seats in the House of Representatives.

In several cases the imbalance between the value of rural and metropolitan votes reached a ratio of four to one or even more. Despite several appeals to Japan's Supreme Court there was no legal remedy. The LDP's long reign led, in effect, to a confusion between its governmental authority and that of the supposedly non-partisan state. No independent boundary commission could ever be set up under the LDP, and no general redrawing of the boundaries was ever seriously attempted until they were voted out of power.

In this context the other political parties came to represent either die-hard opposition for its own sake – as was often the case with the JSP – or else limited sectoral interests. Among the other long-lived opposition groups, the Democratic Socialists (formed in 1959 as a right-wing splinter group from the Socialists) are an alternative business voice; the *Komeito* or 'Clean Government' party is allied to the *Soka Gakkai* neo-Buddhist movement and represents mainly under-privileged urban workers; and the Japan Communist Party attracts a mixture of the urban working class and left wing intellectual vote.

The opposition parties, curiously, behaved as if they accepted the hierarchy in which they were destined to play a minor role. The explanation lies in the peculiar dynamics of Japanese group competition. Despite the LDP's commanding strength in the Diet, the other parties could often wring limited concessions from the ruling party on policy matters by applying moral pressure. They frequently used the threat of a joint boycott of Diet business (an affront to the prized idea of consensus), or else offered tactical deals. The opposition parties were never entirely devoid of leverage of their own, as they have always been fairly well represented in the local tier of government, and indeed ran the local administrations in Tokyo, Osaka and other big cities for much of the 1960s and 1970s. In other words, the opposition parties were offered a secure place – albeit a subordinate one – in the order of things.

The Japanese media played an important role, too, in sustaining the LDP in power. The means by which it did so have little in common with the pattern in Britain, where media tycoons – mostly backers of the Conservative party – own and control the great majority of newspapers. In Japan the main newspapers are self-owned, and their publishers and editors pride themselves that theirs are products with wide appeal, and very little, if any, political 'colour'. All of them, especially, the most influential, the *Asahi Shimbun*, have regularly criticised aspects of the LDP's conduct of affairs. Yet the media were drawn into being an integral and key part of Japan's conservative, LDP-dominated Establishment.

During the Second World War the state-controlled press had been organised into *kisha* clubs (reporters clubs) to receive and dispense the information its members received from official channels. It was a system of complete censorship. After 1945 the Newspaper Publishers and Editors Association built on this framework, this time in the name of press freedom, supervising the growth of vast network of many hundreds of such *kisha* clubs, with premises inside government ministries in Tokyo and town halls across the country.

The reporters clubs' stated purpose was 'the social benefit' of their members. But, in keeping with the habits of secrecy and organised privilege in other fields of Japanese life, in reality the clubs took over, as far as they could, the exclusive right to report information from their own 'patch'. They even took over from the official press officers the responsibility for arranging news conferences. Membership of the clubs was jealously reserved for the leading media organisations. With membership went close access to powerful politicians and officials, which was explicitly closed to freelance journalists, as well as those from magazines and 'non-Establishment' journals, and members of the foreign press. The policy of excluding foreigners has only gradually been relaxed, under pressure from foreign media organisations, starting with the more internationally-minded *kisha* clubs such as that covering the Foreign Ministry.

The effect is widespread self-censorship on the part of the Japanese news media. Political figures have been able to take privileged journalists into their confidence, feeding them information on a 'background' basis and demanding in return the suppression of embarrassing facts. No-one from outside the club – not even another journalist from one of the newspapers represented – has the right to be there. Thus a clannish sense of loyalty to a closed group was fostered among the kisha clubs and their 'licensed' journalists whose job was to report almost 24 hours a day on the prime minister and other top figures.

Overt patronage by politicians has allowed dozens of journalists to enter the Diet as LDP members themselves, working loyally in the faction of their own particular sponsor. And senior journalists are regularly recruited into government commissions and think-tanks, making the media an organic part of the governmental process rather than an independent purveyor of it.

Thanks to this near identity of interests between reporters and public figures, the mainstream press has failed to play a consistent role in exposing incompetence or wrong-doing in public life. Often the organised reporters clubs proved an obstacle to public exposure, instead of being its agent. When the Minamata mercury poisoning tragedy came to light in the 1950s, the mainstream economic reporters succumbed to the built-in pressures to avoid writing articles that would damage the interest of industrial concerns, in this case the chemical firm Chisso. Only some years later did a new breed of general reporters (from the newspapers' *shakai-bu* or 'social affairs sections') report the full scale of the disaster.

In the political field the same pattern obtained. It was an investigation in the monthly magazine *Bungei Shunju* which in 1974 first exposed the seamy financial empire behind the then prime minister, Kakuei Tanaka. The mainstream press studiously ignored the scandal, until articles on the same theme in the American press made it 'politically correct' for responsible Japanese media to cover it too. There is evidence that Mr Tanaka had earlier warned Japanese political 'lobby' correspondents that he would use his influence to make sure they lost their jobs should they write ill of him. Later, when Mr Tanaka was recuperating from a stroke at his Tokyo home, numerous elite political journalists were among the hundreds of well-wishers invited in to pay their respects.

The systematic collusion between the press and the public figures whom it followed caused discomfort to many Japanese journalists. But it was not until after the LDP was thrown into opposition that strong pressure built up within the press to loosen its close ties with those in power and seek more independence. The press has itself become the object of harsh public criticism for its past habit of deference to vested interests.

The LDP's decline was not sudden but progressive, from the mid-1970s on. The main symptoms were uncontrollable financial scandals, and the mass disaffection of voters as the party became more and more identified with unpopular vested interests. The twin scandals surrounding Kakuei Tanaka (prime minister from 1972 to 1974) – the first in 1974 over the disclosure of vast personal 'slush funds' and the second the Lockheed bribery scandal of 1976 – brought the first signs of real decay. A small group of younger LDP Dietmen defected from the party to form the so-called New Liberal Club. In the ensuing 1976 election the LDP failed to win an outright majority alone, but was able to put a majority together thanks to an alliance with the would-be rebels, who later re-joined the Liberal Democrats.

The so-called Recruit ('shares-for-favours') scandal, which broke out in 1989, exposed cynical manipulation of the stock market, and corrupt patronage on the part of senior ministers in the (1982–87) government of Yasuhiro Nakasone. That year public disillusionment with the LDP led to the near-collapse of its support, even in rural areas, in regular elections for half the seats in the House of Councillors. New splinter parties standing up for the interests of tax-payers and *salariimen* (white-collar workers) made a surprisingly strong showing, as did the Socialists, led by a woman, Takako Doi. The LDP's resulting loss of overall control of the Upper House was an embarrassment, but not crippling. But more damning exposures of corruption were to follow, this time involving an aged but powerful *kuromaku* (puppeteer) in the party, Shin Kanemaru, which symptomised the party's inability to reform itself. The economic recession which began in 1991 soured the public mood, as did the LDP's foot-dragging in tackling long overdue reforms in politics, trade liberalisation and the tax system. The party's punishment was defeat (it won 227 seats, 30 short of an overall majority) in the July 1993 election.

Characteristics of Contemporary Political Life in Japan

On the outside, the post-war Japanese political system looks remarkably similar to the British one. Both countries have a parliamentary system, with a cabinet whose members are usually appointed from the legislature, and a constitutional monarch as a state figurehead. But when one examines the way in which politically important decisions are taken, any close comparison fails.

In the United Kingdom, if one wished to show an interested visitor something to convey the essence of the political system, one might choose the 'Queen's speech', which is written by the prime minister and sets out the government's legislative programme for the parliamentary session, generally giving clear signals as to the government's plans.

By contrast the casual visitor to Japan, at least up to the very recent past, would have learned little of interest from business in the Diet. Policy speeches by the prime minister were extremely vague about future plans, relying on hazy generalisations about working, for example, to make Japan 'a nation of welfare and cultural vitality', and making only the most general references about, say, continuing the (very slow) privatisation programme begun in the 1980s. Important announcements by the prime minister or his chief spokesmen are made, more often than not, outside the Diet, as separate, televised events.

The great bulk of parliamentary business takes place anyway in committees. The debating is generally lacklustre and the results of voting have for the past four decades been tediously predictable, notably the no-confidence motions which brought down the governments of Masaru Ohira in 1980 and Kiichi Miyazawa in 1993. But these rebellions were not primarily parliamentary occasions: they were rather factional revolts against the current party leadership, not battles over principles or policies.

For an insight into how things really work, the visitor ought rather to be taken behind the scenes to the *ryotei*, the classy restaurants in the Akasaka area of Tokyo, near the Diet, where the political bosses cement the loyalty of their factional supporters, or mould deals with their rivals or even the opposition in such a way that open confrontations are unnecessary.

It would also be instructive to attend one of the fund-raising parties regularly thrown by politicians, especially those of the Liberal Democratic Party. The visitor would there see the stock in-trade of Japanese politics in action: envelopes with money contributions being handed over by many hundreds of guests, much bowing and exchanging of name-cards (but little or no substantial exchange of views), and formulaic speeches intended to boost the fortunes of the host within his faction or party. There the visitor would perceive what is the vital ingredient of Japanese politics – personal bonds of loyalty between the politician (addressed as *sensei* or 'teacher') and the members of his personal support group, known as the *koenkai*.

As the British scholar Ronald Dore has argued, modern political attitudes in the West have been strongly influenced by the Christian concept of original sin. Consciously or not, the idea lies behind the restless demand for proof of moral integrity among politicians, and numerous forced resignations, such as that of David Mellor in 1992 and Timothy Yeo in 1994. The same motivation leads to a confrontational pattern of relations between the government on one hand and both the opposition and the press on the other. Japan, Professor Dore says, is in a wholly different tradition. That is the neo-Confucian tradition of 'original virtue' on the part of the ruler. That concept was invoked and refined during the long Tokugawa era to reinforce respect for authority. And although Japan has gone through many changes since, strong traces of the underlying attitudes of deference survive. It is easy to see how one tradition helped to produce the institution of Prime Minister's Question Time in the House of Commons, and the other the politics of the puppeteer and the kingmaker.

One can summarise the functions of the main features of Japanese political life as follows:

Leadership: the prime minister (until now always the leader of the LDP) is expected to lead not from the front, but 'from the middle'. Henry Kissinger was right when he wrote in his memoirs: 'High office in Japan does not entitle the holder to issue orders, it gives the privilege of taking the lead in persuasion.' The limited power of individual prime ministers was all too obvious in recent years, as they clearly lost the initiative to the collective power of the internal LDP party factions. Cabinet building became a more or less dreary question of rewarding loyalties, and maintaining the needed balance among the four or five important factions within the party. Under Japan's 'consensus politics' the room for manoeuvre of any leader must remain severely circumscribed.

In Britain a great deal more is normally expected of the individual who happens to be prime minister, and he (or she) has much more constitutional room to manoeuvre. It is impossible to imagine a single figure dominating Japan's political scene and agenda for a decade, as Mrs Thatcher did in Britain. Yet strong personalities have certainly played a part in Japan, too. Shigeru Yoshida's personal convictions set the country on its conservative but pro-western course after the war. And Yasuhiro Nakasone, adeptly appealing to the public over the heads of the faction chiefs, succeeded in moving Japan towards more self-reliance in defence as well as towards market reforms, using the expedient of government commissions which he brought into being himself. While in office, he used this technique to out-manoeuvre the other more or less degenerate factions, led among others by Noboru Takeshita and Kiichi Miyazawa, not only to stay in power but to set a policy course of his own. As for the first post-LDP prime minister, Morihiro Hosokawa, he has firmly presented his own ideas for sweeping policy changes as well as fundamental electoral reform. In the face of strong resistance from some of his own allies, his path may be a steep one. But the collapse of the previous LDP gerontocracy may bode well for the appearance of more 'men (or women) of ideas' as leaders of Japan in future.

Factions and parties: The tradition of separate factions *(habatsu)* coalescing around several strong figures in particular parties can be expected to endure, at least in some form. The LDP factions were, as long ago as the 1970s, widely condemned as the root of all evil – that is, various forms of association such as 'policy study groups' – and continued to flourish, both for cultural reasons (the Japanese propensity to form closely-bound groups) and for financial ones (the factions were the conduit for collecting vast sums in political funds).

The reform of Japan's electoral system which has lately been proposed could dent the internal party faction system badly. In place of multi-member constituencies usually electing a total of three to five members of the Diet, the key Lower House would be elected by a combination of first-past-the-post and proportional representation. This could remove an important *raison d'etre* of party factions, which has been to win as many seats as possible within a system where in practice up to three different LDP candidates could be elected in a single constituency.

It could be, though, that in place of party factions, Japanese politics is now destined to go on being characterised by a myriad different political parties, also founded around more or less magnetic political figures. If so, the business of forming coalition governments will indeed be confusing, and the demerits of the faction system may be transferred to the national, party political stage. There is no tradition of strong but constitutional leadership to save Japan from such a prospect. Yet the country and its people stand to gain enormously from the current shake-up, if they can find a new political pattern of behaviour which allows the society to mature without violent ructions, while maintaining Japan's economic strength.

The positive lessons of Japan's experience in terms of maintaining social order, carrying out large-scale social engineering, and husbanding a nation's financial and industrial resources, are plain to see. The warning lessons from a society which cedes arbitrary power to an unaccountable, technocratic elite, and fails to keep adequate checks on its political masters, are equally transparent.

5

Government and Administration under Liberal Democrat Rule

Katsuya Hirose

For the thirty-eight years between 1955 and 1993, the Liberal Democratic Party (LDP) was the governing party of Japan. For most of the post-war period the LDP was regarded as the natural party of government. A parallel factor for stability has been Japan's bureaucracy, which has played a great role in her government-led modernisation since the late nineteenth century, and which survived the radical post-war reform brought about by the American occupation force and continued to be a major player in Japan's political process. Its role in promoting Japan's rapid economic growth is regarded as critical by many observers.

What made it possible for the LDP to retain its rule for such a long period? Was the existence of the strong bureaucracy a condition for one party dominance? How did the long tenure of the LDP alter the relationship between governing party and the bureaucracy? This chapter tries to answer these questions by analysing three aspects of Japan's politics.

The first aspect is party politics. The conditions of party politics which enabled the LDP's long tenure will be explored. The role of the LDP in Japan's political system as a comprehensive interest mediator will be a central point. The second aspect is the history of bureaucracy in modern Japan. Its history made the bureaucracy a highly autonomous organisation. The social expectation of its active role is generally high. That made the bureaucracy an independent major actor in the political process in its own right.

The third aspect is the relationship between the natural ruling party and the bureaucracy. While its long tenure let the LDP attain a significant influence upon the bureaucracy, the latter used sophisticated skills to utilise the LDP's political position in order to strengthen its own role in promoting policy. This mutual penetration was an outcome of one party dominance, as well as a factor which made the one-party dominance stable and sustainable.

Party Political Aspects of One-Party Dominance

After its formation in 1955 the LDP retained its unity until 1993, although preceding conservative parties had been continuously splitting and merging from 1945 to 1955. Apart from the New Liberal Club, which was formed by a small number of young ex-LDP politicians in 1976 and remained small, there was no other major conservative political party other than the LDP in the period. On the other hand, opposition parties became more and more divided. In 1955, there were only two opposition parties: the main opposition Japan Socialist Party (JSP) and the small Communist Party of Japan (CPJ). In 1960 the Democratic Socialist Party (DSP) was formed by politicians split from the JSP, then in 1964 the Clean Government Party (*Komeito*) was established. Thus, the LDP's dominance was based on the combination of a united conservative camp and a divided progressive camp.

Generally speaking, political institutions in post-war Japan have tended to promote a multi-party system. Elections for the House of Representative are in multi-member constituencies (the so-called medium-sized constituency system). One constituency returns three to five members while each voter can cast only one vote.[1] As one seat in a five-member constituency can be won by much less than 20 per cent of all the votes cast, a new small political party has a good chance of winning a significant number of seats. So the electoral system tends to promote a multi-party rather than a two-party system. This institutional bias made the party fragmentation of the opposition camp possible. But in spite of the institutional setting, and despite a fierce internal power struggle which sometimes put the party on the brink of breakup, the LDP managed to keep its unity until 1993. Why did it form a single party in the first place and how did it avoid major splits for as long as thirty-eight years?

At first, the Cold War played a critical role. Without it the LDP might not have been formed at all. During the early 1950s the basic direction of Japan's foreign policy was on the agenda. The conservative parties argued that Japan should be an ally of America and have its own defence forces, while the JSP insisted that Japan should be a neutral state without an army. Because support for the JSP was continuously growing at that time, conservative politicians became anxious about the possibility of a JSP government. If the conservative camp continued to be divided, they feared the JSP would become the largest party. Rival conservative politicians had a common anti-communist ideology, and decided to form a unified large conservative party to prevent the JSP becoming the ruling party in the foreseeable future. After the formation of the LDP, support for the JSP continued to grow until the early 1960s.

Thus the LDP's formation and its success in avoiding an early break-up were results of the Cold War.

Secondly, the nature of conservative politicians should be examined. Judging from their articulated policy preferences, there has been variation in the beliefs of LDP politicians. Some advocated the preservation of traditional social authority and order; others supported rapid industrialisation and economic growth at the cost of destruction of traditional rural communities. If most of them had been ideologically rigorous, the LDP would have soon split into a conservative and a liberal party. But in reality most of them were practical rather than ideological politicians. During the decade of continuous re-alignment of conservative parties, their political groupings tended to be based not on political ideology but on personal trust or rivalry. For example, a small party called the National Co-operation Party (*Kokumin-kyodo-to*) had two future LDP prime ministers, Takeo Miki and Yasuhiro Nakasone, among its members. The former represented the leftmost part of the LDP, while the latter represented the rightmost part, showing what a small role political ideology played in organising conservative political parties. Anti-communism was one of the few things they had in common, and in the face of the practical objective of preventing the neutralist JSP becoming the ruling party, ideological differences within the conservative camp seemed not to be a serious problem to conservative politicians.

Stability of one-party dominance

After its formation, the LDP kept united for thirty-eight years. How was this possible for a party consisting of a broad range of politicians whose policies and personal preferences were quite different?

One factor was the internal organisation of the party. Control by the central party leadership on each MP is very weak. Because all but one constituency return more than two members of the House of Representatives, the LDP stands more than one candidate in almost all constituencies. Naturally each LDP candidate organises their own supporters virtually independently of the party organisation, and this personally organised supporters group plays a central role in the election campaign. Few if any LDP candidates are dependent on formal party organisation to win their seats. In fact most of the local LDP organisations were confederations of personal supporters groups. Sometimes those candidates who could not get the LDP's recognition nevertheless win an election and only later become parliamentary members of the party. Given this condition, the authority of the party central organisation is very limited and each member has great freedom to express and pursue policy preferences which may be inconsistent with the official party line.

Internal opposition can exist within the LDP, and rebels against the party leadership can remain in the party.

Another point concerns the established structure of political careers in the LDP. As a governing party for so long, the LDP developed a pattern of promotion for parliamentarians, covering key posts in both government and party, which combined seniority and a factional quota. Most LDP members of parliament belong to a faction within the party. In essence the faction is an organisation for personnel matters: it helps a politician become elected as an MP, it recommends some of its members for appointment as cabinet ministers, and fights for its leader to be prime minister. In order to be appointed to a key position in the government or party, an MP should have some experience proper for the position – 'experience' being measured by how often the member was re-elected. Three or four successful re-elections were, for example, required to be a parliamentary vice-minister, and at least six to become a cabinet minister. A prime minister would usually have been re-elected ten times. There were some exceptions, but generally these unwritten rules were applied quite rigidly.

Each faction had its quota of cabinet posts according to its size and its relationship with the party leader. When a cabinet was organised, each faction recommended some of its qualified members as cabinet ministers. Being a member of a strong faction gave a good chance of re-election because of the faction's political resources which could be utilised in the election campaign, and gave a good chance of promotion because of its large quota of key posts. At the same time, most qualified MPs were appointed cabinet ministers at least once in their careers. The rigid application of the seniority rule gave politicians an incentive to serve for a long time as LDP members of parliament.

The third reason was that major social and economic breaks did not become major party political issues. Tensions between modern and traditional industry, and between employers and employees, were dealt with in a non-political way. Issues of employment and wages were dealt with by corporate unions and the spring campaign of wage negotiation. Most of the trade unions are organised by corporation, not by type of job. Wages and security of employment are usually negotiated in a decentralised manner at corporate level. Negotiations take place roughly at the same time each spring across the nation. The standardised result, secured simultaneously, is to some extent similar to the politicised national negotiation in corporatist states. But the negotiation at each corporation/union is non-political in essence. The government avoids involvement in industrial relations, and no attempt at party political mobilisation of the tension between the employer and the employee was successful.

The split between the growing advanced industrial sectors and the ones lagging were not dealt with in a co-ordinated way. There was no exclusive representation of a particular industrial sector's interests by a single political party. Both the LDP and the opposition parties tried to represent interests of any vulnerable sector, competing with each other to secure positive government action to protect them. In such competition the governing party has great advantages, and as a result the LDP became a comprehensive mediator of virtually every industrial sector's interests. In this way, party politics in post-war Japan had very little to do with major social and economic issues. And these major issues did not become a serious contributing factor to the split of the LDP.

The final, related point, is that the LDP is a group of politicians who act as mediators of various kinds of particular interests. People support these politicians not because of their political principles but because of their competence to deliver benefits from the government. The ruling position is more significant than the party line. Splitting the party and risking its ruling position is the last thing LDP politicians wanted. Conflicts between incompatible interests were settled within the party preferably.

Dispersed policy activities within the LDP

The LDP is not an organised mass party, but very much a parliamentary party. Within it, MPs are organised in two ways. One relates to policy, the other to personal power struggles. Hence most LDP MPs are specialised in one or a few policy areas, and also belong to a faction.

Policy activities of the LDP are led by politicians who specialise in particular areas. The LDP's Policy Research Council exists to formulate policy. The Council is divided into seventeen divisions and numerous research commissions and special committees. The divisions are organised along government ministries and Parliamentary standing committees. Each MP belongs to one or a few divisions and one parliamentary standing committee normally covering the same policy area. They usually select that policy area according to the interests of their supporters and constituency. An MP tends to be active in that specialised policy area for their whole political career. Those politicians acquire detailed knowledge and build up contacts in the field, so becoming key people in the policy area and a key communications channel between the government ministry and those with interests in the field. They are called *Zoku-Giin*, which literally means 'tribe politicians'. Each policy area has its tribe politicians who are key members of the policy community.

Most of the organised socio-economic interests are covered by tribes, with the exception of the trade unions. As a whole, the LDP was able to mediate between virtually all socio-economic interests, so the party could win political support from a broad range of social and economic sectors. However, the interests mediated by LDP tribes are limited to those politically well-organised with plenty of resources. Generally speaking, the producers or suppliers are politically well-organised and regularly mobilised, while the consumers or minority groups are rarely well-organised and their political mobilisation is very volatile. As a result the former's interests were well represented by the LDP, while the latter's interests were not well represented by the party.[2]

Factional dynamics and pseudo change of government

Viewing the LDP's internal power struggle, the party is an alliance of several internal political factions. The selection of the LDP's leader is the outcome of competition among internal factions. At first factions were very informal and rather *ad hoc* groupings of personal supporters of individual leading politicians. Personalities of leaders rather than their political views or policy preferences played a central role in organising the factions. Eventually, factions became well organised and started to play pseudo-formal functions in the party. The distribution of key posts in government and party by quota among factions is one of the most important aspect of factional politics. In short, elections and personnel matters were dealt with by factions, while the policy matters were dealt with by tribes.

As a result, affiliation to a faction has been very important for an LDP politician's career. As outlined above, support from the faction is significant in their election campaign, political promotion is largely determined by the faction, and if they want to be prime minister, they should be a capable factional politician and succeed the leadership of the faction. So, most LDP MPs belong to factions and loyalty to the faction is strong.

Power struggles among factions constantly revitalised the LDP. There has always been competition, explicit or latent, among faction leaders who want to replace the prime minister. Hence whenever a political crisis emerged, there was always an alternative prime minister prepared within the party. When a prime minister had strong public support, other leading politicians within the party usually behaved loyally to the prime minister and his faction. But once his public support faded away, other factions started to challenge the party leader, because they could legitimise their leadership challenge as necessary means to revitalise the party and regain popular support. They would say that a prime minister should be sacrificed to maintain the LDP's ruling position. As the organisational bases for the challenge were always prepared as factions, intra-party political mobilisation could be very quick and heated. As a result, intra-party factional dynamics played a great role in the changing of prime ministers. For example, from 1972 to 1982 when inter-factional competition was particularly fierce, prime ministers were replaced every two years. Candidates for the next prime minister would articulate themselves as different and appealing new leaders in order to win the leadership competition. They would have a new style of leadership and new preferences in policies.

Thus, in spite of the continuity of the LDP's ruling position, there was frequent renewal of prime ministers and government policies. Facing very strong criticism from the public or from influential interest groups, the change of leadership within the LDP was an effective way to overcome political crisis. In 1960, facing a political crisis of large scale popular protest against the revision of the Japan-US Security Treaty, the then prime minister Nobusuke Kishi, who handled ideologically motivated policy with a confrontational leadership style, was replaced by Hayato Ikeda who concentrated on economic development policy with a soft style of leadership. In 1974, when prime minister Kakuei Tanaka was strongly criticised for his corrupt handling of money, he was replaced by Takeo Miki, who was renowned for being scrupulously clean on money politics. These replacements of prime ministers and their policies were examples of the LDP successfully overcoming political crises.

The renewal could be cosmetic. But continuity of policy can be better than unnecessarily frequent fundamental change in policies which often accompany the adversarial two-party system. And 'cosmetic' changes in policies were enough to provide the chance of the practical modification of existing policies to reflect real needs, and so give the LDP flexibility in its direction.

Recently, factions came to play some role in policy-related activities. Factional leaders had strong control over the faction's members through their dependence on the groups for political funding in election campaigns. This control came to be used during the 1980s to suppress internal rebels against some official party policies. Within the LDP there are many groups representing a variety of socio-economic interests. So internal splits over policy were quite usual. Younger, inexperienced politicians whose electoral basis was weak and thus had to be thoroughly loyal to supporters would rebel against party policy which sacrificed their supporters' interests. On the other hand, experienced strong politicians like leaders of factions tended to have strong electoral bases and felt free to behave against particular interests. Their senior positions required them to behave like national leaders rather than representatives of particular interests.

As a result, policy formation within the LDP often became a process of persuasion of young politicians by senior ones. Because a faction usually consists of many tribes, the representatives of any particular interest were rarely a majority within a faction – so the suppression of rebels representing particular interests could be effective and the LDP could co-ordinate, to some extent, conflicting interests. This was one reason the LDP was able to prevent uncontrolled expansion in public spending despite its position as a comprehensive mediator.[3]

Money, politics and corruption

There were negative aspects accompanying the LDP's self renewal. The most severely criticised, and most incurable, was political corruption. Repeated scandals about funding provoked many political crises and brought down many prime ministers. But no effective measures were adopted to prevent such scandals during the thirty-eight years of LDP rule.

One reason for this was the way the problem was built into the political structure. With the medium-sized constituency system, each individual LDP politician needs a large political fund to cultivate the constituency and organise personal supporters' groups. A large part of the fund is supplied by the candidate's faction, and so faction leaders need huge sums of money to maintain faction members. Leading politicians needed to be capable of fundraising, and some did so in illegal ways.

Recurrent scandals did not lead directly to the ending of the LDP's dominance. As some empirical research showed opposition parties succeeded in developing a role as mediator,[4] although they had a weaker influence on government policy than the LDP. And so the same system of political corruption existed for the opposition parties and some opposition politicians were prosecuted. Voters were not therefore motivated to cast votes of disapproval. The result of recurring scandal was not the collapse of LDP dominance but the decline of voters' trust in politics.

Japan's Bureaucracy and the Dominant Party

After the change of polity in 1868 a centralised national government was established which led the country's rapid modernisation. A variety of western systems – government, justice, education, industry, and so on – was imported. The bureaucracy, or civil service, was among these, and it proved to be one of the most important agencies of Japan's modernisation. A meritocratic system was adopted before the turn of the century. Appointment by examination began in 1888, then in 1894 the appointment of higher civil servants was limited to examination.

Most of the dominant group in the higher civil service were graduates of the Tokyo Imperial University who studied German public law.[5]

During the late nineteenth and early twentieth century, there was confrontation between the governing elites who promoted state-led modernisation and political parties who sought to protect social interests threatened by this. At the time the government was not selected by parliament, and the government tried to prevent party political penetration into the bureaucracy by adopting a rigid meritocratic system. Political appointment was rejected. After 1907 almost all vice-ministers were career civil servants who had passed an examination: only one person in the ministry, the minister, had a political background. After 1912, many cabinet ministers were appointed from former vice-ministers: by this time, the meritocratic bureaucracy had risen above party politics but at the same time had become directly involved in it. In short, the bureaucracy was both highly autonomous and very political.

During the 1920s, party politics developed to form cabinets based on the majority party in parliament. There were two major parties and the government often changed. The bureaucracy could no longer rise above the growing articulation of a variety of social and economic interests which lay behind the development of party politics. Higher civil servants formed two groups supporting each of the major parties. When a party gained power, supporters of the other party were temporarily suspended from their jobs. When the other party came back to power, the higher ranking officers were in turn replaced by those who had been suspended. Although the merit system was retained, party politicisation was extremely developed among career civil servants. The autonomy of the bureaucracy was weakened.

However, the dominance of party politics was short-lived. In the 1930s party politics collapsed because it was unable to overcome either the economic crisis or political corruption. The military and the bureaucracy became the major agents for renewal. Democratic elements of the 1920s system were replaced by a corporatism based on unelected elites. But because of the fragmented nature of the governmental system, as I shall explain, the government became a kind of totalitarian state with no overall leadership. During this period the bureaucracy regained its autonomy from party politics: the status of the higher civil servant was regulated administratively and temporary suspension eliminated.

One distinguishing characteristic of Japanese bureaucracy was its parochial sectionalism. A higher civil servant was appointed to one ministry for which he would have worked throughout his career with perhaps some exception of short-term secondment. Sometimes all civil servants in a ministry, from the minister down to fresh graduates, were life-long members of the ministry. The ministry became regarded as a fate-sharing body by its members. Sectionalism developed. Critics alleged sectional interests came before the national interest. Strong political leadership was required to overcome the fragmentation, but under the Meiji Constitution the prime minister's formal authority was very weak. His control over cabinet ministers was limited, and he had no formal control over the military. While the political system helped each ministry maintain its autonomy, the ministries had to act politically because there were no political actors to lead but themselves. The autonomous and political bureaucracy was in part a product of the fragmented constitutional structure of pre-war Japan.

Bureaucracy in post-war Japan

After 1945 American occupation forces carried out a variety of institutional reforms including the dismantling of the military, the dissolution of the *Zaibatsu* and the purge of war-time political leaders from public office. The bureaucracy experienced limited change and survived virtually intact. The basic intention of reform was the establishment of an efficient, politically neutral civil service. Political appointment was restricted, and the merit system upheld. These measures made possible the survival of the bureaucracy's autonomy.

The fragmentation of the government structure was overcome, at least at the constitutional level. Under the current Japanese constitution, introduced in 1947, parliament is the highest organ of state power and the prime minister who is appointed by parliament has the authority to appoint and remove cabinet ministers. This gives a constitutional base for the prime minister's leadership over the government ministries.

The most important task facing the government of post-war Japan was economic reconstruction. At the early stage, the process was based on very limited resources: effective targeting was necessary. The bureaucracy was at the very centre of the process. It allocated natural resources, foreign currency – even information about the world economic situation – according to its economic reconstruction plans. Private businesses, dependent on government-controlled resources, had no alternative but to follow the bureaucracy's lead: thus the superiority of bureaucracy over the private sector was established. The image of Japan Inc or Chalmers Johnson's characterisation of Japan as a developmental state are based on this kind of role played by the bureaucracy.

But the situation has gradually changed. Rapid economic growth means most resources are no longer scarce. Private businesses can behave more independently from the control of the bureaucracy. In government for so long, the LDP came to have its own policy-making and channels for mediating interests. The superiority of the bureaucracy is no longer secure. The elitist model of Japan's government centred on the bureaucracy ceased to fit the reality of Japan's political economy by at least the latter half of the LDP's rule, from the middle 1970s to the early 1990s. Different views emerged on the role of the bureaucracy, to which I will turn in the next section.

The relationship between the bureaucracy and the LDP

From the early 1980s the commonly accepted theory that the bureaucracy superseded party politics came to be re-examined. Analyses of Japanese politics employing pluralist[6] and corporatist[7] models challenged the conventional image of Japan as a state controlled by the bureaucracy or by an elite coalition of the bureaucracy, business and conservative politicians.

Neither the pluralist nor neo-corporatist analyses deny the active involvement of the bureaucracy in the political process. At the centre of their argument was the role of politicians and the dispersed nature of the political process. Both neo-corporatists and pluralists pointed out that LDP politicians play a significant role in the political process in their own right. They are neither controlled by the bureaucracy nor its natural ally with basically the same values and priorities: they act independently and have a strong influence on outcomes. Unlike the corporatists, the pluralists see the process as competitive, believing that the autonomy of *Zoku-Giin* (tribes) is so strong that they have a counter-vailing power against the bureaucracy.

It is commonly pointed out that the political process of Japan is sectional. What differs is the interpretation of the dispersion of power that results. From the traditional elitist perspective, the sectionalism within Japanese government was seen as a cause of its lack of political responsibility and one of its most serious defects. In each sector the elite coalition controls public policy. But no-one controls the overall political process and no-one has responsibility for the outcome of policy as a whole. For the new type of elitist who stresses the dominant role of economic ministries in successful management of the national economy, the dispersion across various sectors is of little importance.

Pluralists see the dispersion of political power as an important element in the Japanese political process. This process usually involves many different organised interests. As a result, horizontal dispersion made the policy process plural. Pluralists also argue that Japan's political process is dispersed not only horizontally but vertically. In many cases, politicians whose specialisation was developed by the bureaucracy worked to prevent particular policy interests jeopardising the bureaucracy's objectives. During the process, the original policy prepared by the bureaucracy is often modified, but it is not a bad deal for the bureaucracy to sacrifice some of its autonomy in order to ease the difficult task of curbing the interests arising from various socio-economic sectors.

One-party dominance and the bureaucracy

This mutual penetration and interdependence is closely related to the long tenure of the LDP. As the natural ruling party, the LDP could be relatively free from political short-termism. Many senior leaders in the party, secure in a safe seat in their local constituency, tended to promote generally rational policy options rather than pursue goals related to the more immediate benefit of their re-election. In reality, the 'generally rational policy options' were those prepared and promoted by the bureaucracy. It could build close ties with senior LDP politicians without any fear of political revenge from the next governing party, as there was no expectation of change in the foreseeable future.

Finally, I would like to mention briefly the collapse of LDP rule in the summer of 1993. As I mentioned earlier, political corruption eroded people's trust in party politics. In spite of this, the LDP could not change its ways because money politics was entwined with its primary political activity, comprehensive interest mediation. The LDP's senior leaders were beneficiaries of existing political practices. At the same time, the effectiveness of the inter-dependent system of politicians and bureaucrats came to be doubted because it failed to handle some politically salient issues like international trade or military security.

Frustration accumulated towards the existing political system for its inability to remove corruption or to resolve pressing issues. But it was neither organised nor mobilised. While the younger politicians in the LDP, who tended to sit in marginal seats, were sensitive to the popular mood, the established leaders based in safe seats did not share the sense of crisis. When the gap between the two groups combined with factional political tactics of some groups within the party the party formally split. In short, the limitations of the system of bureaucratic and political inter-dependence marked the end of the long rule of the LDP.

Notes

1. There are a few exceptions. One constituency returns only one member, while another returns six, and a few return two.

2. This does not mean the LDP did not attempt to win political support from consumers or minority groups. During the 1980s, the LDP tried to mobilise urban white-collar *salariimen*, a group significant in size but politically ill-represented. But so far well organised and continuous party political mobilisation of this group has never been successful.

3. This kind of policy rationality of senior LDP politicians seemed to be a result of indoctrination by the bureaucracy. See 2 (2).

4. Michio Muramatsu, and Ellis, Kraus, 'The Dominant Party and Social

Coalitions in Japan', in T.J. Pempel (ed), *Uncommon Democracies: The One-Party Dominant Regimes*, Cornell University Press, Ithaca 1990.

5. The historical background of modern Japanese bureaucracy is based on Masaru, Nisio, *Gyoseigaku Nyuumon*, (Introduction to Public Administration), Yuhikaku, Tokyo 1993.

6. See for instance Michio Muramatsu, and Ellis, Kraus, 'The Conservative Policy Line and the Development of Patterned Pluralism' in K. Yamamura and Y. Yasuda (eds), *The Political Economy of Japan*, Stanford University Press, 1987; Inoguchi, Takashi 'The Political Economy of Conservative Resurgence under Recession: Public Policies and Political Support in Japan', in T.J. Pempel (ed) *op cit.*

7. See for example T.J. Pempel, T.J. and K. Tsunekawa, 'Corporatism without Labor', in Schmitter P.C. and G. Lehmbruch (eds) *Trends towards Corporatist Intermediation*, Sage, 1979.

6

Permanent Opposition: the Japanese Socialist Party

Ryoichi Nishida

The July 1993 general election ushered in a new era of Japanese politics by ending thirty-eight years of single party rule by the conservative Liberal Democratic Party (LDP). For months or years to come while the political map is being redrawn, there may be a period of instability and uncertainty. What is certain, though, is that the long-standing opposition parties will once again fail to capitalise on a golden opportunity.

The present turmoil was triggered not so much by the activities of those opposition parties, but by the rebellion of groups of LDP members in the more powerful House of Representatives, the Lower House. A no-confidence motion, carried because the rebels either voted for it or abstained, forced the then prime minister Kiichi Miyazawa to dissolve the House and call an election.

In the formation of the new coalition government, the newly established conservative parties took the lead. At this critical moment of political re-alignment the traditional opposition parties merely rallied around these major players. This latest election is only one more episode in the catalogue of failures of the Japanese opposition parties. So what is wrong with them?

The long-standing opposition parties span a very broad spectrum, ranging from the Japanese Communist Party on the far left, to the centre-right *Komeito* or Clean Government Party. In between are the Social Democratic Party of Japan (still known by its old name, the Japan Socialist Party or JSP), the centrist Japan Democratic Socialist Party and the smallest party, the United Social Democratic Party. The largest of all, in terms of the number of seats held in the Lower House, has been the JSP which has undoubtedly been the dominant opposition force since the immediate aftermath of the Second World War.

In 1945 all the non-Communist proletarian parties of the pre-war period agreed to amalgamate under the banner of the JSP. Naturally their various pre-war legacies, including ideological differences, died hard. As a result, the JSP's history has been riddled with internal struggles and bickering, which from time to time ended in divorce.

Only once did the JSP come to power. In the first Lower House election called under the new constitution in 1947, it was returned as the single largest party. It formed a coalition government with the conservative parties, and Tetsu Katayama, leader of the JSP's right wing, became the first ever socialist prime minister. But this 'cohabitation' regime was brought down just ten months later due to Katayama's weak leadership, and by the conservatives' dominance in the cabinet that enabled them to impose their own policies on the Socialists. The coalition was too short-lived for the JSP to consolidate its power base.

The JSP was dealt another serious blow in the 1949 election when it lost two-thirds of its seats in the Lower House. There followed fierce ideological disputes over whether to support the San Francisco Peace Treaty and the Japan-US Security Treaty, disputes that led to the first divorce. In 1951 the JSP split into two parties. The Left JSP objected to the Peace Treaty on the grounds that it would stand in the way of a formal end to the state of war with the Soviet Union; the Right JSP regarded the treaty as the only practical way of restoring Japan's sovereignty.

Within four years though, this split was reversed. In 1955 the Right JSP and Left JSP merged into one party. This re-unification spurred a similar move within the conservative arena. Two major conservative parties, the Liberal Party and the Democratic Party, joined forces and launched the Liberal Democratic Party (LDP). In the 1958 Lower House election, the LDP and the re-unified JSP together won 91 per cent of the popular vote and gained 97 per cent of the seats (the LDP had over 60 per cent of total seats, the JSP just over a third).

Dubbed the '55 structure' after the year of its birth, the political regime that emerged from this re-alignment of both right and left was expected, at least for a while, to pave the way for a two-party system. In the early 1960s one LDP magnate even predicted that socio-economic changes accelerated by rapid growth would erode support for the LDP and sweep the socialists to power within a decade.

Splits, the Cold War and Living in the Past

This prediction turned out to be badly wrong. The '55 structure' had produced a dominant party system. Far from building on the gains of its re-unification, the JSP yet again found itself engaged in bitter right/left ideological conflicts. Personal rivalries and inner-party power struggles further complicated the situation. The confrontation came to a head when the party congress, dominated by Marxists critical of the right-wing faction leader Suehiro Nishio, decided to refer his case to the party's disciplinary committee. Nishio, together with his followers, finally broke away from the JSP and founded a new party, the DSP. The JSP lost thirty-seven members in the Lower House.

Even trade unions could not escape the left/right confrontation. The JSP-affiliated General Council of Japanese Trade Unions (*Sohyo*) came under the control of left-wingers soon after its foundation. In 1954, an unhappy right wing-group bolted and formed a more moderate organisation, which was later renamed the Japan Confederation of Labour (*Domei*) and aligned with the DSP. From then on the *Sohyo* relied heavily on the unions in the public sector, while the *Domei* had the major private sector unions under its umbrella.

A further split, although a minor one, took place in 1977 when a small right-wing faction of the JSP formed the Social Citizen's League, the antecedent of the United Social Democratic Party. But what had the biggest impact on the JSP after the breakaway of the DSP was the foundation of the *Komeito*, the first religious-based party in Japan. Founded in 1964 by *Soka Gakkai*, the lay organisation of a sect of Japanese Buddhism, it appealed to the lower middle classes, factory workers and petty traders who were not enjoying the benefits of economic growth. No doubt the *Komeito* undercut more of the JSP's support than that of the LDP.

Of all the political developments in the three decades after 1955, perhaps nothing is more telling than the steady decline of the JSP, albeit with occasional ups and downs. Its share of the popular vote gradually declined from 32.9 per cent in the 1958 Lower House election to 20.7 per cent in 1976. In the 1989 election, the JSP gained only 17.2 per cent of the popular vote, little more than half its 1958 share. What was behind this decline?

The main factor in the erosion of the JSP's influence was its inability to overcome ideological and policy differences. The JSP inherited these rifts from the pre-war non-communist proletarian parties, along with other negative legacies mentioned earlier. For example, a small pre-war socialist group called the Labour Farmer Faction developed into one of the most seriously divisive elements, the Socialist Association.

The Socialist Association, formed in the early 1950s, fully committed itself to the Soviet line. It grew to be the most powerful stronghold of left-wingers in the JSP in the 1970s when Japanese society was changing very fast with its rapid economic growth. It influenced leadership elections and the formulation of the party programme at party congresses, as well as the selection of candidates for the Diet. Furthermore, it placed the JSP's youth organisation under its control, and at one point in the 1970s became virtually a party within a party.

Alarmed by signs that the Socialist Association was trying to take full control of the party out of their hands, the faction leaders in the Diet started fighting back. They successfully repulsed the offensive of the Socialist Association and contained its influence in 1977. The product of this fierce battle was the Socialist Citizen's League formed by right-wing reformist members disillusioned with the party. The main casualty was the JSP itself.

Another legacy of the past was the JSP's revolutionary Marxist tradition. Until recently it clung to the idea of peaceful revolution. It was quite natural for such a party to attach disproportionate importance to extra-parliamentary movements, such as the struggles against the Security Treaty and against nuclear power plants. In so doing, it has been rather half-hearted about winning elections, in stark contrast to the LDP which set election victory as its primary goal and used all necessary means to retain power – including corruption!

Unique Japanese circumstances during and after the Second World War enhanced this tendency. Under the nationalistic military regime during the war no resistance movement was organised by the leftists. After the war, some socialists were even regarded as militant nationalists and purged from public office by the American Occupation authorities. Moreover, post-war democracy and the Peace Constitution were prescribed by the Occupation authorities. The socialists went back to pursuing their dream of peaceful revolution.

The 1950s and 60s were characterised by ideological polarisation. The issues at stake were Japan's re-armament, constitutional reform, and revision of the Japan-US Security Treaty, a treaty which would eventually incorporate Japan more firmly into a military alliance with the United States. The JSP, backed up by mass movements including the university students' demonstrations flaring up nationwide, confronted the LDP head-on. It fought fiercely against re-armament, reform of the constitution and the Security Treaty.

Even after struggles over these issues died down, the Cold War structure continued to polarise Japanese politics, with the LDP playing the role of defender of the Security Treaty and the American military presence in Japan, and with the JSP on the other side. With the party in this role the JSP left-wing's strength and its preference for mass action more or less continued, making it all the more difficult for the JSP to wake up to changing realities and to respond to them.

Although quite a few JSP politicians, needing to appeal to the voters, have recognised that something must be done, party officials and activists have not. Hence the JSP has often been the subject of quips like, 'the JSP goes left at conventions and right at elections', or, 'left at the centre (i.e. party headquarters), right in the constituency'. In fact unlike the British Labour Party, which jettisoned unpopular policies and militancy under Neil Kinnock, the JSP's limited attempts to make itself electable have been very slow.

Where does the JSP stand on major issues? In the draft platform entitled the '93 declaration', submitted to the party executive committee in May 1993 for approval later in the year, the JSP finally abandoned socialism altogether to create a Japanese version of western social democracy. It belatedly discarded the policy of regarding the Japanese self defence forces as unconstitutional, on condition that such forces were to be reduced. It grudgingly recognised the Japan-US security treaty until such time as a collective security regime based on the United Nations and a regional forum has been established. It accepted the nuclear power plants that provide 30 per cent of Japan's electricity supply as 'transitional energy'.

Although the draft platform recognised the 1965 normalisation treaty with South Korea, the JSP still embraces the pariah state of North Korea. Officially the JSP has not recognised the Japanese national flag or the national anthem, which are more or less accepted by the general public, on the grounds they were symbols of Japanese militarism. Regrettably the JSP's policy review was too little too late. It is true that this position represents the ideas and interests of a certain quarter of Japanese society, including JSP hard-liners. But far from captivating the majority of the population, it has alienated most voters.

The discussion held by senior party officials on the draft platform illustrates how hard it is for the JSP to change its unrealistic policies and party line. The right-wing reformist secretary-general Hirotaka Akamatsu reportedly pleaded with others to agree to the draft by saying, 'Once in government how can we appoint a Director General of the Defence Agency (Defence Minister) if we continue to regard self-defence forces as unconstitutional?'.

It might seem like a bad joke in a different organisation or country, but this is the situation in the JSP where leftist hard-liners always resist any practical reforms. In 1991 the JSP dropped 'Socialist' from its name in favour of 'Social Democratic' to improve its image. But this was only as far as the English name was concerned. Strangely enough, the party kept the old name in Japanese.

The situation in one northern prefecture in the 1970s and early 1980s demonstrates the JSP's failure to adapt to reality. This prefecture is divided into two Lower House constituencies, the total quorum of which is seven seats. At that time these two constituencies returned at best only one JSP candidate. But in their heyday, in the 1960s, the JSP had three Lower House members from these constituencies. All three were charismatic leaders of peasant movements. Those politicians left the scene as the peasant movement lost its momentum. And with its disappearance, the opposition parties lost their political base.

The last 40 years have seen rapid industrialisation, and with it fundamental changes in the occupational and industrial structures in Japan. There has been a shift from agricultural to factory workers; from manual to non-manual and professional work; from employment in manufacturing to employment in the service sector. As the economy has grown, workers' incomes have grown tremendously. The middle class has expanded and the majority of the population now have something to lose: houses, cars, property, savings, etc. They have become more and more conservative.

This affluent society had been achieved under the virtual one-party rule of the LDP. The LDP's consistent basic policy has been to stick to the Security Treaty. Here the interests of the US and the LDP converged. The LDP government had in a sense taken advantage of the US policy of building up and maintaining bulwarks against communism's expansion in Asia. It placed Japan under the US defence umbrella, enabling it to curb defence spending and pursue economic growth. The policy paid off. And as a result of economic expansion, LDP politicians could pour massive 'pork barrels' back into their constituencies and count on continuous donations from big business to keep up their costly election campaign machines which included support groups in the constituencies.

By contrast, the JSP continued to put forward policies anchored in the past. And, strange though it may seem, it failed to exploit various problems created by rapid economic growth. For example, it was very slow to set industrial pollution near the top of its agenda, and to translate into votes the anger of residents of affected areas. The apparent hesitancy of the JSP to address these issues could partly be attributed to the concern of its main backer, the trade unions, that investment in prevention of pollution or compensation for victims might weaken their companies' competitiveness and cause job losses. The JSP was also ineffective in absorbing the urban and rural population that had been left outside the creation of wealth. Some of these dissatisfied electors eventually turned to the *Komeito*.

Any observer of the JSP's performance would be tempted to ask its members if they were resigned to their fate. Through repeated failure and continuous decline in elections, a sort of defeatism seemed to have seeped into the hearts and minds of politicians and supporters alike. They sometimes gave the impression that they did not care about winning power. The only power they could get hold of was power within the party. Such a desperate situation, accompanied by ideological differences, further intensified infighting. That, in turn, further undermined the confidence of the voters. The party had alienated itself from real power. It was a vicious circle.

Another major reason for the JSP's failure to gain power is its overdependence on the trade unions. The relationship between the JSP and the *Sohyo*, and that of the DSP and its unions, was far stronger than the British Labour Party's union links. You could even say that in Japan these parties and their trade unions were two sides of the same coin. Trade unions were not only the single most important financial source for these parties, they also had a very big say in the selection of candidates.

The membership of the JSP, and that of the DSP for that matter, is very small compared to the large numbers of union members. During election campaigns, the unions mobilised into a strong campaign machine in the same manner as the LDP candidates' personal support groups. Union activists became campaign managers and 'foot soldiers'. They were dispatched to various parts of a constituency as canvassers or election rally organisers.

Trade unions usually imposed on member unions a quota of votes to be cast for their candidates. Member unions did likewise on their local chapters, and chapters did the same for each member. Union members were advised by the chapter head not only to vote for those candidates, but also to persuade relatives and friends to do the same. This method was especially effective in Japan, where wives and children tend to be influenced by the husband's voting intentions.

Trade unions were extremely caring. Support for the JSP politicians included their financial well-being. When the chairman of a JSP local association lost the prefectural councillor election and was deprived of his income (Japanese councillors are relatively well paid), the union chapter paid generous income support to this unlucky union baron turned politician. (This particular chairman, by the way, later became a Diet member). The JSP politicians, once elected, repaid such loyalty and support by putting the interests of the unions before almost everything else. Moreover, unions had been the sole recruiting ground for the JSP for a long time.

But only two and a half decades ago, things were totally different. Regarded as a party of the future by many political aspirants, the JSP could attract talented candidates from various walks of life. Take, for instance, the 1958 general election, the first one ever fought under the '55 structure'. Journalists, lawyers, local politicians, and even quite a few senior national government officials, ran as official JSP candidates and were elected. Union leaders accounted for less than 30 per cent of successful JSP candidates.

As the JSP gradually lost its popularity and credibility, the young, educated, politically ambitious Japanese turned their backs on the JSP and leaned more and more heavily toward the LDP. Consequently the JSP seats in the Diet were heavily dominated by former union barons. The trade union dominance in turn further distanced potential supporters from the JSP, especially in urban areas. Its share of the popular vote in Tokyo in the 1976 general election was reduced over the previous decade by approximately ten per cent, to merely 17.2 per cent.

On the whole, strong trade union links isolated the opposition parties, such as the JSP and the DSP, from the mainstream of Japanese society where, increasingly, people do not look to the unions to improve their lives. It was against this background that the LDP government, under prime minister Yasuhiro Nakasone, implemented the controversial privatisation and division of the Japanese National Railways as part of the general privatisation of public corporations in the 1980s.

It is ironic that one of the by-products of this privatisation scheme was to accelerate the long awaited re-alignment of trade unions. Faced with a crisis of diminishing power, the JSP-affiliated *Sohyo* and the DSP-affiliated *Domei* finally merged in 1989 to create an eight million strong national federation of trade unions called the Japanese Trade Union Confederation (*Rengo*). But the *Rengo* has not been so loyal to its masters. The parties' links with the trade unions have become looser and looser since then, to the point where the *Rengo* fielded its own candidates, or selectively supported candidates other than those of the JSP and the DSP. Observers see the historic defeat of the JSP in the 1993 election as partly due to this selective support. It seems that its over-dependence on trade unions backfired.

Chances were nevertheless given to the opposition parties. A rare opportunity came in 1989 when the JSP leapt forward by doubling its number of seats in the House of Councillors (Upper House) election, helping to deprive the LDP of its overall majority there. The JSP capitalised on nationwide resentment against the LDP government's introduction of VAT, and on the personal popularity of its first woman leader, Takako Doi. In the following Lower House election, where the pros and cons of VAT were at issue, the JSP once again dramatically increased its number of seats from 83 to 136. But this time it was at the expense of all the other opposition parties, not the LDP.

The euphoria was soon over. As the anti-government mood generated by the VAT debate subsided, so support for the JSP ebbed away. In the 1992 Upper House election (half its seats are elected every three years), the LDP resurged with a majority of half of all seats. The advance of the opposition parties, including the JSP, was dented. In the end the JSP's election gains turned out to be inflated by a huge, but temporary, protest vote.

Certainly, the JSP, as the second largest party, was the only force to be reckoned with when it came to taking over from the LDP. But the JSP proved to be incapable of winning elections and halting the LDP's continuation in government. After failing to be the main alternative party on its own, the only option left for the JSP should have been to rally behind it all the smaller opposition parties (apart from the Japan

Communist Party which is too far to the left to join the centre parties). That was the theory. In practice it didn't work. Post '55 structure' history shows us that things went the other way. Why was this? As always, ideological differences. The opposition parties could not clear that hurdle.

The various attempts there have been to forge an electoral pact, apart from limited seat pacts or tactical voting have failed, as have alliances of the opposition parties led by the JSP. In the aftermath of the LDP's astonishing defeat in the 1989 Upper House election, for the first time in decades a situation arose where the opposition parties acting in unity might have been able to force the government to resign by blocking all bills passed through the Lower House. But they lost the chance. When compromise was most badly needed, the JSP refused to concede over issues such as security and the military. Unlike the LDP, which, unbounded by a strong ideology, was able to respond flexibly to the demands of the times, the JSP was often dragged into an unrealistic stance by the strong resistance of a left wing obsessed with old dogma.

Therefore it was not so surprising that the trade unions were ahead of the trailing opposition parties when it came to the re-alignment of left and centre forces. As if the tail were wagging the dog, the newly formed national federation of trade unions, the *Rengo*, embarked upon an ambitious plan to unite the opposition parties under the leadership of the politically astute Akira Yamagishi. As the first step, the *Rengo* fielded its own candidates for the first time in the 1989 Upper House election. Its aim was to be a stronger magnet to bring together the JSP, the DSP, and the united Social Democratic Party by building a foothold in the Diet. Initially it was a great success. Out of twelve endorsed candidates, eleven were elected. Encouraged by this, the *Rengo* ran twenty-two candidates in the next Upper House election in 1992. But in contrast, the second attempt was a disaster in which all their candidates were defeated.

The reason why the *Rengo*'s scheme ended in tears shows clearly how difficult it is for the opposition parties to join forces. In the run-up to that election in 1992, the very controversial Peace Keeping Operation Co-operation Bill was passed after a long period of heated debate. This measure paved the way for the sending of self-defence forces to foreign soil as non-combatants for the first time. The LDP government, wanting to see Japan play a bigger role in proportion to its economic might, had tried very hard to push the bill through both houses. The JSP, regarding the self-defence forces as unconstitutional had fought strenuously against the passage of the bill, even resorting to delay tactics known as the 'ox walk'. The DSP, confronting the JSP fiercely, backed the bill.

The anger and frustration lingering on both sides opened old rifts

within otherwise more or less monolithic *Rengo* camps. In some constituencies, the former JSP-affiliated trade union group openly challenged the *Rengo* by running another candidate. Adding to its woes,
such a division among the opposition parties caused disillusionment
among the anti-LDP floating voters and alienated them from those
parties. From then on, the prospect of an alliance of opposition parties
rapidly receded.

Summing up, the traditional Japanese opposition parties, above all
the JSP, were simply unable to adapt to the rapidly changing political
and economic realities since the Second World War. The end result is
that the JSP has become a party of 'permanent opposition'. In retro-
spect, no single Japanese opposition party has been a genuine opposition
party in the sense of a government in waiting, a scenario seen in a two-
party system like the British one. Instead, as is often pointed out, in
Japan it was the power struggle among factions of the LDP that changed
governments, not a struggle between two parties vying for power. There
is some truth in such an argument. Under the '55 structure', whenever
there was a change of prime minister from one factional leader to
another, a slight shift in policies and leadership style accompanied it.
And that was the case until the 1970s.

Change from Within: The End of
One-Party Dominance?

The 'Japanese style' of change of government – the only remaining 'life
support system' for parliamentary democracy under a single dominant
party – altered in 1974 when Prime Minister, Kakuei Tanaka, leader of
the biggest faction of the LDP, was forced to resign after an exposure
of his corruption. Tanaka was arrested and indicted on charges of
involvement in an international bribery case, the Lockheed scandal in
1976.

He nevertheless continued to control his faction and desperately
expanded it in the hope that he might be able to get a 'not guilty'
verdict by maintaining his political influence in the LDP. No factional
leaders could become prime minister without his backing. He controlled
the party as leader of the dominant faction, and controlled the government through successive prime ministers and cabinet members who
were under his influence. By this strange mechanism called the 'structure
of dual power', he tried to perpetuate his power.

One of his potential successors who could wait no longer for the
hand-over of the Tanaka faction, mounted a palace coup in 1987 taking
over the almost intact faction. He became prime minister, but was forced
to resign due to suspicions of his involvement in another corruption
case, the Recruit scandal in 1988. Another traditional LDP politician

Shin Kanemaru, emerged as the influential elder figure in the faction, and then in the party as a whole. So the situation in which the predominant faction of the LDP kept the government indirectly under its control continued until the end of 1992, when the faction split in two. In such an extraordinary situation, many problems had piled up within the LDP and the government.

First, the government and the LDP had completely run out of steam and ideas, typical signs of the fatigue of a long reign. Graft and corruption scandals, as mentioned earlier, had repeatedly shaken the LDP. Election fraud, including vote-buying, had been rampant. To run as a conservative Diet member, especially to be successful, requires such an astronomical amount of money that few independent first-time candidates could afford the cost. The door to the Diet seemed to be open only to hereditary politicians, who account for 40 per cent of LDP members, or to high-ranking bureaucrats or union barons. It had become more and more difficult to infuse new blood into politics. The LDP politicians had heavily relied upon unaccountable bureaucrats who had virtually formulated policy.

The Japanese way of politics did not change so easily. But the end of the Cold War began to change the international landscape. Suddenly the old approach to economic growth under the US security umbrella became untenable. Japan's relationship with the US necessarily changed with the reduction of the American military presence in Asia, and with the escalation of the trade war between the two countries. Demands for a greater Japanese contribution to the international community grew among the major powers. Aspirations that Japan should assume a larger role on the world stage were also growing inside Japan. But the new world opened up by the end of the Cold War turned out to be an unstable, unknown territory. Traditional 'out-of-touch' politicians mired in graft and corruption, or precedent-blinded bureaucrats, can no longer live up to expectations. To cope with the new situation, Japan needs new directions and visions, a new political leadership based on genuine democracy, and, to say the least, clean elections. All these are vital if it is to be fully accepted by the international community.

The establishment of a healthy two-party system that ensures a sound change of government has been seen as the first viable step, with electoral reform a vital means of approaching that objective. The attempts at political reform have targeted the multi-member district system which has taken much of the blame for Japan's political ills. This system, whereby each party can field as many candidates as the quorum of the constituency, has encouraged futile and heated competition among LDP candidates and the conservative independents. It has brought huge election expenses, which candidates have tried to recover after being elected – fertile ground for graft and corruption. Under this system, elections have been fought not so much on the basis of party policies, as on the personalities of the candidates, and on 'pork barrels'.

In the run-up to the July 1993 election, several parties put forward various ideas for electoral reform. When inter-party and inner-party negotiations to overcome differences became deadlocked, the former prime minister Kiichi Miyazawa reneged on his promise to implement reform within the session of parliament. Seeing that the LDP leadership were not going to face up to their irresponsibilities, disgruntled reformist groups within the LDP openly revolted against Miyazawa in a no-confidence motion. True, the motion was introduced by traditional opposition parties including the JSP, but it was the rebellion from within the LDP that precipitated the election.

In the election, the LDP completely lost its overall majority by the biggest margin since 1955. The JSP suffered a humiliating and historic defeat, almost halving its seats from 137 to 70. All the newly formed, reform-minded conservative parties leapt forward and spearheaded post-election political changes. Whatever the outcome, the implication must be the emergence of Japanese politics from the Cold War era and the demise of the whole '55 structure'. The electorate's verdict on the JSP was especially severe, suggesting further marginalisation for its left wing and perhaps the party as a whole. Sadly, though, this was no more than the party deserved.

7

Comparing Japanese and British Politics: Some Basic Data

Helen Margetts

Table 7.1 Population and population density

	Population 1988 (millions)	Population density 1991 (people per sq km)
Japan	122.6	350
UK	57.1	250

Source: Statistical Handbook of Japan, 1993 and the *Economist Book of Vital World Statistics*, Hutchinson, London, 1990.

Table 7.2 Electoral Systems

	Japan (until 1994)	UK

Lower House	House of Representatives 511 members elected every 4 years in 130 multi-member constituencies.
	  Each voter has one single non-transferable vote within a multi-member constituency. Holds legislative power.
		House of Commons 651 members elected every 5 years in single-member constituencies.
		  Each voter has one single non-transferable vote within a single member constituency. Holds legislative power.

Upper House	House of Councillors 252 members. Half of members elected every 3 years for six-year term: at each election, 50 elected from whole electorate; 76 in single member constituencies. Voters cast 2 votes, one for party list in national constituency and one for candidate in a single member constituency.	House of Lords 1034 members. Unelected. Members are divided between: hereditary peers (58%) created life peers (40%) and bishops (3%)
Head of State	Emperor	Queen/King

Table 7-3a (Japan) Percentage of valid votes and number of seats by parties before 1993

	LDP		Democratic Socialist Party		Komeito		Japanese Socialist Party		Communist Party		Other/ Independent		Shinseito		Japan New Party		Sakigake		Total
	Votes	Seats	Votes	Seats	Votes	Seats	Votes	Seats	Votes	Seats	Votes	Seats	Votes	Seats	Votes	Seats	Votes	Seats	Seats
1958	58	287					33	166	3	1	7	13							467
1960	58	296	9	17			28	145	3	3	3	6							467
1963	55	283	7	23			29	144	4	5	5	12							467
1967	49	277	7	30	5	25	28	140	5	5	6	9							486
1969	48	288	8	31	11	47	21	90	7	14	6	16							486
1972	47	271	7	19	8	29	22	118	10	38	6	16							491
1976	42	249	6	29	11	55	21	123	10	17	10	38							511
1979	45	248	7	35	10	57	20	107	10	39	10	25							511
1980	48	284	7	32	9	33	19	107	10	29	7	26							511
1983	46	250	7	39	10	58	20	112	9	26	8	27							511
1986	49	300	6	26	9	56	17	85	6	26	11	12							512
1990	46	275	5	13	8	45	24	136	8	16	9	26							512
1993	37	223	4	15	8	51	15	70	8	15	8	34	10	55	8	35	3	13	511

Source: Calculated from data contained in *The Japanese Party System*, by Ronald J. Hrebenar, Westview Press, Colorado, 1992 and *The International Almanac of Electoral History*, by Thomas T. Mackie and Richard Rose, Macmillan, Basingstoke, 1991. Information also provided by the Japanese Embassy.

Note: Percentages are rounded up to the nearest whole number.

At the 1993 election in Japan, the LDP lost power for the first time since 1955. It was replaced by an eight party 'rainbow' coalition consisting of:

Social Democratic Party (formerly Japanese Socialist Party)
Japan Renewal Party (*Shinseito*)
Clean Government Party (*Komeito*)
Japan New Party (*Nihon Shinto*)
Democratic Socialist Party (*Minshato*)
New Harbinger Party (*Sakigake*)
United Social Democratic Party (*Shaminren*)
Japanese Trade Union Confederation Group (*Rengo*)

The coalition government is pledged to introduce electoral reform. The system that has been chosen is a proportional system similar to that used in Germany, were members are elected in single-member constituencies with top up seats allocated via party lists. This system, *Heiritsusel*, was approved in the National Diet on March 4, 1994.

Table 7.3b (Britain) : Percentage of valid votes and number of seats before 1993

	Con Votes	Con Seats	Labour Votes	Labour Seats	Lib Dem Votes	Lib Dem Seats	Welsh/Scot Votes	Welsh/Scot Seats	Others Votes	Others Seats	Total Seats
1955	50	345	46	277	3	6	0	0	1	2	630
1959	49	365	44	258	6	6	0	0	1	1	630
1964	43	304	44	317	11	9	1	0	1	0	630
1966	42	253	48	363	9	12	1	0	1	2	630
1970	47	330	43	288	8	6	1	1	2	5	630
1974 Feb	38	297	37	301	19	14	3	9	3	14	635
1974 Oct	36	277	39	319	18	13	4	14	3	12	635
1979	44	339	37	269	14	11	2	4	3	12	635
1983	42	397	28	209	25	23	2	4	3	17	650
1987	42	376	31	229	23	22	2	6	3	17	650
1992	42	336	34	271	18	20	2	7	4	17	651

Source: David Butler and Dennis Kavanagh, *The British General Election of 1992*, Macmillan, Basingstoke, 1992 pp 284–5.

Neither Britain nor Japan (before 1994) have proportional electoral systems. In the tables below, deviation from proportionality (DV) is calculated by adding up the differences between the percentages of votes and the percentages of seats of the major parties (ignoring positive and negative signs) and dividing by two. This figure is included because it gives some indication of the extent to which the electoral system

Table 7.4a (Japan): Percentage of valid votes and seats by parties and deviation from proportionality before 1993

	LDP		Democratic Socialist Party		Komeito		Japanese Socialist Party		Communist Party		Other/ Independent		Shinseito		Japan New Party		Sakigake		DV
	Votes	Seats	Votes	Seats	Votes	Seats	Votes	Seats	Votes	Seats	Votes	Seats	Votes	Seats	Votes	Seats	Votes	Seats	
1958	58	62	9	4			33	36	3	0	7	3							6
1960	58	63	7	5			28	31	3	1	3	1							10
1963	55	61	7	6	5	5	29	31	4	1	5	3							8
1967	49	57	8	6	11	10	28	29	5	1	6	2							9
1969	48	59	7	4	8	6	21	19	7	3	6	3							12
1972	47	55	6	6	11	11	22	24	10	8	6	3							11
1976	42	49	7	7	10	11	21	24	10	3	10	7							10
1979	45	49	7	6	9	7	20	21	10	8	10	5							7
1980	48	56	7	8	10	11	19	21	10	6	7	5							9
1983	46	49	7	5	9	11	20	22	9	5	8	5							7
1986	50	59	6	5	9	8	17	17	6	5	11	2							11
1990	47	54	5	3	8	9	24	27	8	3	9	5							11
1993	37	44	4	3	8	10	15	14	8	3	8	7	10	11	8	7	3	3	10

Source: Calculated from data contained in *The Japanese Party System*, by Ronald J. Hrebenar, Westview Press, Colarado, 1992 and *The International Almanac of Electoral History*, Thomas T. Mackie and Richard Rose, 1991, Macmillan: Basingstoke and information provided by the Japanese Embassy. Percentages are rounded up to the nearest whole number.

translates the votes cast into seats in parliament; the extent to which parties are over-represented or under-represented in parliament. It has a maximum of around 50 and a minimum of zero for perfect proportionality so the lower the figure, the more proportionally the electoral system is operating.

There are various ways of estimating disproportionality: this method uses the Loosemore-Hanby index (taken from Loosemore and Hanby, 'The Theoretical Limits of Maximum Distortion: Some Analytic Expressions for Electoral Systems', *British Journal of Political Science*, 1 (1971), pp 467–7). Tables 7.4a and 7.4b show that before 1974, the electoral systems in the two countries demonstrated similar levels of proportionality. Since then the Japanese system remained fairly constant while the British system has showed increasing levels of disproportionality.

Table 7.4b (Britain) Percentage of valid votes and seats and deviation from proportionality before 1993

	Con		Labour		Lib Dem		Welsh/Scot		Others		
	Votes	Seats	Votes	Seats	Votes	Seats	Votes	Seats	Votes	Seats	DV
1955	50	55	46	44	3	1	0	0	1	0	4
1959	49	58	44	41	6	1	0	0	1	0	8
1964	43	48	44	50	11	1	1	0	1	0	11
1966	42	40	48	58	9	2	1	0	1	0	11
1970	47	52	43	46	8	0	1	0	2	1	8
1974 Feb	38	47	37	47	19	2	3	1	3	2	19
1974 Oct	36	44	39	50	18	2	4	2	3	2	19
1979	44	54	37	42	14	2	2	1	3	2	15
1983	42	61	28	32	25	4	2	1	3	3	24
1987	42	58	31	35	23	3	2	1	3	3	21
1992	42	52	34	42	18	3	2	1	4	3	18

Source: David Butler & Dennis Kavanagh *The British General Election of 1992*, Macmillan, Basingstoke, 1992 pp 284–5.

Table 7.5 Turnout at general elections in Japan and Britain (percentage of eligible electorate)

	Japan	Britain
1945		73.3
1950		84.0
1951		82.5
1955	75.0	76.8
1958	76.9	
1959		78.7
1960	73.5	
1963	71.0	
1964		77.1
1966		75.8
1967	74.0	
1969	68.5	
1970		72.0
1972	71.8	
1974 Feb		78.1
1974 Oct		72.8
1976	73.5	
1979	68.0	76.0
1980	74.6	
1983	67.0	72.7
1986	71.4	
1987		75.3
1990	73.3	
1992		77.7
1993	67.2	

Source: *Elections Since 1945*, Macmillan, Basingstoke, 1992; David Butler & Dennis Kavanagh, *The British General Election of 1992*.

Economic Indicators

Table 7.6 Unemployment rates for Japan and Britain compared internationally (% by ILO/OECD guidelines)

	1989	1990	1991	1992
Canada	7.5	8.1	10.3	11.3
Italy	10.9	11.1	11.0	10.7
France	9.4	8.9	9.5	10.2
UK	7.1	5.9	8.3	10.1
Germany	5.5	6.2	6.7	7.7
US	5.2	5.5	6.7	7.4
Japan	2.3	2.1	2.1	2.2

Source: *The Guardian Political Almanac 1993–94*, David McKie (ed), Fourth Estate, London 1993, p. 49.

Table 7.7 Percentage of expenditure by government for Japan and Britain compared internationally (total outlays of government spending as % of GDP)

	1988	1989	1990	1991	1992
Italy	50.3	51.3	53.2	53.6	53.2
France	50.0	44.1	49.8	50.6	52.0
Canada	42.5	43.2	45.9	48.8	49.7
Germany	46.3	44.8	45.2	48.7	44.4
UK	38.0	37.6	39.9	40.8	44.1
US	32.5	32.4	33.3	34.2	35.4
Japan	31.6	30.9	31.7	31.4	32.2

Source: *The Guardian Political Almanac 1993–94*, David McKie, (ed), Fourth Estate, London 1993, p. 49.

Table 7.8 Defence expenditure 1987

	$millions	% of GDP/GNP 1987
US	1,061	6.4
UK	402	4.7
France	395	4.0
Canada	307	2.1
Italy	194	2.4
Japan	125	1.0

Source: *The Economist Book of Vital World Statistics*, Hutchinson, London 1990.

Table 7.9 Economic growth: growth of real GNP/GDP (percentages)

	1989	1990	1991	1992
US	2.5	0.8	-1.2	2.1
Germany	3.4	5.1	3.7	2.0
Japan	4.7	4.8	4.0	1.3
France	4.3	2.5	0.7	1.3
Italy	2.9	2.1	1.3	0.9
Canada	2.3	-0.5	-1.7	0.9
UK	2.1	0.5	-2.2	-0.6

Source: *The Guardian Political Almanac 1993–94*, David McKie (ed), Fourth Estate, London 1993, p. 50.

Working Life

Union membership in Britain shows a picture of steady decline, whilst in Japan it has been fairly constant since 1975. In Japan the unionization rate is about half the size of that in Britain when differences in population size are taken into consideration.

Table 7.1 Trade union membership in Britain and Japan

	Japan		Britain	
	Unions	Membership (millions)	Unions	Membership (millions)
1979			453	13.3
1980	72,693	12.4	438	12.9
1981			414	12.1
1982	74,091	12.5	408	11.6
1983	74,486	12.5	394	11.2
1984	74,579	12.5	375	11.0
1985	74,499	12.4	370	10.8
1986	74,183	12.3	335	10.5
1987	73,138	12.3	330	10.5
1988	72,792	12.2	315	10.4
1989	72,605	12.2	309	10.2
1990			287	9.9
1991			275	9.6

Source: *Japanese Working Life Profile 1990*, Japan Institute of Labour, Tokyo, 1990 and *The Guardian Political Almanac 1993/4*, David McKie (ed), Fourth Estate, London 1993.

Table 7.11 Female labour force participation rate by age group

Age	Japan	United Kingdom
15–19	16.6	56.5
20–24	73.6	69.2
25–29	56.9	62.6
30–34	50.5	62.6
35–39	61.3	71.4
40–44	68.4	71.4
45–49	68.4	69.9
50–54	61.8	69.9
55–59	50.8	51.5
60–64	38.5	18.8
65–69	26.5	2.7
Total	48.6	54.2

Source: Japanese Working Life Profile, Statistical Aspects 1990, Japan Institute of Labour, Tokyo, 1990 p 57.

Table 7.12 Industrial Disputes in UK and Japan 1977–89

	No of disputes		Involving > 1,000 persons	
	Japan	UK	Japan	UK
1977	1,707	2,703	692	1,166
1978	1,512	2,471	660	1,042
1979	1,151	2,080	449	4,608
1980	1,128	1,330	563	830
1981	955	1,338	247	1,513
1982	944	1,528	216	2,103
1983	893	1,352	224	574
1984	596	1,206	155	1,464
1985	627	887	123	643
1986	620	1,053	118	538
1987	474	1,004	101	884
1988	498		75	759
1989	362		86	727

Source: Japanese Working Life Profile, Statistical Aspects, 1990, Japan Institute of Labour, Tokyo, 1990 p. 57.

Table 7.13 Life in Japan and the UK (1986–88)

	Japan	UK
Life expectancy	**yrs**	**yrs**
Life expectancy (men)	75	72
Life expectancy (women)	81	78
Consumer spending	**%**	**%**
food/drink	20.6	18.5
clothing	6.1	7.1
energy, housing	18.4	19.8
household goods	5.5	6.6
health	10.6	1.3
transport	9.3	15.9
communications		
leisure, other	29.5	30.8
Newspapers		
No of newspapers	124	105
Circulation per 1,000	566	421
Consumer durables	**% of households owning**	**% of households owning**
TV set	99	98
Video	53	61
Microwave	57	35
Washing machine	99	83
Fridge	98	93

Source: The Economist Book of Vital World Statistics, Hutchinson, London 1990.

THREE

Government and Opposition in the United Kingdom

Factions and Tendencies in the Conservative Party

Philip Norton

The Conservative Party has been in power continuously since 1979. It also has the distinction of being the only major party in Europe with a record of political success spanning more than 150 years. It emerged in the 1830s as the successor to the Tory Party. It inherited the basic values of the Tories but later in the century took on board other beliefs, especially during the leadership of Benjamin Disraeli. Disraeli transformed the party from a party of landed interests to a national party, appealing across class divisions and emphasising that which unites rather than divides the nation.

There are several core tenets of Conservative thought: a belief in society as an organic and evolutionary entity, a belief in the maintenance of order and discipline (stemming from respect for the institutions of the state, underpinned by the rule of law), a belief in the ownership of property, in limited government, in wealth creation, in the maintenance of 'one nation' at home and 'one nation' abroad. Disraeli was responsible for the concept of 'one nation'. At home, this entailed an acceptance of some measures of social reform. Abroad, it meant the expansion of empire and the defence of British interests. Underpinning this corpus of beliefs is a basic scepticism as to the power of human reason and a disposition to favour society as it presently exists. There is a reluctance to espouse grand and untested schemes, preferring instead that which has derived from the wisdom of generations.

These tenets provide a framework of Conservative thought. They also provide the basis for tensions between Conservatives. There is the potential for tension between continuity and change. Society is evolutionary, not static. But at what stage does one accept the need for some particular change? There is the potential for tension between the emphasis on wealth creation and the 'one nation' emphasis on maintaining social harmony. And there is the potential for tension between those who place the emphasis more on maintaining order and standards in society and those who emphasise limited government.

The potential for such tension has variously been realised throughout the party's history. The party split badly in its early years on the issue of the Corn Laws, resulting in it being the 'out' party in British politics for the next forty years. It suffered another disastrous split at the beginning of the twentieth century, again on the issue of free trade versus protectionism. It has witnessed more recent tensions on economic policy and Europe. Those more recent tensions will form the focus of this chapter.

However, three preliminary points can be made about the nature of the party in relation to dissent that, in combination, set it apart from its Japanese counterpart. Two of these are longstanding, the third is of more recent origin.

A Party of Tendencies

The Conservative Party in Parliament is most aptly characterised as a party of tendencies rather than one of factions. That is, there are different strands of opinion within the party, but the strands do not find reflection in consistent and organised expression. The strands of thought are several. They precipitate responses that differ depending on the issue. Consequently, dissenters on one issue are not necessarily dissenters on another. Those who emphasise the importance of one nation abroad may make common cause with those who emphasise the imperatives of wealth creation on one issue (for example, to join the European Economic Community in the 1960s) but depart from their stance on another (for example, avoiding large-scale redundancies in the armed forces), making common cause instead with those who stress the importance of one nation at home.

Thus there are shifting tendencies within the party. The fact that they shift means that there is little incentive to develop an organisation – a party within the party – to pursue a particular line. However, the shift is not so frequent that different configurations cannot be identified. These configurations change over the decades, though recent years have seen some movement towards factionalism on particular issues, notably that of Europe.

An Emphasis on Leadership

In his chapter, William Horsley has noted the extent to which Japanese prime ministers are expected to lead 'from the middle'. This is in sharp contrast to British parties and it is especially in sharp contrast to the expectations, and largely the practice, of the Conservative Party. The party is hierarchical and stresses the importance of leadership. The leader is, in the words of one party report, 'the fount of all policy'. The leader ultimately determines the policy of the party: he or she may draw on other bodies in the party to assist in formulating policy, but such bodies are advisory only. The leader also enjoys powers of appointment not enjoyed by other party leaders. In office, the leader – as prime minister – enjoys the formal power of appointing members of the cabinet. The equivalent power, though, applies when in opposition: the leader appoints members of the shadow cabinet. Whether in government or opposition, the leader appoints the principal officers of the party, notably the party chairman, deputy chairmen, vice-chairmen, and treasurers.

Though leaders often try to achieve some political balance in the appointment of ministers, they can and frequently do appoint loyal supporters to key posts. As prime minister, Margaret Thatcher appointed like-minded ministers to the key economic ministries. As prime minister, Edward Heath – who exercised greater power over his Cabinet than Margaret Thatcher did over hers – appointed virtually a whole Cabinet comprising of personally loyal ministers.

Though the leader is constrained – arguably more so since 1975, when the parliamentary party introduced the principle of annual election of the leader – the party nonetheless looks to the leader to give a lead. In giving that lead, the leader may anticipate reaction from different tendencies within the party, but the emphasis is nonetheless on leading, not on following. So long as the leader looks likely to bring success (measured usually in electoral terms), the party defers to the leader and, if the party enjoys an overall majority in the House of Commons, then that majority normally ensures that the measures brought forward by the government – led by the prime minister – are passed.

By leading from the front, the leader may thus encounter dissent from particular tendencies within the party, but deference to the leader – and loyalty to the party – have been employed as important tools in limiting the extent and impact of that dissent.

Greater and More Overt Dissent

When Conservative MPs have harboured doubts about the policies of their leaders, they express those doubts primarily in private – to the party whips, in party backbench committees, or to ministers directly. Party whips are longstanding features of parliamentary life. Since the 1920s, the parliamentary party has developed also a substantial internal organisation. Party committees are an important feature of the life of Conservative MPs. The committees provide a means of discussing topics within a particular sector with experts from outside and with fellow MPs (and peers) interested in the subject. They also provide a valuable means of two-way communication between leaders and led. Ministers can be invited to speak and can be closely questioned on their policies and their stewardship of their departments. The meetings are private and so Members feel they can speak in a way not possible in the partisan environment of the House. The opportunity to vent disquiet, even opposition, at such meetings may be sufficient for some Conservative MPs. As long as the minister has heard what they have had to say, or a whip (normally present at meetings) has heard what they have said, they may be satisfied. The whip will pass on details of any dissatisfaction expressed at meetings and, if necessary, arrange for a meeting between the appropriate minister and the MPs expressing dissatisfaction. If MPs are still dissatisfied, then ultimately they may express their disquiet privately to the prime minister. Even if the prime minister does not accept their argument, at least they have had an opportunity to put their case.

For much of the period from 1945 to 1970, there was relatively little overt dissent by Conservative MPs. When MPs did disagree with government policy, they often preferred to express their dissent privately. They were reluctant to make it public and to go as far as voting against the government in the voting (division) lobbies of the House. To do so was viewed as an act of disloyalty, it undermined the party – the electorate does not reward a divided party – and, if on an issue of importance, it could jeopardise the government's majority and thus run the risk of bringing the government down. This last perception derived from a constitutional myth (that an important defeat required the government to resign or dissolve Parliament – the constitutional convention of collective responsibility actually only requires such a response if defeated on an explicit vote of confidence), but since MPs nonetheless held that perception it affected their behaviour. During the 1950s, there were actually two parliamentary sessions in which not one Conservative MP cast a dissenting vote in the division lobbies.

Recent years, however, have seen a change in the behaviour of Conservative MPs. In absolute terms, the change is not great, but compared with pre-1970 behaviour it is significant. Since the 1970s, Conservative MPs have proved more willing than before to express dissent on the floor of the House and to vote against their own government in the division lobbies. In the Parliament returned in 1970, Conservative MPs voted against the whips on more occasions than before, in greater numbers and with more effect than ever before. On six occasions, the numbers voting in the Opposition lobby were sufficient to deny the government a majority. As one leading dissenter observed, 'after you had defeated the government on one occasion, it became easier to do it a second time'. The experience of that Parliament set a precedent for later Parliaments, with Labour MPs frequently cross-voting in the period of Labour government from 1974 to 1979, and with Conservative MPs maintaining a notable level of cross-voting in the period of Conservative government from 1979 onwards. In the period from 1979 to 1992, when governments had reasonably large overall majorities – especially in the two Parliaments from 1983 to 1992 – most incidents of cross-voting by Conservative MPs could be absorbed by the large majority. However, this was not true on all occasions, with the Thatcher government variously being forced to withdraw proposals under threat of defeat or, occasionally, because of actual defeat in the lobbies. The most notable defeat occurred in April 1986 when the government was defeated on the second reading of the Shops Bill, a measure to de-regulate Sunday trading. Seventy-two Conservative MPs voted with the Opposition to defeat it – the first time a government had lost a second reading vote since 1924 and the first time this century that a government with an overall working majority had done so.

I have argued elsewhere that the triggering mechanism for this sudden change in behaviour is to be found in Edward Heath's style of prime ministerial leadership from 1970 to 1974. He introduced a number of radical measures that encountered opposition from some of his own supporters. What precipitated that opposition being expressed in public form – on the floor of the House and in the division lobbies – was Heath's unwillingness to listen to his own backbenchers. He insisted on the expeditious passage of measures, without amendment and without even giving a hearing to those Conservative MPs who had doubts about the measures. Those MPs concluded that the only way they could express their dissent was in the division lobbies – and that is what they did.

Though Margaret Thatcher set out consciously to avoid Heath's style of leadership, she too eventually succumbed to a similar approach – being too isolated from backbenchers and not taking time to consider disquiet expressed on the backbenches. She ignored various warnings – including a notable warning given in November 1989, when sixty Conservative MPs failed to vote for her in the leadership contest forced by Sir Anthony Meyer. Ultimately, she paid the same price as Edward Heath – she was voted out of her leadership.

More recent years have also seen a relative decline in the significance of the backbench committees. They remain important. A sizeable attendance by backbenchers at a committee meeting can signal trouble. After Michael Heseltine, the President of the Board of Trade, had announced in October 1992 plans to close most of the remaining coal pits, he attended a meeting of the backbench trade and industry committee. A normal committee meeting would usually attract about half a dozen or so MPs. This one attracted about 150. However, most regular meetings suffer from a small attendance. It is a growing problem. There are other demands on the time of MPs and attending backbench committees do not take priority over other commitments. Though the committees remain important as channels for expressing views in private, there is the danger that they will not remain as significant in the future as they have in the past. This development may contribute to a greater willingness to express dissent on the floor of the House.

Contemporary Tendencies

That provides an essential background to the contemporary position within the Conservative Party in Parliament. What, then, of the different configurations that exists within the party's ranks?

The debate within Conservative ranks has taken different shapes in recent years. It has often been expressed in terms of a simple dichotomy: left versus right, Whig versus Tory, and – more especially in the early 1980s – Wet versus Dry. These do not do justice to the richness of opinion within the party's ranks. They do not allow for various sub-sets of opinion. Furthermore, the Wet and Dry dichotomy focuses heavily on economic policy. The debate within the party's ranks has been more subtle and complex than these simple divisions allow. Indeed, in recent years at least seven configurations can be identified.

Those seven groupings within the ranks of the parliamentary party derive from an analysis of Conservative MPs undertaken in 1989. The groups varied in size and, indeed, in the extent of the 'fit' for each Member. They do, though, help explain the nature and the extent of tensions within the party in recent years. The groupings, or tendencies, are:

(1) *Neo-liberals.* They have a principled belief in the supremacy of market forces. Government intervention distorts market forces and denies choice. They are generally opposed to European union and to capital punishment. They are likely to support more open government.

(2) *Tory Right.* They are more concerned with morals than economics. They stress the need to maintain social order, standards and discipline. They are strong exponents of the need for law and order. They support capital punishment and legislation that enshrines social values. They are generally opposed to more open government and to European union.

(3) *Pure Thatcherites.* Led by Margaret Thatcher, they bring together the neo-liberal espousal of a market economy with the Tory emphasis on

maintaining standards. They want to roll back government intervention in economic affairs while maintaining law and order and social standards. They are generally supportive of capital punishment and sceptical of European union.

These three groupings can be considered under the broad heading of 'Thatcherites'. In 1989, they accounted for seventy-two MPs, just under 20 per cent of the parliamentary party.

(4) *Populist.* These are so described, not because of their style, but because they tend to resemble popular stances on issues – that is, to the right on law and order issues (pro-hanging, tougher sentencing, strict immigration policy) but to the left on social welfare issues (pro-National Health Service, emphasising the need to maintain jobs rather than to cut public spending to the bone). They are sceptical about European union and exhibit some scepticism about privatisation.

The populists, perhaps surprisingly, are few in number within the ranks of the parliamentary party. In 1989, only seventeen MPs could be found to fall in this category – just under 5 per cent of the parliamentary party.

(5) *Wets.* The Wets are committed to the concept of 'one nation' at home and stress the imperatives of social harmony. They accept the need for government to act as a creative force in economic regeneration and for government to intervene to help those in need. They are generally opposed to capital punishment and cuts in public expenditure. They are strongly supportive of European union.

(6) *Damps.* They are sympathetic to the stance of the Wets but not as rigorous in expressing their opposition. They are generally pro-European union and sympathetic to government intervention. They were likely but not certain to oppose the poll tax and charges for eye and dental tests. They are generally more amenable than the Wets to persuasion by ministers and the whips on particular issues.

During the Thatcher years, the categories of Wets and Damps could be combined under the heading of 'Critics'. They were most likely to find themselves critical of, sometimes strongly opposed to, policies advanced by the prime minister and her chancellors. In 1989, the Critics comprised sixty-seven MPs – 17 per cent of the parliamentary party.

(7) *Party faithful.* The party faithful comprise MPs whose loyalty is first and foremost to the party rather than to a particular strand of thought within the party. This is not to say that they have no ideological leanings

of their own, nor that their support can be taken for granted by the leader. They may share the views of some of the particular groupings – the Tory Right for example – but their natural inclination is to subordinate the expression of those views for the greater good of the party. On a particular issue, they may feel sufficiently strongly to express an opinion or, if the party looks doomed to electoral disaster, they may then swing against the leader, but their natural disposition is to be supportive.

This grouping is the largest within the parliamentary party. In 1989, there were 217 MPs – 58 per cent of the parliamentary party – who fell in this category. This number includes some who are best described as Thatcher loyalists – those who were essentially loyal to Margaret Thatcher (as distinct from Thatcherism) and her style of leadership.

There is a correlation between these groupings and some of the un-official bodies formed within the party. A number of pure Thatcherites, for example, formed the No Turning Back Group. The Tory Right tend to be predominant, and the key figures, in the right-wing 92 Group, though membership extends well beyond that grouping. A number of Wets in the mid 1980s formed Centre Forward. Wets and Damps are at the heart of the group known as the Lollards. Some of these bodies not only form congenial environments for like-minded Members, they also serve to mobilise support and ensure that some of their number get elected to backbench party offices. The annual election for officers of the 1922 Committee (the body comprising backbenchers) and the various party committees involve campaigning by different groups and the formation of slates of candidates. The 92 Group and the Lollards are especially active in forming slates. In 1993, some of the party faithful also got organised and campaigned for a particular slate of loyalist candidates – or, perhaps more accurately, campaigned against a number of candidates deemed to be disloyal to the leadership.

Figure 8.1 illustrates the correlation between the groupings and the unofficial bodies. It also illustrates the stance taken by the different groupings on a range of issues, especially those that were salient and the cause of tensions within the party during the Thatcher years. From the Table, one can see how some of the different groupings would be inclined to come together on one issue but then form different alliances on other issues. Neo-liberals and pure Thatcherites would be united in wanting to achieve a reduction in government intervention but divided on the issue, say, of capital punishment.

This analysis helps explain the nature and the extent of the Conservative dissenting lobbies in the 1980s. It also helps in explaining the fall of Margaret Thatcher and both the initial success and later difficulties of her successor.

STANCE	Party Faithful	Thatcherites		Populist	Wet	Damp	Party Faithful
		Tory Right	Neo-liberal				
ORGAN-ISATION		── 92 Group ── Selsdon Group 'No Turning Back' Monday Club			Centre Forward ──── ── Tory Reform Group ── ── C.A.R.E. ── (Conservative Action for Electoral Reform)		
POSITIONS ON SPECIFIC ISSUES 1987/88	- - - - - -	── - - - - · anti-EC ───── ── critical of race relations law ── pro-open government anti-hanging		- - - - - -	pro-open government anti-hanging ───── support for Child Benefit	- - - - - - - - - - - - - -	
				- - - - - - Opposed to Community Charge - - - - - - - - -			
		── Opposed to Health Charges - - - - - - - - -					
NOTABLE FIGURES		G. Gardiner Sir R. Boyson Teddy Taylor	J. Biffen Sir R. Body N. Budgen I. Gow	N. Winterton Dame J. Knight A. Beaumont-Dark	E. Heath Sir I. Gilmour N. Scott P. Walker	M. Heseltine William Waldegrave Mrs L. Chalker	

Figure 8.1 Groupings within the Conservative Party
Source: P. Norton, 'Choosing a Leader: Margaret Thatcher and the Parliamentary Conservative Party 1989–90', *Parliamentary Affairs*, 43 (3), 1990, p. 251.

The Fall of Margaret Thatcher

Margaret Thatcher led from the front. She is the only prime minister in British history to generate an 'ism' – Thatcherism. As prime minister she was able to utilise both the powers of the office and her position as party leader to ensure that she usually got the outcomes she wanted. Within the parliamentary party, she was able to call on only a relatively small band of supporters totally committed to her way of thinking. But she had the support not only of the Thatcherites (neo-liberals, Tory Right, pure Thatcherites) but also of the party faithful. They deferred to the leader. The leader looked like being able to deliver success. They appeared to waver in 1981 at a time of recession – and when the party at one point was trailing third in the opinion polls – but the outcome of the Falklands War put paid to any doubts and the party faithful remained loyal to the leader until 1990. Even in the leadership contest in 1989, no more than between five and fifteen appeared to withold their support from her. When the government ran into opposition on the backbenches it was normally from the Critics, joined on occasion by the Populists. Occasionally, there was dissent from the Tory right, but that was because the government was not going far enough – not because it had gone too far. When the Tory right pressed for more radical reform of the trade unions, it did so knowing that the prime minister was sympathetic to their views.

When the Critics did voice their opposition and enter the lobbies against the government, they were never able to maximise their numbers. A disproportionate number of Damps were ministers. Though this created problems for the prime minister in that it meant she never crafted a fully Thatcherite team of ministers, it did have the benefit of reducing overt dissent. The grouping least well represented in the ranks of ministers – the Tory right – was one unlikely to desert the prime minister as long as she stuck to Thatcherite policies.

However, the prime minister's support slipped in 1989 and 1990. A combination of popular opposition to the poll tax, Mrs Thatcher's uncompromising stance on the issue of Europe, and economic downturn combined to make her politically vulnerable. In 1989, the party suffered a major reverse in the UK elections to the European Parliament. In the spring of 1990, there were poll tax riots in different parts of the country. The party trailed the Labour Party by more than twenty points in the opinion polls. In the autumn, Sir Geoffrey Howe resigned from the Cabinet and precipitated Michael Heseltine's challenge for the leadership. In the first ballot, the party faithful failed to support the leader in the way they had the year before. They split roughly down the middle. Given the Conservative emphasis on leadership and loyalty, the defection of half of the party faithful was fatal for the leader. Even without the high hurdle set by the rules for the leadership contest (an absolute majority, plus a majority representing 15 per cent of the parliamentary party) it meant that Margaret Thatcher's leadership was fatally wounded. Members of her Cabinet realised that and told her she was not likely to win the second ballot. To Mrs Thatcher they were engaging in treachery. In reality, they were acting as candid friends. Mrs Thatcher's problem was not the Cabinet. Her problem was the outcome of the first ballot. That sealed her fate. An incumbent could not survive for long without the overwhelming support of the party faithful.

The Premiership of John Major

John Major was elected as leader in the second ballot. He was drawn from the party faithful. As such, he was able to convey a stance that appealed to the different groupings within the party. To Thatcherites he appeared fiscally conservative. To critics, he appeared liberal on social issues. To the party faithful, he was one of them. Drawn from the party faithful, he was also able to promise to modify the party's stance on those issues which were the cause of its unpopularity. In contrast, both Michael Heseltine and Douglas Hurd – the other candidates contesting the second ballot – were drawn from the Damp strain of Conservativism. They both drew their strength from the same political constituency. They had little appeal to the Thatcherite section of the party.

Once in office, John Major was able to move to get rid of the poll tax and moderate the government's stance on the issue of Europe. That, and his leadership during the Gulf War, helped reduce the party's deficit in the opinion polls. He was able to convey the impression not just of new leadership, but of a new government. In April 1992, he was able to lead the party to a narrow, and unexpected, election victory.

The fact that John Major was drawn from the party faithful was one of his strengths in enabling the party to regain its electoral support. As such, it was a notable asset. But it was a notable short term asset. In the long term, it is more of a liability. The fact that Margaret Thatcher was a Thatcherite meant that she had a long-term goal. Being drawn from the party faithful, John Major is more concerned with the here and now of politics. He has no obvious future goal. He thus has difficulty conveying a clear sense of direction. Instead, he has to look for policies that might prove electorally popular as well as suggest a particular sense of direction. Had he succeeded another leader drawn from the party faithful, such as Sir Alec Douglas-Home, the contrast might not have been so sharp. By following Margaret Thatcher, the contrast is stark and obvious. Furthermore, he has to contend with Thatcherite MPs who do have a clear sense of what they want to achieve. And by being drawn from the party faithful, he has no firm support based on commitment to a particular set of beliefs. His loyalty is derived from those who are loyal to the individual and those whose loyalty is to the party. He has to rely on the party faithful and, as we have seen, their support for the leader is likely but not certain.

Furthermore, John Major has had to contend with a division within the party's ranks that has some of the characteristics of a factional dispute: that on the issue of Europe. The negotiations on the Maastricht Treaty were hailed as a triumph for the prime minister and, following the 1992 general election, it looked likely that the resulting bill – the European Communities (Amendment) Bill – would have little difficulty in being passed by the House of Commons. The result of the first Danish referendum in June 1992 put paid to that expectation and unleashed a serious split in the parliamentary party. Sceptics of European union mobilised in opposition to the bill. The bulk of the committed sceptics were drawn from Thatcherite MPs, but their number spilled over to include Populists, and even extended into the margins of the party faithful. (They also, and exceptionally, had one Wet MP – Sir

Peter Tapsell – in their ranks.) Their opposition to the bill was not only consistent but also organised. They met regularly and even had two of their number serve as unofficial whips. The prime minister had not only to contend with this body of sceptics but also with those MPs – drawn principally and notably from the Wets and Damps – who were committed to the principle of European union and were not inclined to support any government concessions to opponents of the bill. The party thus faced an internal split similar to that which had rent the party at the beginning of the century. As with that earlier split, the party had a leader not ideologically committed to either side (though leaning one way rather than the other – in John Major's case more towards scepticism than support) and who sought to reconcile the largely irreconcilable. John Major's handling of the issue at times seemed maladroit but ultimately he got the bill passed and the Maastricht Treaty ratified. Margaret Thatcher, an opponent of the bill, would clearly have handled it differently. Had she still been leader, there is the possibility that she would have led the party to an irrevocable split.

For John Major, the challenge now is to unite the different party groupings behind new issues – or at least old issues on which the party is basically united. European union is likely to remain an issue. If it remains a central issue, there is the danger of the parliamentary party becoming factional. If it is but one of the many issues exercising the minds of Conservative MPs, then the prime minister has a greater chance of leading a party of tendencies, with the configurations of support varying from issue to issue. The challenge remains a daunting one. The Japanese prime minister has to mobilise support among seven different parties. The British prime minister does not have that problem. He has to mobilise support among seven separate tendencies within his own party.

9

Bluehall? The Civil Service
Since 1979

Peter Hennessy

The setting is a comfortable-looking house somewhere in England some time in 1993. Kenneth Baker, Margaret Thatcher's former party chairman and sometime Environment Secretary and Education Secretary, is in conversation with Sir Charles Powell, a retired Foreign Office diplomat who served as her Foreign Affairs Private Secretary in No 10 Downing Street throughout the middle and late 1980s.

The conversation goes like this:

POWELL: She did feel that you either belonged or you didn't belong ...
BAKER: Did you ever feel that she felt I was 'one of us'?
POWELL: Yes. Oh, yes. But more latterly than earlier.

This was by British standards an extraordinary scene – a career politician asking a supposedly politically neutral career official if he, as a minister, had been politically acceptable to a Prime Minister. According to constitutional practice, Powell should have been able to transfer his services to Neil Kinnock in the course of a Friday afternoon had Labour won the 1987 general election.

Revealed in September 1993[1,] was this yet another piece of evidence that the British Civil Service had become politicised or 'gone native' on the Conservative party and its policies? In short, had Whitehall 'turned Japanese'? The first requirement of an answer is to revisit the genesis of that standard constitutional practice which Charles Powell seemed to flout with such insouciance.

The Durability of the Late Nineteenth Century Model

Behind the late nineteenth century notion of a permanent, politically neutral career civil service were a pair of implicit assumptions. First, that governments would change with reasonable regularity. That is why Gladstone and Lowe, acting along lines laid down in the crucial Northcote-Trevelyan Report of 1854, took such care over the creation of an administrative instrument that would be a piece of transferable technology capable of switching its capabilities from one set of ministers to the next at a flick of the electorate's wrist.[2]

Secondly, that the philosophical and policy differences between the major parties competing for political power would be fairly narrow, and certainly not of a kind which threatened constitutional fundamentals, the DNA of the British system of administration. This was a kind of unwritten contract between the permanent and the temporary wings of policy-making in government – unwritten in that it took no statutory form, its essentials being implemented by orders in council under the powers of the royal prerogative. This was in stark contrast to the money side of central government which has operated on a statutory basis since the Exchequer and Audit Act of 1866 – a strange and unremarked asymmetry in Gladstone's reshaping of the customs and practices of what modern political scientists call the 'core executive'.[3]

Like all reformers, Gladstone was reacting to the perceived abuses of the recent past, not anticipating future changes in the configuration of British political parties or the contents of their programmes, let alone the outcomes of a still-to-develop national political competition based on a fully extended franchise. Yet the late nineteenth century model survived for more than a century after Gladstone's pioneering construction of a job-creation scheme for the nation's best and brightest. It was a century which brought the moves to one-person, one-vote; the transformation in the political battlefield with the decline of the Liberal Party and the rise of Labour; and the changes in the political economy and the scope of the state which this and a couple of 'total' wars brought.

It took a combination of factors after 1979 to place acute stress on the post-1870 structure. One of them – Mrs Thatcher's desire to return to a minimal, 'night watchman' state of a kind Mr Gladstone presided over – placed a large question-mark on the survival of that very same permanent career public service which the Grand Old Man bequeathed his successors. Similarly, the polarisation of the two major parties, symbolised by the great gulf between their 1983 general election manifestos, raised justifiable speculation as to the capacity of Whitehall, especially its foreign and defence policy people, to make the ideological swerve required if a Foot administration had taken office pledged to call the Polaris squadron back to base, dismantle its nuclear missiles, and to negotiate Britain's exit from the European Community.

But the chief cause of the profoundest unease was as simple to explain as it was difficult to measure – the cumulative effect of successive Conservative election victories. Three in a row were within the memory of people over fifty who could recall the elections of 1951, 1955 and 1959 which produced a Tory ascendancy of thirteen years under four premiers. But when the 1992 result made it four victories in a row under two prime ministers it established a political condition unknown since the 1832 Reform Act began the slow, sputtering process of building a fully-fledged democracy. In the often facile shorthand of contemporary political language, Britain, it was widely declared, had become a 'one party state'. This was patently absurd given, on a national scale, that the nationalist parties in Scotland and Wales, and the Liberal Democrats in the UK (Northern Ireland apart) as a whole, gave the electorate a wider choice than it had enjoyed in the 1950s and 1960s. It was, however, arguable that Britain had acquired a 'predominant party system'[4], though, given the rarity of centre/left governments since 1900, this was hardly a novelty in the twentieth century. This, in turn, raised the question of whether British politics, and, therefore, its administration, was 'going Japanese'.

While remaining convinced that our politics, constitutional procedures and administrative practices are so singular, so determinedly *sui generis* that they can only go on being British, I am willing enough to recognise the utility of posing such a question for the purpose of divining how profound and how permanent are the changes wrought in Whitehall by the accumulated reforms and experiences of Conservative government since 1979.

The Thatcher Impact

Margaret Thatcher claimed so often and so firmly to have 'changed everything' that she tended to be believed, not least in Whitehall matters. The Civil Service, after all, is a prime minister's direct labour organisation. She or he is the Minister for it, though day-to-day supervision is invariably delegated to a cabinet colleague. The question must be split into two parts. Did Mrs Thatcher politicise the people? Did she politicise the process?

Process first. Top officials were uneasy about her Cabinet style. Collegiality in decision-taking almost has the status of an ethic in Whitehall. Her dislike of it worried them. One very senior figure put it to me in the mid-1980s, for example, that 'temporarily we don't have Cabinet government ... we have a form of presidential government in which she operates like a sovereign in her court'.[5]

But did Margaret Thatcher infect their processes, their software, with a political virus? I think not. Her managerial reforms were politically conceived but neutral in effect, designed to produce better value-for-money and a better-managed state, not a Tory fiefdom. Certainly she wanted more businesslike methods imported from the private sector.

And her first two Efficiency Advisers came from that background (Sir Derek Rayner from Marks & Spencer and Sir Robin Ibbs from ICI). Though, significantly, her third, Sir Angus Fraser was a retired career civil servant who had finished as Chairman of the Board of Customs and Excise.

It was highly significant, too, that the one important aspect of 'Thatcherism' (a word I dislike as too all-embracing and simple, but one must recognise its universal usage) Labour was not pledged in the run-up to the 1992 election to overthrow was the managerial reforms (both personnel and financial) including the 'Next Steps' agencies into which a high proportion of public service 'business' already had been placed.[6] The process of market testing under her successor, however, is quite another matter.

What about people? Did Mrs Thatcher apply a 'one of us' test not just to her ministers but to the senior civil servants at permanent and deputy secretary level over whose appointment and promotion she had a direct say? I have no doubt that the para-governmental penumbra of 'quangoland', the BBC Governors and chairman, chairmen of regional health authorities, urban development corporations and so on, were substantially, though not wholly, infected by such a criterion to a degree not experienced under previous premiers.

But the senior civil service was a different matter. Some were promoted younger and faster than otherwise. Some reached permanent secretaryships in surprising ministries, Sir Michael Quinlan at Employment, for example. And Sir Peter Middleton is most unlikely to have reached to top slot in the Treasury under a Labour government. Though his name would almost certainly have been on the shortlist produced by the committee of senior officials chaired by the Head of the Home Civil Service. There were casualties. Usually the reasons were temperamental. Mrs Thatcher had a habit of making up her mind about an official in five minutes. Donald Derx talked himself out of the top job at Employment, for example, by standing up to her in a way she didn't care for during her 'state' visit to the department in the early 1980s.[7]

I can think of only two officials out of a senior complement of 4,000 in a profession half-a-million strong who can really be said to have 'gone political'. Both were her so-called 'praetorian guard' in Number 10 – Charles Powell and Bernard Ingham. As a large section of her Cabinet deserted her on the evening of 21 November 1990, after her failure to dispose of Michael Heseltine in the first leadership ballot, Mr Ingham told her, gripping her arm, that whatever others felt, 'we in No 10 were with her'.[8]

It has emerged too, from memoirs, how active Charles Powell could be politically on her behalf, not just on the last days of November 1990 when he urged Douglas Hurd, the Foreign Secretary, to sign her nomination for the second ballot.[9] But even to the point of dining with a prominent newspaper proprietor, Conrad Black, in the spring of 1990 in an attempt to extract a more sympathetic line from the *Telegraph* group.[10] This, it has to be said, almost puts him in the same category as the infamous Sir Horace Wilson in the Chamberlain years – an example treated as one to be avoided at all costs by senior civil servants in the post-war period.[11]

Ingham and Powell, however, were the exceptions. And it remains an open question to what extent Mrs Thatcher was responsible for their conception of their duties as career officials. Both men knew what they were doing and how it differed from established custom and practice even in Number 10, the apex where administration and politics meet.[12] The real problem, however, in the 'turning Japanese' context is not the isolated examples of a pair of 'courtier' officials, but the behaviour of the 4,000 civil servants who may come into direct contact with ministers. And this is generational rather than political. If Labour forms a government in the mid-1990s, lack of familiarity on both sides will be acute given the rules which keep shadow ministers at a distance from the senior civil service until the last year of a parliament or until an election is called.

By then only, perhaps, a dozen to fifteen Labour 'shadows' will have had personal experience of ministerial life of any kind. And only officials over forty (mainly those over fifty) will have memories of working closely with Labour ministers. Whitehall was acutely conscious of this in the run-up to the 1992 election. In the Department of Social Security, for example, seminars were held in which old sweats instructed the younger generations on how to deal with Labour ministers, including the vocabulary of politics – which words not to use orally or in written submissions (eg. 'privatisation' and 'market testing').[13]

The Department of Employment took a luxurious central London conference centre for a day for the same purpose. Among the requirements addressed was how to switch overnight from telling the department's 'clients' that the 'social chapter of the Maastricht Treaty was 'a bad thing' to describing it as 'a good thing".[14] Environment was another delicate ministry. In 1992 you had to be in your late thirties to remember a time when local authorities were seen as part of the answer to problems not part of the problems themselves. 'I suppose we need them,' Mrs Thatcher once said of the local councils to Kenneth Baker 'with a resigned sigh'.[15]

So titanic a political force was Mrs Thatcher, so deep the shadow she continues to cast, that it is necessary to remind oneself constantly that Whitehall ceased to be her DLO when she resigned as prime minister on 27 November 1990. If possession of the state passes from Conservative to Labour or to a combination of Labour and Liberal

Democrat after the next election, it will, for all her powerful shaping of it over eleven and a half years, be from hands other than hers.

Major and Beyond

Significantly, traditional Cabinet government was felt and heard to have been restored from John Major's very first meeting. Chris Patten emerged from it on 29 November 1990 saying he and his colleagues were like the prisoners in Beethoven's opera, *Fidelio*; walking, blinking, into the sunshine and singing of freedom.[16]

Similarly the argument about Civil Service politicisation, on the policy-advising side at least, lost much of its vitality after the change of premier. Mr Major's was a much more reflective, evidence-driven approach to policy-making than Mrs Thatcher's 'conviction' style.[17] But Mr Major's drive for market testing, after the publication of the White Paper *Competing for Quality*,[18] in November 1991, revived the accusation in a different form.

The 'Next Steps' agencies had been susceptible to cross-party consensus because, with a very few exceptions, they were destined to remain with the public service and staffed by civil servants. Market testing was based on the premise that value-for-money might require the franchising of formerly central activities of the state (even prisons and tax records) to the private sector as part of what Stephen Dorrell, Financial Secretary to the Treasury, called the 'long march' towards a minimal state, to what he called the 'inescapable core of government'.[19]

The appointment of businessman Derek Lewis to the Director-Generalship of the Prison Service Agency in preference to the career civil servant incumbent, the highly regarded Joe Pilling, in 1993, was widely seen as having been swung by Mr Lewis's enthusiasm for private prisons.[20]

The possibility of politicisation of either the policy-making or the managerial kind led to a renewed stress on the question of ethics in the public service. For example, Mrs Thatcher's own deputy, Lord Howe of Aberavon, laid a special emphasis on paragraph 55 of *Questions of Procedure for Ministers*, the formerly secret guidelines of ministerial conduct.[21] It requires ministers 'to give fair consideration and due weight to informed impartial advice from civil servants as well as to other considerations and advice in reaching policy decisions' and reminds them of their 'duty to refrain from asking or instructing civil servants to do things which they should not do and a duty to ensure that influence over appointments is not abused for partisan purposes.'[22]

Taken together with the so-called 'Armstrong Memorandum' on *The Duties and Responsibilities of Civil Servants in Relation to Ministers*,[23] this is all the protection British civil servants have as they are the creatures of the royal prerogative without statutory definition. The last Labour prime minister Lord Callaghan, was sufficiently concerned by this constitutional gap to call for 'an appropriate code of ethics' to be drawn up by a joint select committee of the House of Commons and the House of Lords.[24]

For his part, the late Labour leader John Smith wanted the traditional Whitehall model to be maintained but had doubts about what he might find should the electorate have propeled him into Number 10. In a radio interview between the 1992 election and his replacement of Neil Kinnock, he said:

> It certainly occurs to us from time to time that there might be a Conservative mind-set that has settled against public sector solutions, for example, and that does worry me that there could be a tradition, tilted so far away from the policies of the [Labour] Government that it might create problems. I hope that is not the case. I very much hope that is not the case. But then, at the end of the day, a government and the head of the government must make it clear that he expects a much wider set of possibilities to be advertised to his ministers.[25]

Might this be the case? Might a future non-Conservative Government inherit a Bluehall, not a Whitehall, which had long grown accustomed to acting as an in-house 'think tank' to Tory governments as has been the case in Japan for the bulk of the post-war period?[26]

Conclusion

The danger is real but it is still potential rather than palpable. It is an attitudinal problem to do with the accumulation of day-to-day experience since 1979, not a question of politicisation. It is all very human and understandable. The former head of the Home Civil Service, Lord Bancroft, captured its essence when he said in the middle of the Thatcher years:

> The dangers are of the younger people, seeing that advice which ministers want to hear falls with a joyous note on their ears, and advice which they need to hear falls on their ear with a rather dismal note, will tend to make officials trim, make their advice what ministers want to hear rather than what they need to know.[27]

The answer? At the very least a code of ethics, agreed by all parties and monitored by the Treasury and Civil Service Select Committee. Even better would be a Civil Service Statute incorporating the core principles of impartiality, integrity and political neutrality.[28] Such a statute could be repealed only by another statute – by primary legislation rather than through changes in custom and practice or by scarcely noticed amendments to orders in council. Only then would the possibility of

Whitehall 'turning Japanese' be properly precluded, especially if Conservative ministers remain in unbroken possession of the state apparatus into the twenty-first century.

Notes

1. *Kenneth Baker's Memoirs: Maggie's Minister*, BBC2, 11 September, 1993.

2. For a fuller exposition of the Northcote-Trevelyan legacy see Peter Hennessy, *Whitehall*, Secker & Warburg, London, 1989, pp 30–50.

3. See *The Role of the Civil Service: Interim Report*, Vol II, Treasury and Civil Service Committee, Session 1992–93, House of Commons 390-II, HMSO London, 1993, pp 80–1.

4. The phrase is Professor Anthony King's.

5. Peter Hennessy, *Cabinet*, Blackwell, Oxford 1986, p 99.

6. See John Smith, 'The Public Service Ethos', lecture to the Royal Institute of Public Administration, 8 May 1991.

7. Jim Prior, *A Balance of Power*, Hamish Hamilton, London, 1986, p 136.

8. Bernard Ingham, *Kill the Messenger*, Harper Collins, London 1991, p 396.

9. Kenneth Baker, *The Turbulent Years: My Life in Politics*, Faber, London, 1993, p 397.

10. Alan Clark, *Diaries*, Weidenfield, London, 1993, p 284.

11. See Hennessy, *Whitehall*, pp 85–6, 238–9, and Public Record Office, CAB21/1638, 'Function of the Prime Minister and his Staff', 1947–49.

12. See G.W. Jones, 'The Prime Minister's Secretaries: Politicians or Administrators?' in J.A.G. Griffith (ed), *From Policy to Administration: Essays in the Honour of William A. Robson*, Allen & Unwin, London, 1976, pp 13–38.

13. Private information.

14. Private information.

15. Baker, *The Turbulent Years*, p 111.

16. 'Bagehot', 'Selling a new spirit', *The Economist*, 5 December 1990 – Mr Patten's authorship of the analogy emerged only in 1993 after his departure for the governorship of Hong Kong.

17. See Peter Hennessy, 'Central Administration' in Peter Catterall (ed), *Contemporary Britain: An Annual Review 1992*, Blackwell, Oxford 1992, pp 21–2. On 'conviction' – famously she had said just before becoming PM in 1979: 'It must be a conviction government. As Prime Minister I could not waste any time having any internal arguments'. Interview with Kenneth Harris in the *Observer*, 25 February 1979.

18. *Competing for Quality: Buying Better Public Services*, Cmnd 1730, HMSO, 1991.

19. See Mr Dorrell's evidence to the Commons Treasury and Civil Service Committee on 13 July 1993, *The Role of the Civil Service: Interim Report*, pp 262–5.

20. Private information.

21. *The Role of the Civil Service: Interim Report*, p 130.

22. *Questions of Procedure for Ministers*, Cabinet Office, 1988.

23. *The Duties and Responsibilities of Civil Servants in Relation to Ministers: Note by the Head of the Home Civil Service*, Cabinet Office, 1985.

24. *The Role of the Civil Service: Interim Report*, pp 142–3.

25. Peter Hennessy and Simon Coates, *Bluehall SW1? The Civil Service, the*

Opposition and the Government during a fourth Conservative Term, Strathclyde Analysis Paper no 11, 1992, p10.

26. See Charles Leadbeater, 'Unusual Show of Strength', *Financial Times*, 13 July 1993.

27. Lord Bancroft interviewed for Brook Productions Channel 4 programme, *All the Prime Minister's Men*, 10 April 1986.

28. I outlined my reasons for preferring this solution to the Treasury and Civil Service Committee in May 1993. See *The Role of the Civil Service: Interim Report*, pp 80–92.

Clinging to the Wreckage

Gareth Smyth

The British Conservative Party is both a ruthless and a radical organisation: much more ruthless, and considerably more radical, than its opponents. (*David Marquand*)[1]

This is not just an intellectual victory won within the Conservative party. It ties in with deeper changes in the aspirations of the electorate. The language of free markets and enterprise has modernised the party and left socialists clinging to the wreckage as their ideology sinks beneath the waves. (*David Willetts, MP*)[2]

I

Towards the end of the 1992 general election campaign, there was a nagging frustration among the press that the Conservatives weren't making a fight of it. 'Why are all your posters so negative?' one sighing hack asked John Major at the morning press conference. The Conservatives, the depressed pack generally agreed, were fighting a lousy campaign.

'The teenage Tories running Central office miss too many opportunities and make too many mistakes,' opined *Sunday Times* editor Andrew Neil in a signed leader recommending the appointment of Michael Heseltine as election supremo.[3] There was evident disquiet in Conservative ranks. Polls and commentators suggested the most likely outcome was a hung parliament, probably stacked in Labour's favour. Labour expected to win. Robert Waller, the only pollster who consistently predicted otherwise, was pilloried in parts of the press.

Indeed Labour had behaved for some time as though it expected to win. The infamous Sheffield rally, praised by many commentators the day after[4] and condemned in hindsight was not the first of its kind:

Margaret Beckett might have only dour arithmetic to convey, but at least she can dress like Father Christmas in drag, complete with blood-curdling stiletto slingbacks.

When the time came for Kinnock the Crusader to swagger, splay-footed, no-necked and iron-shouldered to the dove grey-painted, chipboard-constructed, mock-Romanesque lectern and address the expectant throng, pale pink steam was already bursting out of his ears.

Everybody knows Labour has no ideology. The sums (the way it does them) just don't add up. What it does have is Kinnock the Cocksure, Kinnock the Streetfighter, Kinnock the Prole Who Won't Lie Down. Sure, it's show as much as substance. But just try not shouting – Hurrah![5]

This was January 1992. Labour felt it had come a long way from the 1980s when, as in the 1950s, it had been fashionable to argue that demographic and economic changes made it unlikely that Labour would ever again win a Commons majority. The decline in large-scale production, commentators argued, undermined collectivism. 'Essex man' became a potent symbol under Margaret Thatcher, as the government sold council houses and widened share-ownership through unprecedented privatisation programmes. But by the later 1980s a consensus developed within Labour that presentational problems underlay its demise (social attitude surveys, after all, revealed continuing support for many values associated with Labour, and the 1983 election campaign had been particularly inept). The post-1987 Policy Review, a detailed exercise in revision launched in glitz, gave a real expectation of victory. The defeat in 1992 revealed Labour's problems were more deep-seated.

The party's General Secretary, Larry Whitty, reported to Labour's National Executive on 21 June 1992 in stark terms:

... possibly the most telling statistic is the degree to which the electorate had begun to believe the Labour Party could win. It is difficult to escape the conclusion that at the very end of the campaign the electorate was just too apprehensive about Labour and the more evident it became to them that Labour would either win or there would be a hung parliament dominated by Labour, fears of high taxation suggested by the Tories and the tabloids, plus the general unease about our economic competence or general distrust of the Party and its leadership all took their toll.

Patricia Hewitt, who co-ordinated Labour's election campaign during the last week, reached a very similar instant verdict:

It was the prospect of a Labour government, with or without a majority, that was absolutely terrifying to a lot of those who ten days out from the election looked as if they were going to vote for the Liberals.[6]

Labour's weaknesses were palpable. The party had been shaped decisively by its initial reaction to Thatcherism. It spent the years between 1979 and 1992 trying to recover from its initial failings, while all the time the Conservatives continued to move the agenda and so made Labour's task of recovery more difficult.

In responding to the early years of Margaret Thatcher's government few Labour politicians believed the Conservative reform programme tapped any popular chords or dealt with any deep-seated problems in the post-war consensus that Labour had helped produce. There was much resistance both to Eric Hobsbawm's argument that Labour's 'forward march' had been halted and to the very concept of Thatcherism by which Stuart Hall and Martin Jacques attempted in *Marxism Today* to pinpoint what distinguished the Thatcher government from the Conservatism that had gone before.

Labour's own diagnoses of the failure of the Callaghan government focussed on psychology, emphasising its timidity – its acceptance of IMF conditions, the imposition of incomes control, even the decision not to go to the country before the 1978/9 'Winter of Discontent'. It rapidly became accepted wisdom that the parliamentary leadership had 'lost touch with the rank and file'. In opposition after 1979 the pendulum within the party swung sharply to the left, so prompting the departure of three leading MPs to form, with Roy Jenkins, the SDP and Tony Benn's challenge for the deputy leadership in 1981. By then Labour was completely unelectable. Its 1983 general election manifesto, the 'longest suicide note in history', was a badly-presented, jumbled accumulation of conference resolutions including withdrawal from the European Community and unilateral nuclear disarmament.

Margaret Thatcher's second term, 1983–87, was accident-prone. Despite a majority of 144 the government had great difficulty in managing back-bench unrest over issues as varied as banning trade unions at GCHQ, rate support grants and Sunday shopping (on the last, the government was defeated when as many as sixty-eight backbenchers voted against its proposal). With the 1985 Westland Affair, an apparently innocuous discussion over the future of Britain's sole helicopter manufacturer blew up into a row which cost the scalps of two cabinet ministers, Michael Heseltine and Leon Brittan. But even after that, and despite good local election results in May 1986, Labour was unable to sustain a lead in the polls.

Only very slowly did Labour realise that Thatcherism tapped millions of voters' negative experiences of paternalist, state bureaucracy. The party faithful were not alone in believing that Labour had been the victim of little more than an anti-government swing. The Nuffield College study of the 1979 election stresed that 'since 1959 no British government had won re-election at the end of a full term in office'.[7] The expectation that the pendulum would swing back blinded Labour to the electorate's expectations and so to its own faults.

II

The general election of 1992 was hardly a success for the Liberal Democrats. All the by-election gains of the parliament – Eastbourne, Ribble Valley, Kincardine & Deeside – were wiped out. Paddy Ashdown found his party 17 per cent behind Labour, with 18 per cent of the vote and only twenty-two seats. Outside south-west England, where the party won Cornwall North and Devon North and removed Conservative Chairman Chris Patten in Bath, the picture was gloomy: key targets like Hazel Grove and Richmond & Barnes remained in Tory hands.

Now on a lower base than the Liberal/SDP Alliance had enjoyed in both 1983 and 1987, it was difficult to sustain the argument that the Liberal Democrats could replace Labour as the party of opposition. Yet the obvious alternative was far from straightforward, as Peter Kellner noted:

> Mr Ashdown would be taking an enormous risk were he to advocate realignment with the Labour Party as it is, rather than wait for its destruction. Labour might brush him aside. He might lose the vote of disgruntled Tories.[8]

Ashdown was playing the long game. The 1992 result, he argued, was a structural advance on at least the 1970s: the two-party system had been destroyed.

> Labour can no longer win on their own. They are a drag factor on others who fight the Conservatives. They have now lost their historic role as the sole left-of-centre party capable of winning government. Our role is to be the catalyst, the gathering point for a broader movement dedicated to winning the battle of ideas which will give Britain an electable alternative.[9]

Ashdown's 'long game' continued a march, in the general direction of power, begun by earlier leaders. The fortunes of the Liberal Party had improved surely but very slowly throughout the 1950s and 1960s until February 1974 brought the party over six million votes and a 'hung parliament'. But when Edward Heath offered Jeremy Thorpe a Royal Commission on electoral reform and, reportedly, the post of Foreign Secretary, the Liberal Party, concentrated on the 'Celtic fringe', balked at the prospect of compromise and no deal was possible.

David Steel, who replaced Jeremy Thorpe in 1976, was determined the Liberals would become a party of power, and courted disapprobation in his first speech to the party's conference by arguing forcefully for coalition. When James Callaghan's Labour government lost its parliamentary majority, Steel quickly took his chance: the Lib/Lab pact of 1977–78 brought little tangible policy benefits but took the Liberals into the corridors of power.

The reconstruction of British politics under the shock-waves of

Thatcherism could hardly spare the centre. Steel saw the advantages of hauling on board former cabinet ministers Roy Jenkins, David Owen, Bill Rodgers and Shirley Williams when the SDP was formed in 1981, but the 1983 election result – when the 'SDP/Liberal Alliance' polled only 675,985 fewer votes than Labour – represented a highpoint. As Steel sought to outmanoeuvre the Liberal 'left' epitomised by the bearded Tony Greaves of the Association of Liberal Councillors, David Owen, who succeeded Roy Jenkins as SDP leader, was increasingly contemptuous of the Liberals. The vote for unilateral nuclear disarmament by the 1986 Liberal conference prompted the Alliance's decline in the polls just before the general election and was a body-blow for Steel. *Spitting Image* cruelly caricatured him sitting in Owen's pocket as a lacklustre campaign in 1987 floundered over a joint leadership where Owen appeared to lean towards the Conservatives and Steel towards Labour. Beneath the surface, the personal bitterness between the two was even more acute. The departure of the Owenites and a series of disastrous name changes seemed to portend the demise of the merged party.

Through recovery from the nadir of the 1989 European election results, when the party's share of the vote fell to 6.2 per cent, Paddy Ashdown achieved an ascendency over the party unparalleled since Gladstone. At the same time the party's strength in local government elections gradually increased, so building up outside Westminster the experience and profile of previously unknown politicians. While talk of a massive parliamentary breakthrough remains wishful, the Liberal Democrats by the middle-1990s are an established reality in British politics. Though their political support is lower than was the Alliance's at its heyday, it is certainly firmer.

III

Across the years of opposition to Conservative one-party dominance, several simple themes emerge which help explain the ineffectiveness of the opposition.

1. The role of the international situation

With the election of Ronald Reagan in 1980, an axis developed between Washington and London of two world leaders who believed that communism should be confronted rather than contained. The 'second cold war' made it difficult for the opposition both in the United States and in Britain to articulate foreign policy alternatives. There was opposition in Britain in the 1980s to the siting of US cruise missiles, but there was also deep unease about Labour's policy (adopted in 1980 and on which it fought the 1983 and 1987 general elections) of giving up all nuclear weapons unilaterally. The 1982 Falklands War evoked deep-seated, if confused, emotions and made defence a more tangible issue than at any time since 1945. A large television audience lapped up images of British people, islanders indeed, invaded by a foreign power. The world was a dangerous place. Labour seemed ill-equipped for such a world. In 1987 Neil Kinnock told David Frost on Sunday morning television that, as a last resort, guerilla warfare would be appropriate defence against Soviet invasion. The Tories seized on the image of 'Dad's Army' and their final, most successful, campaign poster featured a soldier with his hands raised beneath the simple caption 'Labour's Arms Policy'.

In no sphere did Margaret Thatcher exploit the advantages of incumbency more skilfully than in her standing as a world leader. She launched her 1987 election campaign with a visit to Moscow where she served up a string of photo-opportunities wearing a succession of stunning outfits. Kinnock's visit to Washington, where he had few friends in the administration, seemed to emphasise his lowly status. Thatcher ended the campaign by attending the Western Economic Summit in Vienna: television pictures of the prime minister in conference with Reagan, Kohl and Mitterand reinforced her status as the longest-serving of the seven heads of government.

2. Divisions in the Opposition

The 'Thatcher revolution' began with an election victory based on 44 per cent of the overall vote. In the subsequent three elections the Conservatives won around 42 per cent, enough to give decisive majorities in 1983 and 1987 and a narrow majority in 1992. The division of the non-Conservative vote was crucial to these results.

In 1983 and 1987 the battle of Her Majesty's Opposition was with the Alliance, not with the government. Labour's initial aim in 1987 was to come second. Campaign chief Peter Mandelson was subsequently pleased that Labour's 'brilliant' campaign 'proved decisive in seeing off the Alliance and re-establishing Labour as the major contender for power'.[10]

Labour believed, in other words, that defeating the Alliance was a necessary condition of returning to 'normal' two-party politics where Labour could expect its turn in the sun, its turn to enjoy a parliamentary majority. 'We have no alternative with the Alliance but war to the knife,' wrote Robin Cook in 1983.[11] Not everyone agreed. As defeat loomed in 1983, and more so in 1987, some opponents of the Conservatives argued that voters should plump for the opposition candidate best placed in any constituency to defeat the Conservative. But some advocates of tactical voting were expelled from the Labour Party.

Even those who gravitated towards restructuring the political system around proportional representation were unlikely to put out feelers towards the centre. Apart from the brave exception of Jeff Rooker, few were prepared to initiate a public discussion about the political consequences of PR, including the likelihood of coalition government. In an interview with me in 1991, after his conversion to PR, Robin Cook refused to discuss even the question of a hung parliament: 'We are seeking a mandate from the country which involves a majority in the House of Commons. The moment one gets involved in discussing any other scenario, two thirds of the press will be jumping up and down saying – Labour thinks it can't win.'[12]

The divisions in the opposition to the Conservatives were geographical as they were political. The geographical dimension to British politics became more pronounced between 1979 and 1992: Labour consolidated its hold on swathes of northern England and Scotland, and the Conservatives' majority was based on its ascendency in southern England, especially the south-east. But the Liberal Democrats, too, found themselves concentrating their efforts, particularly by 1992 in the south west. Proponents of pacts began to point out that Labour and the Liberal Democrats could challenge the Conservatives in a different set of seats, a case made most clearly by Oxford academic Vernon Bogdanor.

But many in both parties continued to insist that such a pact would not work. Newly-elected Liberal Democrat MP Liz Lynne pointed out that an electoral arrangement with Labour could alienate many Lib Dem voters - 'I was voted for by a number of people who were anti-Labour. I got a lot of the soft Conservative vote, and if I said I was in favour of any deal with Labour I would be selling them out.'[13] There was some polling evidence for this view. Harris found in March 1992 that Lib Dem voters prepared to switch to another party split 45 per cent to 39 per cent in favour of the Conservatives. The Lib Dems were probably damaged in the election by John Major's charge that Paddy Ashdown was the 'door-keeper to a Labour Britain'.

But advocates of pacts argued that this problem could be countered if electoral agreement was linked to principle through a common approach to changing the political system. Matthew Taylor, Liberal Democrat MP for Truro, argued the ball was in Labour's court:

> What do the Labour Party hope to achieve by fighting Truro hard? The best they could possibly have achieved would have been the election of a Conservative member of parliament. Why did they put in the effort? Because they don't accept the principle of the multi-party system. They believe that they can still recreate the two-party system, Labour Party and the Tories, and deliver effective majorities for the Labour Party within it. If agreement can include the acceptance that we are headed towards a multi-party system, the Labour Party chooses actively a multi-party route, then just maybe we might begin to see something delivered.[14]

3. A culture of opposition

'Multi-party politics' – seeking compromise with other parties to develop common aims – was not part of Labour's culture. For the bulk of the 1979–83 parliament Labour was pre-occupied with internal matters. A fractious special conference in 1981 introduced a cumbersome electoral college to choose the leader; battles between unilateralists and multi-lateralists raged until the late 1980s; and after electoral defeat, assigning blame became a major preoccupation. To commentator Peter Jenkins, Michael Foot, who became leader of the Labour Party in 1980 at the age of 67, personified Labour's oppositionism:

> The spoilt baby of his distinguished family, he had remained an *enfant terrible* until in 1974 at the age of fifty-eight he had condescended for the first time to accept the responsibilities of office as Secretary of State for Employment. Until that time he had preferred the luxuries of opposition, to which his temperament was suited, and studiously avoided acquiring any of the skills of modern government; he was ignorant of economics, unversed in nuclear strategy or the affairs of the European Community, a stranger to Washington. His interests were literary and rhetorical and it is likely that he knew more about the eighteenth century than his own.
>
> Quite unfitted for the office of Prime Minister and hopelessly ill-equipped to fight an election in a television age, he led his party to catastrophe. His invocations of the 1930s and of 1945 stirred old folk memories but meant little to the electorate of the 1980s. Foot appeared to the country as the walking past.[15]

Neil Kinnock was Michael Foot's chosen successor – indeed Foot timed his resignation in June 1983 to improve Kinnock's chances. Neil Kinnock's strength in his rise to the leadership (he won with 71 per cent of the electoral college) and in subsequently confronting Bennery was precisely that he was not tainted by the experience of 1974–79, when he had refused office. The phrase 'skipping a generation' was used to rule out former ministers like Peter Shore and Roy Hattersley (Tony Benn lost his Bristol East seat in the election and so was ineligible). The reality was that experience of power was seen as a disqualification. Nothing more clearly demonstrated Labour's oppositionalism than 'loony leftism', the policies and antics of local councils, especially in London. As Kinnock went about isolating the hard left and building a majority on Labour's National Executive Committee (NEC), local government became an attractive playground for radicals. During the miners' strike of 1984–5, a group of local authorities sought to open a 'second front' by refusing to set a rate. Their campaign collapsed in internal recriminations and accusations of betrayal, but their focus on 'the local state' was common within the party. Great hopes were placed in the innovations of 'local socialism'. David Blunkett, leader of Sheffield

Council said in 1984 that being in opposition highlighted 'the fact that local government can be a tool for achieving socialist change'

> People have recognised that local government is a far more important vehicle than they had ever believed. What we are trying to do is change a climate of opinion that Mrs Thatcher has very successfully fashioned, to the benefit of her own government. This can only be done from the local level, because you do have to fire people's imagination and commitment.[16]

4. Inflexibility

As Labour nestled in its northern heartlands, there was a temptation to return to old certainties. Margaret Thatcher was seen as a backlash, as someone taking Britain back, rather than as someone creating new realities and new problems for the opposition. Labour's task was to 'defend' the post-war consensus.

Stuart Hall noted how strange this situation appeared to the 'radicals' of the left:

> what is particularly novel is that the new Right succeeded in its efforts to establish itself as the radical political force, the political force that was going to change things. One of most astonishing signs of the reversal in the 1979 election was to hear Mr Callaghan complain that the radical Right meant to tear the old system up by the roots. And we had been foolish enough to imagine that tearing society up by the roots was what socialism was about![17]

Not only did this limit Labour's thinking, it made the party look very old-fashioned. A streak of sentimentality was never far from Labour's sense of identity. Central to this was the ritualistic evocation of 1945. Tony Benn evoked the example at the LSE in June 1992:

> (In 1945) whoever thought we'd defeat Churchill, the most popular man, won the war single-handed with a big cigar, came out of his bomb-proof shelter and sympathised with the East Enders who'd been bombed to hell. But there was a change. And the change was because people had hope. And this whole philosophy from the people, the professional pessimists, they're mainly in the media – there's no hope, come to terms with it.[18]

Sentimentality made it difficult to think afresh. Labour came round gradually to accept the right of council tenants to buy their homes, but only through a series of reluctant policy changes after its 1980 Conference voted for compulsory repurchase of former tenants' homes. It grudgingly came to terms with the need for 'efficiency' in local government, the desirability of secret, postal ballots for trade union elections, and the purchaser/provider split in the NHS: but it did so as a reaction, usually very belatedly, to the reforms driven through by the Conservative government against Labour opposition.

In the wake of Labour's fourth defeat, Neil Kinnock's rapid resignation provoked a leadership contest whose result was a foregone conclusion. It was the same old story, observed Ivo Dawnay in the *Financial Times*:

> As Labour's leadership election grinds on into its second month, the party appears ever more unable to avoid reminding the electorate just how fiercely conservative and anachronistic its basic instincts remain. Rather than spark debate, the leadership race has reinforced traditional positions as candidates have vied for the votes of the party faithful. [19]

Not all within Labour's ranks were satisfied. Patricia Hewitt admitted that Labour's changes had been insufficiently bold:

> We were always much more successful at getting rid of old policies than we were in developing big, new bold ones. There will not be another detailed policy review, and indeed there needn't be. There will I think be clearer positions on a few big questions, one of which will probably be electoral reform. There will be a fresh look at the whole question of social justice and redistribution, and how Labour combines it moral crusade against poverty with some sense of identification with the aspiring working class. What I hear everywhere I go is working-class people, who don't identify themselves as middle-class, they identify themselves as working-class and they say – I've got things, I want more, I'm moving up, and Labour is not for me, because Labour's about people moving down. And unless we know who we stand for, what those people want, and we represent their interests, then I think the results of the next election may look remarkably like the results of this election. [20]

A similar argument was advanced by newly-elected MP Nick Raynsford in a provocative piece in the Fabian Society's newsletter – 'The Party appears to be substituting a state of anaesthetised torpor for the previous mood of hyperactive aggression. If we go on like this, are we not at risk of sleepwalking into electoral oblivion?' [21]

Raynsford advocated tackling 'big strategic issues' including a review of tax and benefit, management structures for public services including health and education, and the economic management of Britain in decline. This theme proved popular with many of the new intake, who sought to ally a radical reappaisal of issues with a re-examination of core Labour values, teasing out distinctions between means and ends. (See chapter 14)

But the likelihood of Labour carrying out such a radical rethink was not increased by the April 1992 election result, which gave the Tories a relatively narrow majority of twenty-one seats despite having a lead over Labour of nearly 8 per cent in votes. 'One more heave' appeared a tantalisingly attractive approach. Struggling with internal dissent over Maastricht and the recession, John Major's government rapidly became unpopular and suffered by-election losses. In the local elections of May 1993 the Conservatives lost control of all the counties bar Buckinghamshire. Labour's 1993 Conference saw victory for John Smith in achieving one-member-one-vote for the selection of parliamentary candidates, but it was also remarkable for triumphalism and the reassertion of the Labour's traditional ideology. The conference voted for the centrality of Clause IV, for 'full employment', for the continuation of first-past-the-post: even the one-member-one-vote was won only by a traditionalist tub-thumping speech from John Prescott.

Furthermore, the parliamentary Labour party remains – even after the gains of the 1992 general election – composed primarily of men elected in the north of England and Scotland. Each of them is a big fish in their own little pond. The resultant inflexibility has worked to place Labour on a political terrain favourable to the Conservatives.

5. Tory Terrain

Evoking the 1945–51 government remains the easiest way to win applause at Labour conference. Even after the adoption of a Euro-socialist manifesto for the June 1994 European parliament elections, Labour's view of British politics emphasises the nation state as the centre of power. After the 1939–45 War the two major parties alternated their hold of the British state through a parliamentary majority assembled through the first-past-the-post voting system. Labour believed the Conservatives would use their hold to either consolidate (as in the 1950s) or to 'turn back the clock' (as under Margaret Thatcher). Labour would use their turn to take steps towards 'socialism', a model centred on economic management and social solidarity and based on the war-time experience of 1914–18 and 1940–51.

Thus Labour was very slow to appreciate the growing importance of the European community, a distraction from Labour's mission to seize the British state. It tended to see the rise of the third party as a temporary aberration – if the 'Alliance' could be seen off it would be back to good old two-party politics. The desire for devolved government and accountable administration in Scotland was seen by many within Labour as a threat, both because the rise of the SNP could remove Labour MPs north of the border and because any reduction of the Scottish contingent at Westminster, through either devolution or independence, would remove Labour's chances of a UK parliamentary majority.

Labour showed a consistent unwillingness to change the rules. In 1990, after eleven years in opposition, a party commission under Professor Raymond Plant was established to look at voting systems. The electoral reformers were growing in confidence, but first-past-the-post retained the allegiance of most of the MPs it had elected. The leadership adopted a strategy of professing an open mind. During the 1992 election, this came across as an indecisive flirtation and proved damaging.

As polls indicated the likelihood of a hung parliament Neil Kinnock's 2 April commitment to 'enhancing' the role of the Plant Commission made headlines. Television commentators outlined various voting systems and people talked about PR in pubs. But Labour had prepared neither itself nor the electorate for the rather different terrain of post-PR, pluralist politics. In a country without peacetime coalition this century, a hung parliament was easily portrayed as chaos. Labour's 'open minded' approach to reform gave the Conservatives a field day – as ministers launched an anti-PR barrage, Neil Kinnock refused to reveal his personal view on *World in Action* three days before polling day. Paddy Ashdown was left alone on the burning deck.

'Kinnock seeks deal with Libs,' blazed the *Evening Standard* front page headline on 2 April. 'Other parties may fiddle and flirt with constitutional change for party political gain,' John Major told a Wembley rally on 5 April. 'This party will not.' In the face of the Conservative onslaught and Labour's dithering, public opinion moved against electoral reform and a hung parliament by the final week of the campaign. The NOP/BBC exit poll found 44 per cent support for first past the post against 37 per cent for PR; the Harris/ITN exit poll found a bigger majority for the status quo – 52 against 43 per cent.

But its stance on PR was symptomatic of a deeper malaise within the Labour party. As the 1993 Conference would show, the vast majority in Labour's ranks did not accept much of the 'new realism' on which Labour fought the 1992 election. Arguably the voters understood this. Harris Research, who polled for the Conservatives in the run-up to the election found in January 1992 that 46 per cent of Liberal Democrat voters and 50 per cent of women believed Labour had 'changed just to win the election'. Hence undermining Labour's credibility was crucial for the Conservatives during the 1992 election. Ministers seized on every opportunity to pounce when Labour spokesmen hinted at additional spending commitments. It paid off in the end. The key slogan of the campaign was simple, but telling: 'You can't trust Labour.'

Particular verve was reserved for attacking Labour's credibility on economic management. There had long been a gap in Harris polling between those saying they would vote Conservative and those saying they would be better off under the Conservatives. I noted the day before polling:

> Conservative managers insist that – regardless of what the pollsters are told – electors will vote with their wallets once in the privacy of the booth. The psephologists call this 'pocket-book voting'. As the campaign draws to a close, Mr John Major, the prime minister, has returned to the theme of tax and insisted that only a Conservative government will end the recession. The

polls still show a Conservative lead on 'ability to manage the economy' and as the party under which people feel they will be best off financially.[22]

Even the defeat of party Chairman Chris Patten could not take the shine off the Conservatives' night of triumph. 'The architects of John Major's election campaign said the Tory triumph had vindicated their election strategy,' observed Colin Brown in the *Independent*. 'After breathing a collective sigh of relief as the final results came in, they took credit for holding their nerve.'[23]

IV

In the local elections of 1993 and 1994 the Conservatives fared badly. Labour was in a healthy opinion poll lead, and in no mood to compromise. But at the same time polls found politicians more unpopular than ever before, and with an unprecedented volatility voters kicked the government in mid-term. Few commentators doubted Conservative MPs would dump John Major if they thought it necessary to win their fifth successive election victory.

Even the newly found hostility of the press to the Conservatives after 1992 reflected ambiguously on Labour. Trevor Kavanagh, the political editor of the *Sun*, explains the newspaper's changing role partly in terms of lack of effective opposition:

> We'd be a very toothless society if we had no newspapers to stand up and represent the views of a lot of readers. Who else is there? The Labour Party doesn't do it. The Labour Party isn't an opposition at the moment. It's so closely allied to the Tories in so many ways you can hardly tell the difference. They don't do much in the way of standing up and shouting anyway, on issues that might be worth opposing.[24]

Even if the press shifted, other facets of the political scene looked familiar, as was observed even before Smith won the Labour leadership by Matthew Taylor, one of the Liberal Democrat MPs who publicly advocated electoral co-operation between the opposition parties:

> What will actually happen in practice? What we will probably see happen is John Smith becoming leader of the Labour Party, inevitably as a new leader seek to rally the troops. As one would normally expect in any democracy, during the mid-term of the government the Labour Party will look likely at various times to be able to at least remove the Tory majority, possibly have a majority of its own. That will lead the Labour Party to feel it is possible to win under the two-party system again, the one-more-heave school will be strengthened in their belief that it can be achieved. In the run up to the general election, the economy will be improving, albeit from a poor base. The Conservatives will fight back and they will probably win again. The debate in the immediate aftermath will be very similar to this one. John Smith I think has himself privately talked about being a one-shot leader, so

there will be a new leadership election and the new leader will come in place. He will feel that he has to rally the troops, tell them that they can make it, and we will be back on to the same old cycle.[25]

Notes

1. 'The Meaning of Major', in Gareth Smyth (ed) *Can the Tories Lose?*, Lawrence & Wishart, London 1991, p. 18.

2. *Modern Conservatism*, Penguin, Harmondsworth 1992, pp 49–50.

3. *Sunday Times*, 29th March 1992. Vincent Hanna wrote in the *Guardian* on 6 April – 'It is hard to escape the feeling that the Liberal Democrat surge owes a lot to the inept Tory campaign, which, I fear, is based on a mis-match between its marketing strategy and its customers.'

4. For example, one observed ' ... Labour, in Harold Wilson's words, owing more to Methodism than Marxism, had put on an alcohol-free show ... . When Neil Kinnock came to the platform to speak, six flags – the EC flag blowing behind the four of the United Kingdom and the Union Jack – in a message as subliminal as any other last night, waved through his speech, blown by a wind machine. It was corny, manipulative and totally successful.' *Independent*, 2nd April 1992.

5. Dave Hill, 'Kinnock the King?', *New Statesman & Society*, 17th January 1992.

6. LSE Public Policy Group/Commons Voice symposium, 'Turning Japanese?', LSE, June 1992.

7. David Butler & Dennis Kavanagh, *The British General Election of 1979*, Macmillan, Basingstoke, 1980, p 339.

8. *Independent*, 24th April 1992.

9. Quoted *Independent on Sunday*, 10th May 1992.

10. Colin Hughes & Patrick Wintour, *Labour Rebuilt: the New Model Party*, Fourth Estate, London 199, p. 34.

11. Robin Cook, 'Getting out of the hole', *Marxism Today*, November 1983.

12. 'Force for Change' (part of the supplement 'The Good Vote Guide'), *Marxism Today*, October 1991.

13. Quoted *Financial Times*, 22nd June 1992

14. 'Turning Japanese?', LSE Symposium.

15. Peter Jenkins, *Mrs Thatcher's Revolution*, Pan, London 1989, pp 120–1.

16. 'Local Socialism: the way ahead', in Martin Boddy & Colin Fudge (eds), *Local Socialism?*, Macmillan, London 1984, pp 244–5.

17. Stuart Hall, 'Faith Hope or Charity', *Marxism Today*, January 1985.

18. 'Turning Japanese?', LSE Symposium.

19. *Financial Times*, 29th May 1992.

20. 'Turning Japanese?', LSE Symposium.

21. 'Sleepwalking into oblivion?', *Fabian Review*, November 1992.

22. Gareth Smyth, 'Polls suggest Labour is increasing lead in marginals', *Financial Times*, 8th April 1992.

23. *Independent*, 11th April 1992.

24. Interview with GS.

25. 'Turning Japanese?' LSE Symposium.

Nightmare on Norm Street

David McKie

On the morning after the Tory triumph, the *Sun* had no doubts. Under the heading: 'It's the Sun Wot Won it', the paper reported on April 11: 'Triumphant MPs were queuing yesterday to say "Thank you my Sun" for helping John Major back into number 10.' The paper quoted David Amess, whose victory at Basildon had signalled Major's victory against the odds, as saying: 'It was your front page that did it. It crystallised all the issues.' The page had shown Neil Kinnock's head encased in a light bulb: if Labour won, said the caption, would the last person to leave the country please turn out the lights?

A leader amplified the message. Headed 'Triumph of Mr Nice Guy', it said:

> Take a bow this morning, Sun readers. It was you who decided the fate of Britain in the General Election. And in our view, decided rightly ... (John Major) had to climb the mountain of grievance over a recession that was not of his making. He did it with integrity, conviction, and above all, courage.

The view that the Tory tabloids, militant for Major, virulent against Kinnock and Labour, and contemptuously dismissive of Ashdown and the Liberal Democrats, had turned the tide in the 1992 Election was not confined to the *Sun*. Some very senior Tories shared it. In the *Sunday Telegraph* of April 12, the former Conservative Party treasurer, Lord McAlpine, wrote:

> The heroes of this campaign were Sir David English (editor of the *Mail*), Sir Nicholas Lloyd (editor of the *Express*), Kelvin MacKenzie (editor of the *Sun*) and the other editors of the grander Tory press. Never in the past nine elections have they come out so strongly in favour of the Conservatives. Never has the attack on the Labour Party been so comprehensive. They exposed, ridiculed and humiliated that party, doing each day in their pages the job that the politicians failed to do from their bright new platforms. This is how the election was won, and if the politicians, elated in their hour of victory, are tempted to believe otherwise, they are in very real trouble next time.

The following Sunday, the same paper's Mandrake column cited an even more eminent source – though one, like McAlpine, with an obvious interest in trying to diminish the contribution of the non-believer who ran the official Tory campaign, Chris Patten. 'She (Mrs Thatcher) told friends that it was the Tory journalists who won the election and that this should never be forgotten' the column said. 'Men like Mr Paul Johnson and Mr Kelvin MacKenzie, the editor of the *Sun*. 'You won it' she said to Sir Nicholas Lloyd, the editor of the *Express*.'

In his valedictory press conference on April 13, the Labour leader Neil Kinnock quoted McAlpine. Kinnock added:

> I make, and I seek, no excuses, and I express no bitterness, when I say that the Conservative supporting Press has enabled the Tory party to win yet again when the Conservative party could not have secured victory for itself on the basis of its record, its programme or its character.

The *Sun*, uncharacteristically, then developed cold feet. It quoted Amess as saying he'd been misquoted. He hadn't said the *Sun* had won the election; only that it had helped. The *Sun* said of Kinnock: 'It is flattering for him to suggest we have so much power. Like so much else he says, it is also untrue.' An acute attack of modesty also occurred at the *Mail*. Its editor, Sir David English, told a reporter:

> I have no doubt that we helped swing a number of people towards the Tory position and equally turned a few more away from Labour. To suggest, as Mr Kinnock has done, that the *Daily Mail* singlehandedly won the election for the Conservatives and brought about a Labour defeat is very flattering but it ascribes far more influence to us than we could give ourselves.

Kinnock himself later admitted that he'd thought from the Friday before the election that Labour had lost its chance. On that basis, the grand finale of the *Sun*'s cheerleading coverage would have made no difference, though the energetic and committed build-up might still have done.

The claim that the Tory tabloids may have swung the result found support in other quarters. Figures compiled by MORI showing shifts from Labour to the Conservatives among readers of different papers up to April 9 found substantial swings to the right among readers of some of the right-wing/cheerleader papers with Labour gaining ground among readers of the neutral *Independent* and near-neutral *Today*. But these figures could have been affected by changes in newspaper readership over the period. And note that there are swings to the Tories among papers which were opposed to them – 3.5 per cent for the *Guardian*, 2 per cent for the *Mirror*.

Why should the *Sun* and *Star* (the *Star* did not formally endorse the Tories, though its coverage was far more favourable to them than to their opponents) have been so much more persuasive than the equally

Table 11.1 Newspaper readers: how they swung/election advice

Paper and party supported	How they would have voted in Jun-Dec 91	How far they swung	How they voted April 9	How they would have voted if typical of their social class
Telegraph (CON)	Con 72 Lab 13 LD 15	1 to Con	72 11 16	50 27 20
Express (CON)	Con 66 Lab 19 LD 13	3 to Con	68 15 15	45 33 19
Mail (CON)	Con 66 Lab 16 LD 15	0.5 to Con	65 14 18	45 32 19
Times (CON)	Con 61 Lab 19 LD 17	3.5 to Con	64 15 19	51 25 20
Today (CON)	Con 51 Lab 31 LD 18	4 to Lab	43 31 23	43 36 18
Sun (CON)	Con 39 Lab 47 LD 11	8.5 to Con	45 36 15	39 40 17
Independent (NIL)	Con 33 Lab 39 LD 25	3 to Lab	25 37 35	55 27 20
Daily Star (NIL)	Con 26 Lab 62 LD9	7.5 to Con	32 53 12	37 39 17
Mirror (LAB)	Con 20 Lab 67 LD 12	2 to Con	20 63 14	39 40 17
Guardian (LAB)	Con 12 Lab 59 LD 22	3.5 to Con	15 55 25	49 28 20

Source: Martin Linton, *Guardian Guide to the House of Commons*, based on MORI analysis.

fervent *Express* and *Mail*? Professor Bill Miller of Glasgow argues that *Sun* and *Star* readers are less likely to be committed to a political party and less likely to start the campaign with an interest in politics. They are therefore more likely to be open to influence.

There is other supporting evidence from the pollsters. Harris's final poll for ITN found that voters who in fact would not have been hurt by the Labour budget or would even have gained from it believed it would harm them. That supports Labour's belief that the constant reiteration of the dubious Tory claim that Labour would put £1,250 on every tax bill, in the press as well as on billboards, helped turn the election against them. But some of these respondents might have feared for their fate when they had climbed higher up the ladder, rather than what would happen straightaway.

There are also scattered findings in the work of those chagrined pollsters who went back to find out what might have gone wrong with their final projections. ICM quoted these sample reactions:

> I read in the paper about Neil Kinnock having a light bulb in his head and I had strong fears. I also thought Arthur Scargill would raise his ugly head again.

> I read the Sun ... Arthur Scargill, what he was going to do with the unions if Labour got in.

> I read two or three articles about Labour's tax plans and the implications they would have on me. I had never before seen them so specifically printed. (The *Mail* and *Express* had both printed detailed projections of Labour's tax effects based on material compiled in Conservative Central Office.)

All had one thing in common: the frighteners had worked.

None of this is conclusive. But it chimes with other findings from Martin Harrop of Newcastle University and Bill Miller. Harrop reported that Tory voters are more likely to stay loyal if they read a Tory paper (12 per cent more in February 1974, 14 per cent more in October 1974, 15 per cent more in 1979) while uncommitted voters were more likely to choose the Tories if they read a Conservative paper. Miller calculated the tabloid effect as equivalent to a 2 point advantage for the Conservatives. In the year up to the 1987 election, there was a 5 per cent overall swing to the Conservatives; among persistent readers of Tory tabloids it was 12 per cent; among persistent readers of Labour tabloids only 1 per cent. In a pattern similar to that of MORI's findings, *Express* and *Mail* readers swung right by 8 per cent, *Sun* and *Star* readers by 17 per cent.

Some argued against this thesis that the Tory papers have always behaved like this, yet Labour was still elected when it deserved to be. But Labour have only had two clear victories in the past sixty years, 1945 and 1966. In 1945 Labour had been in coalition, and its leaders were known not to be demons; coverage was also restricted by newsprint regulations. In 1966 people had seen a Labour government at work over 18 months: again, that diminished the effect of the demonology. In 1966, in any case, Labour had a far bigger share of newspaper backing

than it did in the years of Tory supremacy from 1979 onward. Since
then, newspaper readers have overwhemingly tended to be told the
story as seen through Tory eyes.

Table 11.2 Election advice of papers by circulation:

	1966	1970	1974(F)	1974(O)	1979	1983	1987	1992
Con	56	55	68	47	66	75	73	66
Lab	43	44	30	29	28	22	25	25
Lib	4	5	5	5	0	0	3	0
Gap	13	11	38	18	38	53	48	41
Majority of winning party	L 97	C 31	none	L 4	C 44	C144	C 101	C 21

Perhaps the shrewdest comment on the second-thoughts claims of
the *Sun* and *Mail* that they didn't make that much difference came from
the journalists' trade paper, the *UK Press Gazette*. 'To claim that they
have no influence over the decisions, opinions and attitudes of readers
would be a suicide note sent to all advertisers, and it would also mean
that their anti-Labour campaign was a preconceived exercise in futility.'

The tabloid campaign began well before the calling of the election.
Indeed in a sense it had been under way for years. Even outside election
periods, these papers tend to put their characteristic spin on events –
as the *Mirror* did for Labour.

The way the system works was described in the *Independent* of
February 3 1992 by its then political editor Tony Bevins, a graduate of
the *Sun* and the *Mail*. He wrote:

The anti-Labour, pro-Tory bias permeates every level of the Tory tabloids;
to the point that political reporters see it as their task to generate their own
propaganda ... . Having worked for nine years as a political correspondent
of the *Sun* and the *Daily Mail*, I count myself as something of an expert on
the insidious nature of the process. To survive and rise in, or on, 'the game',
you pander to the political prejudices of your paymasters, giving them the
stories that you know will make them salivate. That means putting a spar-
kling gloss on anything to do with the Conservatives and their policies, while
denigrating, or 'ratting', Labour. When I was on the *Sun* and *Mail*, for example, that task included taking every possible opportunity to hype every threat
from the Labour left in general, and Tony Benn in particular. The direct
assistance of Conservative Central Office was not needed then, any more
than it was needed by the *News of the World* yesterday, when it headlined its
report on the latest anti-Labour wheeze from Rupert Murdoch's Wapping

power-base: 'Kinnock and the Commies.' … Their (the rat packers') friends recognise their skill as professionalism, their critics as prostitution. The best are rewarded with salaries between £40,000 and £50,000, generous expenses and big cars. Those who fail do not survive; the attrition rate is high.

As the *Guardian* and *Independent* noted at the time, the *Mail* and *Express* were conducting a kind of phony election at the start of the year. (See on this point the chapter on the Near Term campaign in Butler and Kavanagh, *The British General Election of 1992*, Macmillan). Attempts would be made on a Monday to supply a theme for the week. This was the *Mail*'s contribution in January:

Monday 6: Labour plans eight new taxes. (Followed on Tuesday by: Labour double budget blow; including tables on estimated effects derived from Conservative Central Office calculations and based on a 10p increase in basic rate).

Monday 13: Leak of planned Tory attack on Labour defence claims.

Monday 20: Labour part-time tax shock.

Monday 27: Ford chief: Labour's crazy tax plans. (The Ford chief was Ian McAllister, who repudiated the story. A similar story presenting Labour as a threat to the car industry led the *Mail* on April 4). A second story charted projected effects on Courtaulds and Coates Viyella of Labour's minimum wage. The story was only partially confirmed by Coates Viyella and repudiated by Courtaulds. (Patrick Wintour, *Guardian*, 29 January 1992)

As their architects hoped, some of these stories were taken up by the broadcasters, prompting Labour Deputy Leader Roy Hattersley to lodge the year's first complaint. 'Here is a serious democratic problem' he said, 'when one newspaper can tell a lie and the BBC can report it as fact.'

As the campaign for the April election developed, the tabloids deployed a battery of tactics old and new in support of the Tory party. Stories favourable to the Government or unfavourable to Labour were given a prominent showing: Labour successes and Tory embarrassments were played down. (The *Mirror*, for Labour, applied the same principles the other way round). It was even suspected by Labour that the *Mail* published its world exclusive on the break-up of the marriage of the Duchess of York when it did to ensure that a clutch of bad economic statistics, due for publication in the opening week of the campaign, would be lost amid the excitements of a belting royal story. As they largely were.

When on the night of March 31, three opinion polls appeared giving Labour winning leads and suggesting the first break in the logjam, the

Tory tabloids were curiously unenthralled. The *Star*, exceptionally, led with a foreign story (Libya), the *Sun* on a multi-home-owning shadow minister, and the *Mail* on Labour's allegedly 'coy' response to its splash of the previous day. Next day, however, the *Mail* and *Express* made much of these polls, even though subsequent figures contradicted them, as exemplifying the danger that a Liberal Democrat surge might put Labour in.

Open partisanship was sometimes supplemented by a kind of spurious even-handedness. The most blatant example here was the *Mail* of April 6, which opened its pages to the three party leaders to answer *Daily Mail* questions. Neil Kinnock refused to take part: his questions were printed, and the space for answers left blank. A leader condemned his pusillanimity: 'how arrogant of him' it said 'to turn down this perfectly civil request to clarify his views'. Still, reading the questions you could see why he'd been suspicious. Sample questions to Major: 'Can I ask whether you think Mr Kinnock was wise to admit to grave errors of judgment?'; 'Why don't you make the point that the other two parties will pull us into a federal Europe, and the Tory party won't?' Sample questions to Kinnock: 'Socialism has been ditched in Eastern Europe and discredited here in the West. What makes you think Britain wants or needs another dose of it?' 'Your manifesto is stuffed with spending promises which Labour won't cost and the nation cannot afford. Is not this manifesto a fraud?'

Even that perhaps was a little more subtle than the *Daily Express*'s strategy for destabilising Labour's leader. It called home its Moscow correspondent Peter Hitchens, whose pursuit of Kinnock had plainly discomfited the Labour leader in 1987, to resume his harrying.

The Tory campaign, newspapers had predicted, would concentrate on fears about Labour's tax proposals and distrust of its leaders. That, together with a package of dire predictions about the economy (mortgages up, a shrinking pound, the return of roaring inflation) was also the Tory tabloid agenda throughout the campaign. But towards the end other issues were worked up too. One was the fear of reviving union power. For instance:

March 24, *Sun* – threat of return to picket terror. *Star* – strikes will be back, and secondary picketing will be legalised.

March 25, *Star* – Remember the winter of discontent.

March 31, *Mail* – Labour's secret plans to pay unions more. Plus a leader: Public sector would rule the roost under Labour.

April 1, *Mail* – The kickback: this secret tax which will allow Labour to reward its union paymasters, by Eric Hammond. *Express* – Union paymasters in the wings, by Lord Tebbit.

April 8, *Sun* – Unions will expect Neil to cough up. Lest we forget: the winter of discontent in words and pictures. Polling day, *Mail* – Demon King Arthur (Scargill) waits in the wings. The winter of shame: this was the face of Britain last time Labour ruled. *Express* – Give sacked miners their jobs back, says Scargill: Arthur is back, waiting in the wings.

Immigration also surfaced. For instance:

March 26, *Mail* – Kinnock won't curb flood of bogus refugees. Plus a leader quoting Douglas Hurd as saying there was no sign the Labour Party understood the problem or could be trusted to deal with it.

March 30, *Express* – leader: Labour is soft on terrorism and immigration.

April 2, *Express* – Fake immigrants- an explosive problem (Kenneth Baker warns). Feature: Open door to chaos – stricter controls needed as immigration threatens to swamp Europe's cities. *Mail* – Migrant madness – asylum switch 'would open door to refugees' (Baker warns).

April 4, *Sun* (front page spread) – Human tide Labour would let in: bogus refugees will grab state hand-outs. We risk sowing the seeds of fascism, says Garry Bushell.

April 7, *Express* – Baker's migrant flood warning: 'Labour set to open doors'. Leader: dangers of uncontrolled immigration. April 8, *Mail* – Major stands firm against migrant flood ('John Major stood alone yesterday as the only serious party leader to reject any relaxation of immigration control'.) *Sun* – Labour's lukewarm stance on immigration will weaken European resistance to the threat of massive immigration.

Also Electoral Reform. For instance: April 7, *Mail* – PR has helped the fascists march again in Europe, warns Baker. *Express* – Baker describes PR as 'pact with the devil': could have terrible effect on Britain, he warns. Feature: the politics of chaos – under PR, Nazis and even porn stars have a say in government. April 8, *Mail* – Italians want to dump PR and adopt First Past the Post.

The culmination of all these processes, and possibly the most perfect specimen yet in the history of this art form, was the *Sun*'s penultimate paper on April 8. Across the top of page one was a comment piece asking who would best run Britain. 'Who would you choose?' it demanded. 'A solid dependable man with a cool head who has been Chancellor, Foreign Secretary and Prime Minister. An experienced world statesman whose friends criticise him for having the style of a bank manager? Or Kinnock: look at his public image. A nice man, but someone who could be drawn into a punch-up at a curry house.' Readers were then turned loose in a journalistic theme park called 'Nightmare on Kinnock Street' on pages 2, 3, 4, 5, 6, 7, 8, 9 and 34.

This assaulted Labour policy on housing, the EC, energy prices, the unions ('Unions will expect Neil to cough up'), inflation, the NHS, immigration, planning ('Gays to rule on planning applications: even loft conversions, home extensions and garages will have to be approved by gay and lesbian groups if Labour are elected'.) Elsewhere a report headed 'It's Mao or never for Neil' revealed how a psychic had asked some famous dead people how they would vote in this election. The line up was: Conservative – Churchill, Field Marshal Lord Montgomery, Queen Victoria, Elvis Presley, Sid James. Labour – Mao, Marx, Stalin, Trotsky, Brezhnev, Andropov, John Lennon and Robert Maxwell ('I see a lot of me in Neil Kinnock'). Incongruously there appeared in the midst of all this a full page advertisement placed by the Conservative Party.

The most crucial issue of all, however, was the choice between Kinnock and Major. 'Our position is clear' the leader announced. 'We believe by a long, long, long way that only John Major can take us out of recession. Only John Major is strong enough to lead us in the dangerous world of the nineties.'

From the very start of Major's new government there were those on the right who shook their heads and prophesied doom. The coven of former Thatcherites camped out at the *Sunday Telegraph* and *Spectator* never believed John Major was fit to fill Margaret Thatcher's shoes. They would never forgive her assassins, of whom, some believed, Major, even if passively rather than actively, was one. It was not to be long before the starting signal was fired for wider hostilities. On July 24, just fifteen weeks after Major's much acclaimed triumph, the *Mail* ran a piece by Paul Johnson headed: 'Is Major becoming the Harold Wilson of the nineties?' It disparaged the PM's handling of the David Mellor affair, described his cherished Citizen's Charter as 'boring, and just a teeny bit ridiculous', and compared his economic policies with those of Mr Micawber. 'Major,' Johnson wrote, 'has the makings of a great Prime Minister. To be one, however, he must accept constructive criticism in the spirit it is given – good-tempered friendship.'

It was no doubt good-tempered friendship which inspired the *Times* to run a leader on October 16 deploring Major's 'destructive stubbornness', especially over Europe, and declaring: 'He is struggling to keep up with the onrush of events. He gives no sign of even trying to get ahead.' And good-tempered friendship again which drove the same paper to run on October 21 a feature suggesting that Major had come close to breakdown over Black Wednesday. A two page spread in the *Sunday Times*, reflecting on events since Black Wednesday, was headed: 'The Major Mess.' 'Muddling along with Major' it labelled a leader on November 1 comparing the prime minister with President Jimmy Carter. The *Daily Telegraph* too, though less virulent than its Sunday counterpart, was unfriendly reading for Downing Street. A leader on October 20 condemned the ERM debacle and the 'insouciance' with which the Government had handled the economy since the election. 'This news-paper' it said 'was among the first to highlight the scale of the crisis; the response of ministers was to complain bitterly in private about the *Daily Telegraph*'s "disloyalty". Almost since the General Election, the state of industry and the economy has been at the heart of most people's fears. Yet from the Prime Minister down, the Government has seemed scarcely to listen to the public, to the real world – an impression highlighted by some almost insultingly cheerful platform speeches to the Conservative Party conference.'

The waves, for a time, receded, but soon they were back again, crashing higher on the shore. Economic mismanagement, infatuation with Europe, a weakness for standing by ministers who ought to be sacked – these and other offences were condemned with mounting vehemence by those who had once been the party's most steadfast Fleet Street friends. By the summer of 1993, as Major clawed his way out of Commons defeat on Maastricht, and disaster at Newbury was capped by disaster at Christchurch, patience was wearing thin. The *Mail*'s feature writer Ann Leslie, who had written gushing accounts of Major's leadership qualities at the election, now reported Conservative fears that they'd chosen 'a weak and confused political midget, utterly lacking in the kind of ideological bearings needed to guide them through the forest and back to electoral safety again.' His continuation in office, the *Mail* declared in a leader on July 24, was 'ever more problematic'; beneath it, a year to the day since his comparison of Major with Wilson, Paul Johnson speculated on how Major might be removed, and sug-gested a successor (Kenneth Clarke) had now emerged.

The greatest disillusionment, though, was that of the *Sun*, which increasingly looked like the Paper Wot Won It And Now Wished It Hadn't. Its attack was developed in a curious two-barrelled process with its columnist Richard Littlejohn banging away at targets which the leader column had yet to get in its sights. The initial assault was on Chancellor Norman Lamont: Major (often described in leaders as 'Honest John') remained a hero. 'John Major' wrote the *Sun* in May 1992 after the local elections 'is on a winning streak. He is monarch of all he surveys. He has all the authority and prestige he needs to trans-form Britain. So get cracking, honest John.' The *Sun*'s complaint was the level of interest rates. On June 5, the dam burst. It said:

> Look down any High Street and you'll see the legacy of Lamont. Shop fronts boarded up, offices closed down. Small businesses are still going bust at an alarming rate. What the hell is the Chancellor going to do about it? Sit with his fingers crossed and hope something will turn up? You'll have a long wait, Norman.

The Tories, the paper said, were supposed to back the little guy as he made his way in the world. But how could businessmen prosper, or householders survive, when interest rates were so crippling? Six days later, it came back again. 'For God's sake, wake up, Norman' it told the Chancellor. 'Businesses are going under, crippled by High Street interest rates. High Street shops are deserted. Car sales are poor despite the Budget price cuts. People are scared to spend.' 'If Norman Lamont will not act' it added two days later, 'then John Major should. And find himself a new Chancellor.' When the National Economic Development Council was axed, the *Sun* gave the credit not to Lamont (though he, it conceded, had 'helped') but to Major. 'This quiet man' it predicted 'could be our greatest revolutionary since Oliver Cromwell cured Charles I's sore throat.'

But where Major was held to be blameless on the economy, he wasn't on Europe. Major's belief in the Maastricht settlement, and his refusal to allow a referendum, produced the first signs of editorial doubt. 'We beg John Major not to get lost in the European bog' the *Sun* wrote on June 27. 'He is a prime minister of high promise. We want him to carry that into happy reality. But at present the signal is: danger.'

Littlejohn's disillusion was by now marching well ahead of his paper's. Under the heading 'Major getting too big for his boots' his weekly column declared on July 2 – not quite three months after the Tory election victory: 'The nastiest thing anyone could think of to say about him was that he resembled a suburban bank manager.. So come the election we voted for A Nation At Ease with Itself and gave the man from the listening bank his own mandate. Then he stopped listening. John Major came into office looking like a man who would not make a drama out of a crisis. Instead he has turned a crisis into a catastrophe.'

'If you took away the adulterers, the drinkers, the liars, the terminally lazy and the egomaniacs' the *Sun* wrote of politicians on July 25 'you'd only have John Major and half a dozen others left.' 'Major and Lamont' the less forgiving Littlejohn wrote on the 30th, 'have betrayed the very people who voted them back into office on the promise of economic recovery. John Major and Norman Lamont are doing to Britain what David Mellor did to Antonia de Sancha.'

Disenchantment grew with Black Wednesday. The *Sun* was now beginning to turn against the Major government the repertoire it had long deployed against Labour. 'Nightmare on Lamont Street' it proclaimed after Black Wednesday, with sub heads announcing 100,000 to join the dole; 'misery on the cards'; thousands of homes in peril; motor trade crash; tourist bosses rocked; and a blow for builders. 'Let's pretend Labour won the last election' Littlejohn wrote on September 18 'and for the past six months had pursued exactly the same polices as the Conservatives. Tory backbenchers would be demanding a military coup, never mind a recall of Parliament. What a bloody mess. John Major asked us to trust him. He has betrayed us.' Yet a leader on the previous day had drawn a different conclusion. Two things were clear, it ordained. Lamont must go, and Major mustn't.

The *Sun*, even so, was by now a paper of opposition. So were almost all of them. Only the *Express* remained loyal (with some lousy circulation figures, its rivals chortled, to show for it.) Some put this down to cool calculation, and especially the *Sun*'s hopes of exploiting the *Mirror*'s post-Maxwell difficulties and coaxing over readers whom a daily diet of Toryism was more likely to drive away. Such calculations clearly existed. The Murdoch paper *Today*, which had gone though the April election proclaiming its even-handedness with the slogan 'Proper News, Not Propaganda', had recruited a stable of old *Mirror* hands and increasingly looked like the *Daily Mirror* in exile. But the *Sun*'s shift was different. The reasons behind it were essentially those which had influenced Littlejohn. He wrote on September 18:

> I care about the people who read my newspaper and who are suffering through no fault of their own. In April people voted Tory – on the advice of this newspaper I have to say – for a number of reasons. 1. We trusted John Major. 2. We didn't want to pay higher taxes. 3. The prospect of the Kinnocks flying the ANC flag over Downing Street was simply too horrible to contemplate. And what have we got to show for it? 1. Major has betrayed that trust. 2. What's the point of low income tax if you haven't got an income? 3. Still, it could be worse.

You could not call the *Sun*'s behaviour remorse. But it did reflect an awareness of the feelings of thousands of readers, not least in places like Basildon, that effectively they'd been conned. The *Sun* in a sense had been accessory after the fact. If it now tried to pretend all was well under Honest John, its credibility would collapse and its readership possibly dwindle.

For a time it seemed to toy with the notion of recalling Lady Thatcher. 'An amazing sign that Margaret Thatcher is poised to return to power emerged last night from one of history's greatest prophets' it proclaimed in Conservative conference week 1992. The source was Nostrodamus. On October 6 it ran a MORI poll showing 28 per cent backing Major as prime minister against 45 per cent for Thatcher. It lauded Lord Tebbit's straight talk on Maastricht at conference and, though it still believed Major was 'the honest patriot to lead this country back to the good times', even suggested that if anyone now had to quit it might be Major rather than Norman Lamont. 'Dear Mr Major' it wrote on October 13 'Do you have a plan to get us out of this bloody mess?' This, it explained, was the letter the *Sun* hoped it would never have to write. But with the country plunging ever downwards, four serious questions had to be asked. 'What on earth is going on? Where the hell is this once-great country of ours heading? When will you tell us your master plan? Do you even have one?' It concluded: 'The *Sun* has always said you are the best man to lead this country. We still believe that. The only trouble is you seem hopelessly wedded to your faltering European dream. Why not stop the phone calls to Paris, Bonn and Copenhagen and start worrying about Plymouth, Bolton and Colchester? Trust the people, Mr Major. Tell us the truth. We're running out of time and patience.'

The mishandling of the pit closure issue brought a new burst of rage. Page 1 of the October 20 election was blank except for a caption which read: 'This page is dedicated to Michael Heseltine. It represents all he understands about the worries and fears of the ordinary working people in depression-hit Britain. Nothing. Absolutely nothing.' 'Are you going bonkers in a Major way?' it asked its readers on October 23, two days after the *Times* allegation that he'd almost cracked up on Black Wednesday. 'Doubts are being expressed about the sanity of the Prime Minister. And many of the people who voted for him are beginning to believe they must have been off their rocker too.' Soon after they portrayed him, like the England football manager Graham Taylor before him, as a turnip.

The continuing rejection of a referendum on Maastricht (the *Sun* believed Major feared he would lose it) stirred the paper to further frenzies. Phone polls and petitions were organised. Lamont's 1993 budget was 'nightmare on Norm Street' and 'a Vat lot of good.' 'Time Lamont saw a doctor' said a leader headline on March 18. 'Norman Lamont' it argued 'has finally taken leave of his senses. The Chancellor should sit down in a darkened room for a few hours. Seek medical advice. He's gone off his rocker.' 'From muddle to farce, from shambles to outright fiasco, the Government's handling of the Maastricht Treaty has become a national disaster' said a leader on May 6, the day of the Newbury byelection. 'Shambling to disaster' the *Sun* said of the Government as the results came in from Newbury and the shires.

This was abuse of a Tory government by a Tory paper on a scale which few could remember. But still the sentence of death was withheld. 'John Major has some admirable qualities. He is a decent man. But he presides over an administration which is held in contempt for its mistakes, its broken promises, and the atmosphere of political sleaze that surrounds it.' (Leader, May 8). On June 3, the paper invited its readers to 'help John make up his mind' on five outstanding issues he apparently couldn't resolve. Next day they were asked to ring in with responses to the question: who's doing the worst job for England? John Major or Graham Taylor?

At last he dropped Lamont, but it came too late to mollify his persecutors. With Norman gone, he became number one in the firing line. 'Everything we have suspected about Major is confirmed by Lamont' the *Sun* announced.

> There is too much reacting to events, and not enough shaping them. With recovery poised on a razor's edge, this country needs a leader with vision and stature. That man is no longer John Major. If he must go, then he should go early. The lions can no longer be led by a donkey. Especially a lame one.

'It is clear that even if he wins, Mr Major is mortally wounded' the paper declared in July when the PM had to come back to the House to reverse his defeat on Maastricht. 'His stubborn stance on Maastricht, on which he has now staked his political life, has split his party asunder.' 'A nice guy not up to his job' said a leader headline on July 24. John Major, the *Sun* regretfully reported, was 'an honest, decent, likeable man.' He had done his best. But sadly he was not up to the job. This was the theme to which the *Sun* would return, time and again, and with growing vehemence.

The *Sun* reached a new pitch of anger on January 14, 1994. If the *Sun* was indeed the paper Wot Won It in April 1992, it now repented of having done so. 'What fools we were to believe this lot' it moaned. 'Today our eyes are wide open. We can see we have been conned.' Complaining of 'immorality, deceit, incompetence and hypocrisy' the paper said John Major was showing 'all the leadership of a lemming.' 'The way *Sun* readers vote determines the government we get' it warned. 'If the Tories want to remain in power they have got to clean up their act. And they must do so right now.' But again the richest moral outrage came from the paper's alter ego, Littlejohn. 'John Major' he wrote 'has forfeited the right to lead the Conservative Party and the nation. He is a weak, mediocre man, surrounded by unprincipled spivs and chancers … This is a sleazy, dishonest Administration led by a political pygmy.'

The sheer contempt of the *Sun*'s indictment was by now provoking a question which two years before would have seemed inane. Was it possible that at the next election the Tories' most cherished ally would swing behind Labour? In the case of *Today*, that seemed decidedly possible. It was now more or less a Labour paper. But you couldn't even now begin to say that of the *Sun*. In Japanese style politics, where one party has endless hegemony, a change of government becomes not a switch between parties but a switch within the party of government. Thus Major for Thatcher: thus one day, perhaps, Clarke (or Heseltine or Portillo) for Major. Throughout its war on the Government, the *Sun* found space every now and then to insist that Labour was not the answer. Not at least till it totally changed its ways. At first it welcomed the change from Kinnock to Smith. 'If the Labour party had been led by John Smith over the last nine years' it said on April 24 1992 'perhaps it would have been in power today'. Labour, the paper explained in a leader on June 19, had lost the election because of socialism. 'People want something different' it said, 'the chance to help themselves with minimal interference from the state. Labour has to change into a party that encourages self-reliance instead of handicapping it, that welcomes enterprise instead of condemning it. Until they do, there will be no realistic alternative to the Tories. That is bad for Labour. Bad for the Tories. And bad for democracy.'

So John Smith knew what he had to do to gain the *Sun*'s support; and he didn't do it. Soon they were writing him off. Labour, a leader said in January 1993, had sent its two brightest hopes (Blair and Brown) to Washington. What would they learn? That to secure victory, you needed an outstanding leader. 'Not a dead loss like John Smith.' 'The dead hand of socialism' the paper announced on May 3 'has been thrown off all over the world – but it still lies heavy on the opposition benches ... Unless John Smith learns the lesson, his party will not only crash to another disaster at the next general election. It will become just like the brontosaurus. Extinct.' 'It is now nearly 20 years since Labour last won a General Election' the *Sun* mused on June 28. 'Maybe Mr Smith should ask himself why. Because with leadership like his, he and his wretched party are likely to languish in the wilderness for another twenty.' 'Dinosaurs aren't extinct after all' it proclaimed in July at the height of the row over OMOV. 'They're alive and pulling the strings of the Labour Party.' The analogy with primaeval creatures entranced it. 'You don't need to watch Jurassic Park to see what dinosaurs look like' it crowed in September. 'There are whole herds of them on display at Labour's conference.'

What the *Sun* continued to crave, in other words, was an electable Conservative party. It no longer thought it could get it from Major. That in a sense was a risky position; but only if you assumed that the Tories would hang on to Major. And the Tories had been given plenty of notice that unless they dumped him, they were unlikely to get full-hearted support from the *Sun*. Could they ignore such a signal? Once more what the paper's leaders implied was plainly stated by Littlejohn. He'd been watching the Scargills and Skinners at Labour conference and asking himself what people like Tony Blair – by now a *Sun* pin-up – were doing in the same party. 'Once the Tories dump John Major' he wrote on September 30 'Labour will lose the next election. Don't forget you read it here first.'

British Politics in the Doldrums

Patrick Dunleavy

The comparison with Japan highlights some central problems of British politics since 1979. Under the sway of successive Liberal Democratic Party governments Japanese society and the Japanese economy have reaped some benefits in terms of policy consistency and institutional certainty. Economic growth has been very impressive since the late 1950s, when the LDP first established its hegemony by winning absolute majorities of the popular vote. As the LDP's vote declined, and party fragmentation grew in the intervening decades, Japanese society none-theless continued to enjoy some benefits from the pattern of 'creative conservatism' established in the post-war recovery.[1] The historic central-ization of power in the bureaucracy created strong ministries,[2] and in the post-war period they were able to act as partial counterweights to the growing factionalization and corruption of the LDP. Corporatist linkages between the bureaucracy and large industrial firms produced biased but still effective concertation mechanisms. They allowed the state-led bureaucratized economic development of the early recovery years to transmute into more flexible, 'multi-valued' interventions suited to dealing with 'post-industrial' technologies and 'post-modern' changes in the world's consumer markets. And the presence of strong pulls towards social consensus preserved some valuable pre-capitalist elements of Japanese tradition – such as the strength of family ties, looking after the elderly in extended families, moral prohibitions against crime, and lifetime employment traditions inside major companies. All of these 'feudal' elements have somewhat moderated the degenerative impact of market forces and profit-led modernization on pre-modern social mores and values, and partly offset the absence of a developed Japanese welfare state.

Under LDP dominance, Japanese society got the worst of some worlds but the best of others. It suffered from one party governance and centralization. But long-term policy-making was consistent and large-scale resources were committed to coherent industrial strategies and to building up public sector infrastructures. Japanese households experienced low and probably falling levels of housing amenity and environmental quality, but also record-breaking levels of nominal GDP expansion and consumer-goods purchasing. And while public life was polluted by extensive political corruption over several decades, at least in the 1990s there were some impressive elite efforts to implement genuine reforms and a public insistence on the need for change.

By contrast, developments in Britain reveal a pattern of more diffuse political malaise, mostly unrelieved by mitigating achievements elsewhere. Britain thus seems to have got the worst of all worlds – one party governance hand-in-hand with a permanent pattern of volatile multi-party politics; strong executive action, historically rapid changes and unparalleled centralization carried out ruthlessly against opposition, but all to no long-term plan, without policy consistency or strategic direction; and the development of a coarse and cynical *realpolitik* substituting for statecraft and social consensus. I explore these three themes in more detail below.

One-Party Dominance, Multi-Party Politics

Political scientists define 'dominant party systems' in different ways, but at root their definitions refer to those polities where one party enjoys a 'preponderant influence' electorally, ideologically and governmentally. However, some authors also note that: 'Dominant parties should not be identified with parties which are perennially in government'.[3] The British situation is rather odd. We have a single party perennially in government, the Conservatives. And yet despite the Tories' partisan use of power for nearly a decade and a half, despite a severely distorted mass media system, and despite the fragmentation of opposition to the Conservatives, British electoral politics (and citizens' political attitudes generally) remain resolutely multi-party, and have been so for more than two decades now. The Conservatives are dominant because of their hold on national power, but in little else.

The roots of the Conservatives' 'natural party of government' mantle lie far deeper in British political history than most journalistic or academic observers (and virtually all Labour politicians) recognize. In the twelve elections held since December 1918, when Labour first entered nationwide competition, the Conservatives' median score has been 44 per cent of the popular vote, Labour's 38 per cent, and the Liberals 13 per cent. Thus in 1992 Conservative support was just below their historical record. Labour's 1992 vote was still considerably below its median level, and Labour's 'party identification' score dropped sharply as John Curtice notes above (p 15). And the Liberal Democrat's performance comfortably beat their historical average.

In a plurality election system this gap of six per cent between the two largest parties has tremendous long-term consequences for their respective ability to direct state power. Table 12.1 shows the record of party control of government from December 1918 to the end of 1993 (when this chapter was written).[4] The simpler statistics in the first three rows suggest lower estimates of Tory preponderance. Thus in the top row (where the percentages sum to more than 100 per cent because of coalition governments) the data show that Tory ministers have been in office more than twice as often as Labour politicians. Excluding the coalition government, formed because of the special circumstances of the Second World War, increases the Tory-to-Labour ratio slightly, to 2.4 to one. But some predominantly Tory governments, notably 1918–22 and 1931–35, were coalitions with sections of the Liberal party, so that if we focus on the Tory to Labour ratio of access to sole governmental power it drops again to 2.2 to one. However, Labour's record in government also shows some important periods without working majorities in the Commons, notably in 1923–24, 1929–31, February to October 1974, and 1977–79. In all of these periods Labour ministers controlled only a Commons minority, while in 1964–66 and 1974–77 Labour had tiny overall majorities which could not ensure them passage of their controversial bills. The Conservative record shows no such periods, however. So the Conservative-to-Labour ratio of access to governmental power *with a secure majority* is radically different, 4.3 to one, as the last row of the table shows. In modern Britain then Conservative ministers have exercised state power with an overall majority more than four times as often as Labour politicians. And if the Conservatives retain office until the end of 1996, under John Major or another leader, this ratio will carry on rising past 4.5 to one.

Table 12.1 The major British parties' record in government, 1918–93

Percentage of months	Con	Lab	Lib/Lib Dem etc.
Total months in government	72	34	12
Total months excluding wartime coalition	70	29	6
Months as sole government	64	29	0
Months with secure majority government	64	15	0

Notes: From December 1918 to the end of 1993 there are 901 months. Excluding the wartime coalition reduces the N for the last three rows to 841 months. Secure majority government is defined as an overall Commons majority of 10 seats or more.

The origins of this situation lie essentially in the fact that during the 1920s Labour never really erased the basis for Liberal or third party voting in modern Britain – reflecting a deeper truth which political science increasingly recognizes, that political party loyalties are often surprisingly durable.

Yet if the roots of the Conservatives' governing hegemony stretch deep into the past, so too does their inability to turn their dominance of state power into a lasting hegemony over political attitudes and debates. To see the fragility of the Tory position consider the following configurations of party support, and the likely governmental outcomes which would result from them (Table 12.2). The striking thing about these situations is how little separates them one from another. There is a range of eight per cent or less in the parties' shares of the vote across the scenarios. Yet the differences in the parliamentary and governmental outcomes which could result are radical indeed. In the top row of the table, the Conservatives' current governmental hegemony would be transformed into thorough-going predominance by virtue of outstripping all rivals, should they top 45 per cent of the vote. The second row reflects a return to the 1987 situation, when a divided opposition created a huge Tory majority. By contrast, the bottom row shows that the likely maximum loss of Conservative support (down four per cent on their 1992 score) could precipitate a hung parliament where a radical re-appraisal of the electoral system might result – paralleling the changes which took place during 1993 in New Zealand and in Italy, and the changes proposed (but not yet finalized at the time of writing) in Japan.[5]

Table 12.2 Hypothetical three party vote distributions, and probable governmental consequences

| Party support levels (%) | | | Resulting government |
Cons.	Labour	Lib Dem.	
45	36	15	Large Tory majority, strong lead over all opponents
42	32	23	Secure Tory majority, divided opposition
41	37	18	Narrow Tory majority, or hung Parliament
39	39	19	Hung Parliament, variable 'lead' party in government
37	39	21	Hung Parliament, with electoral reform likely?

Notes: These figures assume that 4-5 per cent of votes will go to Northern Ireland parties, nationalist parties in Scotland and Wales, and the Greens or other minor parties.

Thus the British body politic is no less sensitive than the human body. Just as small changes of temperature can tilt the human body between normality and a dangerous fever, so a difference of plus or minus 4 percentage points can still swing British politics into radically different pathways. And between elections, just such swings, indeed far greater swings, do take place. For example, the public reaction following the 1992 election belies the view of Anthony King that: 'Britain no longer has two major political parties. It has one major political party, the Conservatives, one minor party, Labour, and one peripheral party, the Liberal Democrats'.[6]

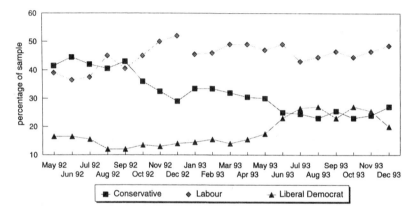

Figure 12.1a Voting intentions 1993–3

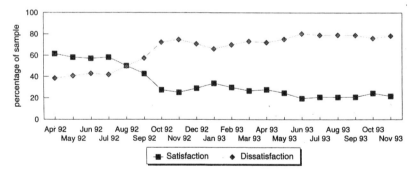

Figure 12.1b Satisfaction/dissatisfaction with Major as prime minister 1993–3

Note: Figures vary across polling agencies; most notably, ICM introduced a secret ballot technique in September. Since that time, ICM has produced Labour leads typically half or less than half of those recorded by other polling companies using traditional techniques.

Source: Gallup Political Index April 1992–December 1993.

Figure 12.1a shows that public support for the 'major party' slumped dramatically within months of the election result. In early 1994 support for King's 'minor party' in some polls surpassed the magic figure of 50 per cent. And Figure 12.1b demonstrates that confidence in John Major's premiership also showed a dramatic reversal of fortunes, rather than the extended honeymoon which might have been expected after the Conservatives' fourth election victory.

Indeed at the only other level where elections take place in Britain, in local government, the years of the Conservatives' unbroken rule at Westminster have seen a long-run decline in Tory fortunes of historic significance. For example, in an estimate made in 1979 I suggested that as a result of local government reorganizations carried out in the 1960s and 1970s by Tory governments, the Conservatives were assured of continuous control of local government areas covering 28.5 million people, compared with 'safe' Labour control of local authorities covering no more than 8.5 million people.[7] The vast bulk of the population I tagged as solidly Tory were in twenty-five English county councils. Yet following the 1993 county council elections, the Conservatives actually retained overall control in only one of these shire areas. The remainder, covering 25.3 million people in 1980, had moved into no overall control, or control by the opposition parties. Thus in rather less than a decade something like four fifths of the previous Conservative 'heartlands' in local government slipped at least partially from their grasp. Although there were some offsetting areas of surprising Tory strength elsewhere, notably in retaining continuous control of many more London boroughs than I predicted, the change in the shire counties is still a striking demonstration of the role that the local government system in the United Kingdom can play as a 'countervailing power' to national government trends.

The response of Conservative governments at Westminster, however, has recognized no legitimacy in such patterns. Local government powers have been circumscribed in historically unprecedented fashion, and their scope for raising revenues in accordance with their own priorities has been virtually eliminated. Large Labour-controlled metropolitan authorities were summarily abolished in 1986, with severely adverse effects in London. Control over public services and public spending has been increasingly passed to quasi-governmental bodies, by-passing municipal elections, while inconvenient large top-tier local governments have been abolished. At the time of writing the Major government seems likely to respond to the Tory loss of control in the counties either by enacting a unitary system of local government at district level, or by simply abolishing a few prominent Labour counties and leaving the remainder untouched.

A Strong Executive, with Nowhere to Go

Every system of government must have built into it a capability for direction by a few central actors. In a liberal democracy the fundamental questions to be asked about this capability concern the numbers of people who occupy roles at its higher levels, and the conditions under which they exercise leverage over the government system as a whole, and hence over the wider society.

The architecture of the Westminster system concentrates a great deal of this directive capacity in only a few hands, and significantly downgrades the constitutional or formal political constraints on its exercise. Conservative pluralists used to hold that the British system rests on 'the absence from our society of overwhelming concentrations of power'.[8] Yet they recognized too that this 'highest form of political development yet seen ... depends upon informal checks and balances and the self-restraint of politicians'.[9] If self-restraint disappears or withers, the Westminster model is uniquely sensitive to becoming unconstrained, as the Thatcher years bear eloquent testimony. The problem is that an unfixed constitution gives British governments the capacity to make 'the fastest law in the West'.[10]

In 1992 John Major released details of the Cabinet committee system for the first time. Research analysing the make-up of committees suggests that a British Prime Minister is a minority share-holder in his or her own government, directly controlling no more than 15 per cent of the influence in the Cabinet committee system as a whole.[11] So to be sure of controlling government business a PM must assemble a group of allies, principally two out of the three other key Cabinet positions (Foreign Secretary, Defence Secretary and Chancellor of the Exchequer), plus the two non-portfolio ministers who chair the Cabinet's domestic committees (the Lord Privy Seal and Lord President of the Council), plus two other loyalist ministers heading substantial departments.

A prime ministerial coalition of seven ministers constructed on these lines can easily control the full Cabinet of twenty-three, and exercise 'majority control' over the twenty-six standing Cabinet committees. The Cabinet in turn controls the other 'members' of the government, the ninety assorted MPs tied into the promotion ladder on lower rungs as Ministers of State, Parliamentary Under-Secretaries, or Parliamentary Private Secretaries – each of whom is 'voiceless', able only to accept and implement prime ministerial or Cabinet decisions or to resign. The government members in total thus constitute more than a third of the 330 MPs needed for an overall working majority. A further third of any parliamentary party will inevitably be loyalist MPs, who will support their current party leadership under almost any conceivable circumstances. So although a numerical minority, the government members normally have no difficulty in controlling the parliamentary party as a whole. And the essence of the Westminster model is that any group of 330 MPs banded together behind a common leadership can do anything they like – for that is what the principle of 'Parliamentary Sovereignty' means in practice. Thus it is that seven ministers can concentrate the power of the whole Chinese box structure, and exercise it in a formally unfettered way, now unique amongst contemporary liberal democracies.

With a prime minister who has no idea why they are in government except that political power is addictive – such as Harold Wilson after 1968, or Jim Callaghan and John Major at any time – the British system creates a debilitating vacuum at its centre. The heart of the machine has the capacity to over-ride other centres of decision within the state apparatus, but no ideas to guide it in doing so, except ephemeral political convenience. 'Strength Without Purpose' might be the guiding motto of such regimes.

By contrast, with a strongly committed, hyperactive, almost maniacal prime minister like Margaret Thatcher, who used a simple ideology and politically appointed staffs as multipliers of her message, the British system concentrates power to a disturbing extent. Thatcher's personality made it progressively more unfeasible for her to continue practising coalition politics, either inside her Cabinet or in the European Community. The two incapacities converged in the six-year feud between the prime minister and her Chancellor and Foreign Secretary over entry to the European Exchange Rate Mechanism, which persisted through half her period in office like a running sore, and finally precipitated Thatcher's downfall in 1990.[12]

Under either kind of regime the potential for centralization always existed. What has realized that potential so strongly since 1979 has been a strange concatenation of forces. The removal of constraint on Conservative partisanship in government after 1981 partly reflected their realization that the divided opposition of Labour and the Alliance/ Liberal Democrats gave them a historically unusual degree of electoral protection. But it also reflected the Conservative reaction to the last Labour government which in 1974–77 passed some of its programme into law despite a tiny overall majority. These years triggered a 'never again' syndrome in Conservative thought, a determination to make irreversible changes in their favour which was sustained by high Tories contemptuous of democracy and local government, and by market liberals committed to a rationalism which the Conservative party had previously always eschewed. The high Tory philosopher, Roger Scruton, openly described democracy as 'this disease' and a 'contagion', scoffing particularly at municipalities which try to mimic the Westminster apparatus of parliamentary practices and governmental power.[13] In his view local government traditions never amounted to more than an

institutionalization of customs, useful for tricking or beguiling an in-
genuous public, but of absolutely no intrinsic value as an area of political
autonomy or decision. For market liberals the test of institutional survival before the 'reform' axe raised by the 'new public management'
was a straightforward cost-efficiency one – anything else was superfluous.

The impetus for centralizing and reorganizing changes reached its
peak under the third-term Thatcher government (1987–90). Where her
first term government made few changes in administrative arrangements, the last did virtually nothing else – inaugurating a sweeping
reform of local government taxation, subsequently scrapped at a cost of
between £2 billion and £4 billion; ushering in a quasi-market within
the National Health Service which has considerably boosted management costs and personnel, for little discernible efficiency gain; pushing
through a national curriculum in order to foment the break-up of local
education authorities and the transformation of schools into micro-local
agencies; carrying the privatization of state enterprises deep into natural
monopoly and public utility industries; and making the most fundamental changes in Whitehall for nearly a century, via 'agencification' of
the civil service and 'market testing'. The Major government (before
and after the 1992 election) has had its hands full coping with the
continuing implementation burden of these changes, but ministers and
civil servants have continually added more of the same to the basic
momentum. In 1993, a key Permanent Secretary involved in this process
summed up the radicalization of civil service attitudes from small 'c'
conservatism to enthusiastic advocates of new public management by
declaring: 'We believe in "permanent revolution"'.[14] Little wonder then
that even some Cabinet ministers began to jib at right-wing demands
for constant change, supported by the civil service (especially the
Treasury and Cabinet Office). In October 1993 Douglas Hurd used a
Conservative Conference fringe meeting to denounce unnamed people
in government and Whitehall who believed in a 'cultural revolution'
every year, pulling up every section of the public services by the roots
to see how they were working.

There is a more fundamental dynamic of self-interest at work here,
as well, consequent on the steady decay of British state power – the
lengthy withering of imperial greatness; the dwindling of British military
capabilities to minor regional power status; successive financial crises
and long-run 'managed decline' in economic life; and finally the loss of
a role in international affairs as the USA's voice in Europe, and the sad
history of Britain's bungled adaptation to being a member state of the
European Union. In an era widely seen as characterized by increasingly
international or globalized policy-making, the UK nation state has faced
a long-run reduction in its scope for effective action, and been poorly
adapted to playing the parts which were still available.

For Westminster and Whitehall elites alike the ebbing of Britain's unilateral capabilities in 'high politics' areas (defence, international affairs and macro-economic policy), and the process of reconciling themselves to dealing co-operatively with other EU countries and other countries in global fora, have both been limiting and painful. Since at least the 1960s national politicians and senior administrators have compensated essentially by first eroding and then progressively displacing all other domestic centres of power in a take-over bid for 'low politics' issues. The politics of micro-economic change, of the welfare state, of local government, of infrastructures and of public service provision have progressively become more attractive to political elites whose traditional spheres of action have been shrinking.[15] Politicians and other elite groups (such as the Tory think tanks) have compensated for the mundane character of the issues with which they now dabble by increasing the amplitude and frequency of the changes they seek to push through, caring little for implementability or policy evaluation.

Late-model Thatcherism was simply an extreme case of a longer-run tendency, a more than usually blatant example of the political urge to hyper-activism, to meddling in half-understood issues and inaugurating schemes of reform as a substitute for genuine thought or sustained innovation.[16] And apparently the enduring lesson which the Major government learned from the Conservatives' revival from the doldrums of 1986 to the election victory of 1987 is that a frenzy of administrative reorganization and government centralization can be used symbolically to demonstrate political 'leadership'. That is, it maintains the grand illusion that someone is running the shop, indeed that 'the shop' can be run at all in contemporary political life.[17] Thus has the pattern of activity which so marked the Heath government, and was early on dismissed by Thatcher as equivalent to rearranging deck chairs on the decks of the Titanic, proved the most enduring characteristic of executive politics in contemporary Britain.

Managing Social Development without Care, or Guile, or Skill

The costs of one party governance and overweening centralization of power affect every British citizen. But for most people the dark sides of these developments are glimpsed relatively rarely, as isolated disturbing symptoms of an elite run out of democratic control. Concentrated costs have been borne by a very particular set of social groups – the additionally unemployed created by economic mismanagement, and politically stigmatized, unpopular or unorganized social groups exposed to government cutbacks of welfare benefits and public service provision. Benefits for young people under twenty-five have been particularly attacked, as have student grants, new construction of social housing, and urban programmes.

A by-product of the electoral changes and the alterations in executive style which they have produced has been a tremendous coarsening of the way that social stability is managed in contemporary Britain compared with earlier post-war periods. The strong and explicit use of force, and the politically controlled granting of state largesse, have both become far more prominent than Conservative philosophers of an earlier period would have dreamed possible, let alone wise. The market liberals have no statecraft, and little concern for the state as such. Their tactics are shaped by a modern Machiavellianism, but it is a *realpolitik* attuned solely to the micro-level, to securing this or that component of a hegemonic project of privatization for its own sake, and devoid of any clear image of how state/society relations can be handled in a long-term way.[18]

The most dramatic and worrying feature of this change has been the development of a clear *electoral/riot cycle* in British society. This idea draws on the large literature in political economy on the 'political/business cycle', where governments deflate immediately after an election in order to create room in the economy for them to stage a reflationary upturn in time for the next election. The hope here is that voters are 'myopic' and are prepared to re-elect the government on the basis of short-term prosperity in the election run-up.

The electoral riot cycle is the obverse side of the political/business cycle. Concerned to deflate early on in their term of office, successive Conservative governments since 1979 have squeezed the economy through high interest rates, over-valued sterling and also repeatedly attacked public spending. After two to two-and-a-half years of deflationary and inegalitarian policies, the upshot is that poor communities are exposed to a peculiarly intense squeeze on income levels and public subsidies. The discontent thus created accumulates in many different places, but finds an outlet in almost random ways, in incidents in particular local areas which spark some form of confrontation between sections of the population and the police force or other representatives of the established order. These confrontations degenerate into riots in a few instances, at which point the extent to which the government has squeezed poor communities becomes the focus of mass media attention. Because the riots occur in the mid-term between elections, at the point when the deflationary or repressive pressure is most intense because of time lags in policy implementation, they also come at the cusp of policy making, when the government is about to reverse direction anyway and begin the run-up to the next general election. The adverse publicity and legitimacy impacts of the riots spur ministers into retargetting and representing their policies, easing the strain on the poorest communities, and beginning general reflationary moves. Together with some 'band-aid' interventions to paper over cracks in riot-torn areas, and in other potential riot sites, these changes cause a relaxation in social tensions, which progressively improve in the election run-up. Once re-elected, however, the government immediately begins deflating again, and the cycle starts to repeat itself.

The evidence for this pattern is fairly clear since 1979. In 1981, the midpoint of the 1979–83 parliament, a wave of riots and disturbances occurred in thirty-one British cities, prompting the Scarman report, the appointment of Cabinet ministers to promote development in the worst-hit areas, and a renewal of significant urban interventions. In 1985, the midpoint of the 1983–87 parliament, there were three serious urban riots, on a larger scale and with more intense violence than four years earlier, including the killing of a police officer. Reportedly in the days after these events, the Department of Environment and domestic policy ministers generally were in something approaching a state of panic about urban policy amelioration. A package of policies relaxing cutbacks on social housing and promoting extra spending on council housing estates was implemented, and the beginnings of economic upturn were accelerated.

In the aftermath of the 1987 election, the government uncharacter-istically maintained an expansionist fiscal policy for eighteen months, until deflation was forced on them by the deteriorating balance of trade and reviving levels of inflation. By 1990, the midpoint of the 1987–92 parliament, the new recession provided a general background to the key focus for civil discontents, which was implementation of the Con-servatives' 1987 election pledge to introduce the highly regressive poll tax. A large-scale campaign of non-payment, obstruction of court ap-peals, and civil disobedience over the poll tax began in Scotland and spread to England and Wales (but not to Northern Ireland where imposition of the poll tax was never attempted). In the summer of 1990 a major riot took place in Trafalgar Square, with the police response being directly micro-managed by the Civil Contingencies Unit in the Cabinet Office just down Whitehall. Police ability to control the situ-ation was finely stretched, and the subsequent pictures of burning buildings in the very heart of London made news pictures worldwide. The riot represented the virtual end of the poll tax, and was a critical nail in the political coffin of Thatcher's premiership.

Although the first task of the Major government was ignominiously and expensively to dismantle the poll tax fiasco, there is not the slightest indication that the lessons of social management have been attended to any more closely this time than in the past. As soon as the 1992 general election was over the government embarked on a turn to the right, announcing public sector wage freezes, a tight squeeze on public borrowing, and large-scale and regressive tax increases (such as the imposition of VAT on fuel, breaking clear election pledges). The Conservatives' 1993 party Conference saw a further radical turn to the right, with reductions in welfare benefits. Although the economic climate was slowly improving in 1993–94, cutbacks in social security entitlements, the scrapping of the urban programme, restrictions on social housing, and ministerial attacks on 'scroungers' and single-parent families (bizarrely blamed for the emergence of a British 'underclass') all increased the pressure in sensitive areas. On past form the occurrence of serious social disturbances in the summers of 1994 or 1995 can be predicted as likely. Whether the upward corkscrew of violence observable in the Thatcher years will be continued is less clear. But at the least it seems inevitable that the electoral/riot cycle will show some new twist.

This history lends powerful support to Marxist and radical critics who portray the Conservative governments of the 1980s and 1990s as motivated essentially by a drive towards class politics. Social inequality has strongly increased throughout the period, and the observable disparities of life chances between rich and poor (measured, for example, by street homelessness in major cities) are starker in contemporary Britain than at any previous time in its post-war history. The UK is not immune from what Galbraith calls 'the culture of contentment', the ability of an employed and housed majority of the population to turn their backs on 20 per cent of people increasingly cut out of the main currents of economic development.[19] Yet the evidence I have reviewed of an electoral/riot cycle in contemporary Britain has become increasingly obvious to all concerned – to the disadvantaged, to the governors, to the police and to the onlooking majority of voters. As Piven and Cloward stressed in their account of poor people's movements in the USA, the message is that civil disobedience is almost the only efficacious way for social groups outside the governing coalition to protect their interests.[20] There is little hope in turning to other social institutions – such as the labour movement, the churches, the Conservative-dominated mass media, or local authorities – for protection against adverse government policy changes.

But a society in which disruptive action increasingly seems a 'rational' course, in which the government apparently listens only to anomic outbreaks of anger, in which the balancing of social interests is permanently out of kilter, is built on perilous foundations. British cities are a whirlpool of ethnic groups, age groups, and class groups, and like all major urban centres they have substantial problems with crime and drugs and the underside of social life. This volatile mix cannot be safely used as a testbed for practising such openly manipulative and coercive modes of managing society as the electoral riot cycle. The long-term effects are likely to be a ratcheting upwards of social dislocation, whose consequences will spill over far more widely than the immediate areas in which civil disobedience flares.

Conclusions

The Conservative philosopher Michael Oakeshott once rephrased Acton's dictum in a memorable way, observing that:

> No individual, no group, association or union can be entrusted with too much power. It is mere foolishness to complain when absolute power is abused. It exists to be abused.[21]

His disciple, Ian Gilmour, amplified the comment in a helpful way:

> Arrangements which at one time promote the dispersion of power may at another promote its concentration. We need to be alert enough to recognize any such change, and energetic enough to deal with it when it is still possible to do so.[22]

As yet, however, there is little sign of sufficient elite or voter alertness to the dangers of one party governance, and none at all of the elite energy which would be needed to correct it. The pattern of Labour leadership following the 1992 election, and in particular the effective sterilization of Labour's Plant Commission on electoral reform, show that the party's *apparatchiks* have learnt few lessons from the last decade and a half. Even with a renewal of party alternation in government and a hung Parliament, Britain's political and administrative elites would have extreme difficulty in coming to terms with change, always supposing that voters could force it upon them in sufficient numbers to break the Conservative's stranglehold. In default of some such shift, paralleling in significance the reform efforts of 1993–94 in Japan, the future for British politics looks depressingly similar to the immediate past – disruptive rather than creative conservatism; slow but persistent and unmanaged economic decline; and a further loosening of the ties that bind British society.

Notes

1. T.J. Pempel, 'Japan's Creative Conservatism: Continuity under Challenge', in F. Castles (ed) *The Comparative History of Public Policy*, Polity, Cambridge 1989, pp 149–91. Pempel observes (p 150) that to comparative public policy analysts 'Japan is especially confounding because many of its policies and their consequences do not appear to follow logically from the overwhelmingly conservative character of its government'.

2. B.S. Silberman, *Cages of Reason: The Rise of the Rational State in France, Japan, the United States and Great Britain*, University of Chicago Press, Chigago 1993, pp 159–222.

3. Hans Daalder, 'Dominant party', in V. Bogdanor (ed), *Blackwell Encyclopedia of Political Institutions*, Blackwell, Oxford 1987, p 180.

4. This table updates the information given in P. Dunleavy, 'The United Kingdom: Paradoxes of an Ungrounded Statism', in F. Castles (ed) *The Comparative History of Public Policy*, Polity, Cambrige 1989, p 259, Table 7.5.

5. See *International Political Science Review*, Special Issue on 'The Politics of Electoral Reform', Autumn 1984.

6. Anthony King, 'The Implications of One-Party Government', in A. King, I. Crewe, D. Denver, K. Newton, P. Norton, D. Sanders and P.Seyd, *Britain at the Polls, 1992* Chatham House, Chatham House, New Jersey 1992, p 224. The quotation is actually from a *Daily Telegraph* story written by King, its headline proclaiming: 'Tory 'Super-Party' Born Out of Last-Minute Switching'. King seems to have had later doubts about it, attributing the quote coyly to 'one commentator' and remarking: 'He may have been exaggerating ... '

7. P. Dunleavy, *Urban Political Analysis: The Politics of Collective Consumption* Macmillan, London 1980, pp 137–8.

8. Michael Oakeshott, quoted by Ian Gilmour, *Inside Right: A Study of Conservatism* Quartet, London 1978), p 95.

9. Gilmour, *Inside Right*, p 226.

10. This phrase was famously used by the reforming New Zealand deputy Prime Minister, Geoffrey Palmer, to characterize his own country's unicameral and Westminster-model system. See G. Palmer, *Unbridled Power?* Oxford University Press, Auckland 1979.

11. P. Dunleavy, 'Estimating the Distribution of Influence in Cabinet Committees under Major' in P. Dunleavy and J. Stanyer (eds), *Contemporary Political Studies 1994*, UK Political Studies Association, Belfast, 1994.

12. H. Thompson, 'Joining the Exchange Rate Mechanism: Macro-Economic Policy Making and the Core Executive, 1979–90' (PhD Thesis, London School of Economics and Political Science, February 1994).

13. R. Scruton, *The Meaning of Conservatism*, Macmillan, London 1980, pp 162–4 on local government, and pp 53–9 on democracy.

14. Participant at the ESRC/LSE Public Services Seminar Series, London School of Economics, Summer 1993. For details of the series see LSE Public Policy Papers Nos 4–7, Department of Government, LSE, 1994.

15. During 1986 I went to a lunch at the Institute of Economic Affairs, where a group of IEA personnel and their guests were discussing the Thatcher government's programme. The level of disillusionment around the table seemed high, so I asked the other diners to nominate one government policy or legislation which truly implemented the IEA's market liberal philosophy. The question provoked many suggestions which were quickly knocked out on one ground or another – for example, the privatization programme had only produced private telecommunications and gas monopolies, not genuine competition; and the Tories' statecraft was far from embracing open government or a determination to tackle public bureaucracies. Eventually, however, the IEA President, Lord Ralph Harris, came up with one government action which everyone agreed met the IEA's requirements – the law which abolished the previous requirement that only opticians could sell glasses, thereby allowing new suppliers to enter the market.

I remarked how peripheral this change seemed to be, set against the big issues facing British society – such as the persistence of mass unemployment, or industrial competition from Japan and the Pacific countries, or decisions on the future of the EC. In what ways could the IEA's approach illuminate these choices? There was little or no response.

16. See K. Minogue, 'On Hyperactivism in Modern British Politics', in M. Cowling (ed) *Conservative Essays*, Macmillan, London 1978, pp 117–30. Originally written primarily as a critique of left-wing politicians, this essay now provides an apt indictment of Margaret Thatcher's executive style.

17. M. Edelman, *The Symbolic Uses of Politics*, University of Illinois Press, Urbana, Illinois, 1964, pp 74–93. The politicians' illusion is sustained by the Opposition and the mass media, who want someone to blame. And it perfectly accords with the 'management' illusions inculcated in administrators by their own experiences and cultures.

18. See M. Pirie, *Micropolitics*, Wildwood House, London 1988.

19. J. Galbraith, *The Culture of Contentment*, Sinclair Stevenson, London 1992.

20. F.F. Piven and R.A. Cloward, *Poor People's Movements*, Pantheon, New York 1977.

21. Quoted in Gilmour, *Inside Right*, pp 96–7.

22. Gilmour, *Inside Right*, p 96.

FOUR

Options for the Opposition

Electoral Pacts: The Lessons of History

Vernon Bogdanor

David Butler once remarked that the two most important figures in British politics were the ghost of Sir Robert Peel and the ghost of Ramsay MacDonald. When Peel repealed the Corn Laws in 1846, the resulting split put the Conservatives in opposition for nearly thirty years: in consequence the Conservatives have always strongly emphasised the importance of party unity. When MacDonald formed the National Government in 1931, the subsequent Labour split led to an almost neurotic fear of coalitions or pacts. It made the Labour Party believe that it was rank treachery even to contemplate any peacetime arrangement with another political party.

The ghost of Peel has proved a more benign figure than the ghost of MacDonald. For although the Conservatives have been in office for much of the past hundred years, this has often been achieved through the co-operation of other parties. Indeed between 1886 and 1951 there were only two general elections which produced independent Conservative majorities – the general elections of 1922 and 1924. Every other Conservative government was in reality a coalition supported by Liberal Unionists, Coalition Liberals, National Labour, or Liberal Nationals.

Conservative administrations were formed with the aid of such leading figures as Joseph Chamberlain, Lloyd George and Ramsay MacDonald, politicians who were certainly not themselves Conservative. In 1975, Harold Macmillan was able to write, with perhaps pardonable exaggeration:

> The last purely Conservative Government was formed by Mr. Disraeli in 1874 – it is the fact that we have attracted moderate people of Liberal tradition and thought into our ranks which makes it possible to maintain a Conservative government today. A successful party of the Right must continue to recruit its strength from the centre, and even from the Left Centre. Once it begins to shrink into itself like a snail it will be doomed.[1]

Certainly the Conservative party has been far more flexible and more willing to share power with other parties than Labour has been. Labour's 'go it alone' policy, on the other hand, has, at such times as the 1920s, and perhaps also since 1987, condemned the party to opposition, when it might have been able to enter government as part of a 'progressive' administration, had it only been willing to share power with the Liberals.

The general election of 1992 was perhaps the most crucial of the four Conservative victories since 1979, and perhaps the most important election since 1945. For it revealed, in a very striking way, the bankruptcy of the strategy of the opposition parties. For Labour, the general election should have confirmed the lesson of 1983 and 1987, that the party cannot, by itself, break into the inner core of Conservative strength in the south east of England. In 1992 Labour won, outside London, just 10 of the region's 157 seats. It is difficult to see how Labour can successfully break into the Conservative heartland in the next general election when the south-east/north-west division of electoral support seems now to be so deeply entrenched.[2]

Labour would seem to need a swing of around 6 per cent to secure an overall majority at the next general election; twice the size of the largest swing that Labour has achieved in any post-war general election, that of 1964. At the next election, therefore, the most likely alternative to a Conservative government is a hung parliament. With a hung parliament, Labour is likely to have to consult with the Liberal Democrats. It might seem more sensible, were it not for the ghost of Ramsay MacDonald, for Labour to consult with the Liberal Democrats now, rather than waiting until after an inconclusive general election.

Yet, Labour remains in its instincts a majoritarian party, believing that 'one more heave' will do the trick. Some believe that this heave should be in the direction of the Liberal Democrats, seeking to win over the Liberal Democrat vote to Labour. If only the division in the 'progressive' vote could be ended, then a strong Labour government could be elected. Similar arguments were heard, of course, in the 1920s, when Ramsay MacDonald saw the Liberals as an obstacle in his path, rather than a potential ally in the creation of an anti-Conservative majority. In July 1924, talking to the editor of the *Manchester Guardian*, C.P. Scott, MacDonald:

> reverted again and again to this dislike and distrust of the Liberals. He could get on with the Tories. They differed at times openly then forgot all about it and shook hands. They were gentlemen, but the Liberals were cads.[3]

Yet in practice the return of Labour was, in 1929, 1964 and February 1974, dependent upon a high Liberal vote, weakening the Conservatives in their southern strongholds. When, in 1951, the Liberal vote seemed anti-Labour rather than anti-Conservative, the Conservatives had no hesitation in arranging local pacts with the Liberals, in Bolton and Huddersfield. They were even prepared, as was Edward Heath in March 1974, to offer the Liberals participation in a Conservative-led coalition, if it meant Conservative retention of power.

Yet, Labour leaders, like Ramsay MacDonald in the 1920s, still seek to benefit from an electoral system designed for two parties, in a political system in which there are three parties competing for power. The Conservatives are likely to prove the sole beneficiaries, just as they were between the wars, when they were able to remain in power for almost the whole of the period.

The attitude of the Labour party is strikingly different from that of similar parties on the Continent. In Sweden, the Social Democrats began 44 years of hegemony in 1932, by forming a coalition government with the Agrarian Party. In Germany, the Social Democrats have only once – in 1972 – secured a higher vote than their Christian Democrat opponents. Yet the Social Democrats have been in power for 16 of the forty-five years of the Federal Republic, in coalition with either the Free Democrats or the Christian Democrats. Finally, in France, the socialists secured only 5 per cent of the vote in the 1969 presidential election. Yet, by skilful coalition politics, François Mitterrand was able to secure electoral victory in 1981, and to provide the first period of socialist hegemony since the Popular Front government of 1936. Why, in a period of increasing contact with similar parties in the European Community, does Labour alone remain so adamantly opposed to electoral pacts and coalition?

The Liberal Democrats have been almost as blinkered as Labour. Since Jo Grimond, the party's aim has been realignment in the sense of replacing Labour as the main party of the Left, a strategy reiterated in Paddy Ashdown's campaign for the leadership of the Liberal Democrats in 1988. But this was always a psephological illusion as the general election of 1983 had shown. For, in that year, Labour's electoral performance proved its worst since it became a mass party. It gained only 27 per cent of the vote, and yet secured 209 seats. A combination of the first-past-the-post electoral system and the concentration of the Labour vote ensured that Labour would enjoy a sizable representation in the Commons even if it gained only one quarter of the vote; moreover, in the general election of 1987, the performance of the Liberal/SDP Alliance was worse in the Labour heartlands than in other seats.

Conceptually the Liberal Democrats may be as much an anti-Labour party as they are an anti-Conservative party. But the British electoral system is a geographical rather than a conceptual system; and, within that system, the Liberal Democrats find themselves situated as an anti-Conservative party, a second anti-Conservative party, complementary to Labour, since the Liberal Democrats are able to win seats in the

Conservative heartlands which Labour cannot win. If there were to be an even 4 per cent swing from the Conservatives to the Liberal Democrats at the next election, the Liberal Democrats would gain 14 seats. But, with an even 4 per cent swing from Labour to the Liberal Democrats, the Liberal Democrats would gain no seats. The Labour seat most vulnerable to the Liberal Democrats is Tony Benn's Chesterfield constituency, which would fall on a 5.2 per cent swing.

Thus the two opposition parties find themsleves deadlocked. Their dog-in-the-manger strategy serves only to benefit the Conservatives. The obvious strategy for two psephologically complementary parties is an electoral pact, enabling the Liberal Democrats to win Conservatives seats in the south, while Labour, with the aid of Liberal Democrat votes, wins Conservative/Labour marginals elsewhere. So it is that political scientists and historians have come to look, with increasing interest, at the history of electoral pacts in Britain.[4]

There have been five national electoral pacts in Britain since 1886.

1. The pact between Conservatives and Liberal Unionists in 1886, a pact which lasted through seven general elections until the two parties merged in 1912.

2. The pact between the Liberal Party and the Labour Representation Committee (LRC), forerunner of the Labour Party, in 1903, often known as the Gladstone/ MacDonald pact. This pact was operative only for the general election of 1906, but it continued in the shape of an informal understanding between the two parties during the two general elections of 1910.

3. The pact between the Conservatives and the Coalition Liberals, supporting Lloyd George, for the 'coupon' election of 1918. The Conservatives refused, however, to fight the 1922 election in alliance with the Liberals, and the two parties fought the general election of 1922 independently.

4. The pact between the parties comprising the National Government – Conservatives, Liberal Nationals, Liberals and National Labour – for the general election of 1931. The Liberals left the government in 1932, but the pact continued with the other parties in the general election of 1935.

5. The pact of 1981 between the Liberals and the Social Democratic Party, creating the Alliance, in the general elections of 1983 and 1987.

Each of these pacts, except the last, secured a period of electoral hegemony for the dominant party in the pact. The 1886 pact ensured the dominance of the Unionist alliance, which remained in government until 1905, except for the interlude of 1892–95. The pact was crucial for the success of the Unionist alliance, since there were voters opposed to Home Rule who would not be prepared to vote for a Conservative candidate, just as there are today anti-Conservative voters who are not prepared to vote for a Labour candidate. 'No one', declared Joseph Chamberlain to his son, Austen, in 1895, 'who has not worked among the electors can be aware how strong are old prejudices in connection with party names and colours and badges. A man may be a good Unionist at heart, and yet nothing can persuade him to vote 'blue' or give support to a 'Tory' candidate.'5

The Liberals would have won the 1906 general election even without the pact with Labour; but the understanding which succeeded the pact ensured that the Liberals remained in government after the inconclusive general elections of 1910. The 'coupon' election of 1918 prefigured the years of Conservative dominance between the wars, while the pact of 1931 meant that there was just one candidate supporting the National Government in the vast majority of constituencies. This helped to secure a landslide victory for the Conservative-dominated National Government. Only the pact forming the Liberal/SDP Alliance failed to achieve its object of 'breaking the mould' of the political system; but the Alliance, in the general election of 1983, came nearer to doing so than any party or grouping since the Liberals in the 1920s. All of the other pacts, except that of 1903, i.e. the pacts of 1886, 1918 and 1931, prefigured long periods of Conservative hegemony, and there can be no doubt that the predominant effect of electoral pacts in Britain since 1886 has been to benefit the Conservative party.

There are, however, important differences between the pacts of the past and the arrangements being discussed today. All past pacts, except for the Gladstone/MacDonald pact of 1903, resulted from party splits, and served to confirm those splits. They were pacts between a long-established party and a new satellite party formed as a result of a party split. In 1886, 1918 and 1931, the Conservatives were able to take advantage of splits within the Liberal and, in 1931 also the Labour party. In 1981, when the Alliance was formed, the Liberals were able to take similar advantage of a split in the Labour party. The 1903 pact, although not the result of a party split, was one between a long-estab-lished party, the Liberals, and the newly formed Labour Representation Committee, still struggling to gain a foothold in national politics. It is clearly much more difficult to arrange a pact between two established parties in the absence of a split.

Moreover, the electoral pacts, again with the exception of 1903, proved to be temporary arrangements leading either to merger or to separation. The pacts of 1886, 1931 and 1981 led to merger, while that of 1918 did not last beyond one general election. The various satellite parties – Liberal Unionist, Coalition Liberal, Liberal National and

National Labour – served merely as a temporary resting-place for MPs who would eventually cross the floor but were unwilling to do so immediately. Similarly, the formation of the SDP in 1981, proved but a prelude to merger with the Liberals after the 1987 general election.

The pact of 1981 was the only one in which two parties, each of whom could have put up a full national slate of candidates, entered into an electoral pact. But parties such as the Liberal Unionists, the early Labour Party, the Coalition Liberals, the Liberal Nationals or National Labour, which were involved in the earlier pacts, were capable of fighting only a small number of seats and it therefore proved much easier to accommodate their demands within the framework of a national pact. Partly for this reason, none of these parties, with the exception of Labour, were able to preserve their separate identity.

Finally, the pact between the Liberals and the SDP in 1981, is the only post-war example of a national pact in British politics. The other pacts occurred before party politics had become nationalised. Moreover, the failure of the Liberal/ SDP Alliance to 'break the mould' of British politics may mean that party leaders will be wary of trying another national pact. Under modern conditions, political parties generally feel that if they are to be national parties, they must contest every constituency. Between 1885 and 1922, however, an average of 138 seats at each general election remained uncontested. To fight every constituency was not then, as it is today, a virility symbol for a political party. The nationalisation of party politics in post-war Britain is one of the main factors which has served to militate against electoral pacts.

The difficulties facing the Labour and Liberal Democrat parties in constructing an electoral pact seem, therefore, on the basis of historical precedent, so great as to be almost insuperable. Yet, there are, in addition, still more difficulties flowing from the mechanics of the electoral system and party organisation.

Under the first-past-the-post electoral system, a pact implies the reciprocal withdrawal of candidates. Yet, in Britain, local constituency parties are autonomous. The decision as to whether or not to run a candidate rests with the local constituency, for whom it is part of its very *raison d'être*. So an agreement between two party headquarters, while it might naturally influence local constituencies, could not of itself ensure the withdrawal of candidates. There is no way in which national headquarters can force a constituency party to withdraw a candidate.

Moreover, even if a constituency party can be persuaded not to put up a candidate, and the candidate can be persuaded to stand down, the whole purpose of the pact might still be frustrated by the arrival of a John the Baptist figure calling himself an 'independent' Liberal or Labour candidate. Such a candidate might well channel away votes which would otherwise be given to the candidate backed by the pact.

This has indeed happened with past electoral pacts in Britain. In 1918, despite the existence of a 'coupon' between the Conservatives and Lloyd George Liberals determining the allocation of candidatures, 83 un-couponed Conservatives stood, of whom 53 were successful. One of the successful uncouponed Conservatives defeated the former Liberal Prime Minister, H.H.Asquith in East Fife, who had been granted the coupon, but was so unpopular among Conservatives that the local party insisted upon putting up a candidate. In 1931, Conservatives were much more willing to stand down for Simonite Liberal Nationals than for Samuelite Liberals who continued to support free trade. Thus, there were contests between Conservatives and Liberal Nationals in only four constituencies, but 79 contests between Conservatives and other Liberals.

A pact will be successful on the ground only if it goes with the grain of local opinion, rather than against it. This need not, however, prove as great a difficulty as it might seem at first sight. For, one of the striking developments in British politics over the past few years has been the growth in Labour/Liberal Democrat co-operation at grass-roots and especially local government level. Of the 12 hung county councils after the 1989 county council elections, 8 were run, in effect, by Labour and Liberal Democrats operating through formal or informal agreements. The Labour Party, which at national level was hostile to coalitions with any other party, was persuaded to alter its stance as a result of repres-entations by local councillors, fearful otherwise of allowing the Con-servatives, by default, to run every hung council. After the 1993 county council elections, Labour, together with the Liberal democrats, controlled such authorities as Essex, Suffolk, Hampshire and East Sussex, while there was no county which was run by Conservatives and Liberal Democrats working together. In the 1992 general election, the feeling that Labour and Liberal Democrats were allies not enemies was, no doubt, one of the factors encouraging tactical voting, which enabled Labour to gain around 10 seats which it would not have won on a uniform swing. Without tactical voting, it has been estimated that the Conservative majority would have been nearer 71 than 21.[6]

These habits of co-operation, may make it easier for pacts to be agreed in the first instance at local level, and then ratified, or at least not obstructed, at national level. Rather than an all-embracing national pact, local constituency parties might be able to agree upon reciprocal withdrawals in adjacent or near-adjacent constituencies. Before the next general election Labour might, for example, agree to withdraw in Oxford West and Abingdon, in return for the Liberal Democrats agree-ing to withdraw in Oxford East; the Liberal Democrats could withdraw in Edinburgh, Pentlands, in return for an agreement by Labour to withdraw in Edinburgh West.

It was a series of such limited local pacts supported by party headquarters which helped the Conservatives regain power in 1951. The general election of 1950 had resulted in an overall Labour majority of only seven. The Liberals had put up 475 candidates in an effort to fight on a broad front, yet all but 100 Liberal candidates had lost their deposit, then fixed at one-eighth of the total poll. Thus, the Conservatives believed that with one more heave, they could oust Labour, while the Liberals were forced to confront the fact that they were no longer a governing party, and indeed faced the possibility of total extinction. There was, therefore, the basis for agreement between Conservatives and Liberals. Yet, a national pact proved impossible. In September 1950, Lord Woolton, the Conservative chairman, wrote to Lord Teviot, leader of the National Liberals, by then indistinguishable from the Conservatives, in the following terms:

> I have had two long talks with Clement Davies [leader of the Liberal Party] who is firmly of the opinion that it would be inadvisable that the headquarters of our parties should seek to enter into any agreement. He thinks that such efforts should be conducted on the constituency level, and it would be best if they arose spontaneously. That is also very emphatically the view of most of those who hold office in the Conservative Party who have discussed this problem with me.[7]

In 1951, there were local pacts in Bolton and Huddersfield, whereby in each of the two constituencies in these cities there was just one anti-Labour candidate: the Conservative stood down in one of the constituencies, and the Liberal in the other. The outcome was that two seats were won by the Conservatives, two by the Liberals and none by Labour. In addition, the Conservatives stood down for Liberals who had voted with them in the 1950–51 parliament, with the exception of Jo Grimond. Churchill himself spoke for an unopposed Liberal candidate, Lady Violet Bonham Carter, in Colne Valley. Moreover, the Conservatives' first list of prospective candidates actually included Liberals in those seats where Liberals were unopposed by Conservatives![8] Of the six Liberal MPs elected in 1951, only one – Grimond in Orkney & Shetland – had been opposed by a Conservative. After the election, Churchill offered the Liberal leader, Clement Davies, a place in his government as minister of education, effectively a formal offer of coalition with the Liberal Party. But the offer was declined. The likelihood is, however, that the various limited local agreements and the atmosphere of co-operation which they created, played a vital role in siphoning off the extra 1–2 per cent of the vote which made a Conservative victory in 1951 possible.

The Conservatives, then, were far more flexible than Labour when they found themselves, after 1945, as Labour was to do after 1983, facing a tide of history, rather than a mere swing of the pendulum. It took Labour the loss of two more elections, in 1987 and 1992, to begin to appreciate the size of the task required to regain power. That is why, slowly, painfully, but surely, a coalition is being constructed on the ground among those unwilling to resign themselves to permanent Conservative rule. The key question which faces the leaders of the Labour and Liberal Democrat parties is not so much whether they favour a pact or not, as whether they are prepared to assist those forces working for co-operation at grass-roots level; or whether, by contrast, the party leaders will act as an obstacle.

A further difficulty, however, in constructing an electoral pact is that political parties do not 'own' the votes of their supporters. Even if the parties at national level were to agree upon such an arrangement, the voters would not necessarily follow it. A party is not a disciplined army which can order its supporters to transfer their votes. As well as being congruent with local *party* opinion, therefore, a pact must also be consistent with local *electoral* opinion.

It is on this basis that some question the rationale of a pact between Labour and the Liberal Democrats. They argue that Liberal Democrat supporters would by no means vote Labour in the absence of a Liberal Democrat candidate. Indeed, survey evidence would seem to indicate that there are as many, if not more Liberal Democrats whose second choice would be Conservative as there are who would support Labour. Therefore, a pact could actually lower the combined Labour/Liberal Democrat vote.

Such an argument, however, underestimates both the psychological consequences and the dynamic potential of an electoral pact. For, there may well be a potential constituency, which includes Conservative voters, prepared to support an alternative majority government of the Left, but unwilling to vote Liberal Democrat or Labour, if the outcome would be a weak minority government. A little-noticed poll of over 1,000 adults, taken just after the 1992 general election, in May 1992, indicated that, with a Lib-Lab alliance, three times as many Liberal Democrats would give their second preferences to Labour as would give them to the Conservatives. In addition, one in 10 Conservative voters would be prepared to switch allegiance to a Labour Party allied to the Liberal Democrats.[9]

There is then a potential constituency, which includes disaffected Conservatives, for an alternative government of the Left. A Labour Party allied to the Liberal Democrats might succeed in attracting such a constituency; Labour fighting on its own might not do so. Thus the dynamic psychological effects of a pact could be very great. Indeed, the main gain from an electoral pact might prove to be not psephological but psychological. As Jessé Herbert, Private Secretary to the Liberal Chief Whip, declared of the Liberal/Labour pact in 1903:

The main benefit would be the effect on the public mind of seeing the opponents of the Government united. It would give hope and enthusiasm to the opposition parties, making them vote and work. It would make the Tories fearful and depressed and rob them of energy and force.[10]

Yet, more than local electoral pacts may be needed if there is to be a convincing alternative government by the time of the next general election. For pacts, if they prove successful, will make a hung parliament more likely. The outcome of a hung parliament would most probably be a minority government which would either seek a tactical dissolution within a few months – as Harold Wilson did in 1974 – or be forced to go to the country – Ramsay MacDonald's fate in 1924. Therefore, the prospect of a hung parliament would arouse fears of instability amongst many voters. There is evidence from survey material that such fears of instability played some part in a late shift of opinion from the Liberal Democrats to the Conservatives in the 1992 campaign. One of the reasons why the Conservatives won was because they seemed to many voters the only party able to offer strong and responsible government.

If they are to deal with the fear of instability, the opposition parties must be in a position to offer an effective alternative government. A pact would, therefore, have to be complemented by a coalition accord between Labour and the Liberal Democrats, comprising an agreed programme for a government lasting for three or four years. There would have to be agreement both on policy and on the distribution of Cabinet posts. In the Irish Republic in 1973 there was a 'National Coalition' of this kind between Labour and Fine Gael which enabled the two parties to break the seemingly permanent Fianna Fail stranglehold on government. In the general election of 1973, both Fine Gael and Labour gained fewer first preference votes than they had done in the previous general election of 1969, but thanks to mutual transfers of later preferences, the two parties were able to win enough seats to form a government.

The argument of this chapter has been radical, calling for local electoral pacts leading eventually to a full-scale national pact, and a coalition agreement between the Labour and Liberal Democrat parties. Clearly such arrangements cannot be brought about in the short campaign or pre-campaign period. Thinking about them must begin much earlier.

After the 1987 general election, Labour continued to act as if it were still a majoritarian party in a two-party system. It therefore resisted any suggestion of electoral pacts or of its natural concomitant, proportional representation. In the 1992 general election campaign, however, Neil Kinnock came to appreciate that he needed the support of Liberal Democrat voters in order to topple the Conservatives and form a government. Therefore, during the last week of the campaign, without preparation, he raised the issue of proportional representation although he was unable to declare himself either for or against it. This appeared opportunistic, and enabled the Conservatives to dismiss the Labour leader as a man without principles.

Since the general election of 1992, some members of the Labour Party have argued that Neil Kinnock's pre-election initiative shows that proportional representation is an electoral liability. Yet this is a complete non-sequitur. What it does show is that an initiative made at the last moment, without adequate preparation or forethought, is highly unlikely to succeed. In 1993, John Smith, the new Labour leader, proposed a referendum on proportional representation. But that, though welcome, is not enough. The Labour and Liberal Democrat parties must at an early stage extend the processes of co-operation which have already begun at local government level. To delay is not to avoid a decision, but in effect to take one against co-operation. That would increase the likelihood of a fifth electoral defeat for the Labour Party.

The historical precedents, and the attitudes and organisation of the political parties, make it clear why a pact between Labour and the Liberal Democrats is so difficult to achieve. The sheer deadweight of inherited party assumptions and institutional inertia constitute the most potent barriers to co-operation between the two anti-Conservative parties. Nevertheless, the psephological facts make such co-operation imperative if voters are to be given a genuine choice at the next general election between a Conservative and an anti-Conservative government. Those who wish to see an end to the period of Conservative hegemony can only hope that reason prevails over party self-interest. But this, in the nature of things, may remain a distant hope.

Notes

1. Harold Macmillan, *The Past Masters*, Macmillan, London, 1975, pp 18–19.

2. See Vernon Bogdanor and William Field, 'Lessons of History: Core and Periphery in British Electoral Behaviour, 1910–1992' in *Electoral Studies*, 1993.

3. Trevor Wilson, *The Political Diaries of C. P. Scott: 1911–1928*, Collins, London, 1970, p 460.

4. See, for more detail, Vernon Bogdanor, 'Electoral Pacts in Britain since 1886', in Dennis Kavanagh (ed) *Electoral Politics*, Oxford University Press, 1992, pp 165–87.

5. Neal Blewett, *The Peers, the Parties and the People: The General Elections of 1910*, Macmillan, London, 1972, p 15.

6. See the Statistical Appendix by John Curtice and Michael Steed, in David Butler and Dennis Kavanagh, *The British General Election of 1992*, Macmillan, Basingstoke, 1992.

7. Woolton Papers, Bodleian Library, Oxford.

8. David Butler, *The British General Election of 1951*, Macmillan, London, 1952, p 94.

9. See the report in the journal *Issues in Focus*, June 1992, p 22.

10. Cited in Philip Poirier, *The Advent of the Labour Party*, Allen and Unwin, London, 1958, p 189.

Back to Basics

Anne Campbell, Calum Macdonald, Nick Raynsford,
Malcolm Wicks, Tony Wright

The State of the Nation

Britain in the 1990s displays evident signs of decline. Economic weaknesses highlighted in 1992 by forced devaluation and ignominious exit from the ERM are matched by political disillusionment as the public grows ever more sceptical of politicians' ability to reverse decline. As real power ebbs away in the international context, Britain clings to the trappings of national sovereignty, pretending to a role which is no longer sustainable. Whether we search for architectural solutions through neo-Georgian pastiche or political solutions through 'Victorian values', our obsession with the past indicates lack of confidence in our present.

This lack of confidence reflects not only economic decline, but an absence of common purpose. Britain in the 1990s is a deeply divided society, riddled with inequalities – in opportunity, education, health, wealth and lifestyle. These inequalities have grown starkly during a period when the Conservative Government and its apologists have argued that greater inequality is a pre-condition of economic recovery. So the highest paid 10 per cent of the population have enjoyed a 50 per cent rise in real income while the lowest paid 10 per cent have seen their living standards fall by 14 per cent. Yet recovery has not followed: Britain's economy is weaker in relation to our international competitors than at any time in the past 300 years.

A large balance of trade deficit acts as a brake on the growth of the British economy. Our financial institutions, set up with a captive market of the old British Empire in mind, are geared to quick returns for the wealthy, not to the long term health of our industries. Britain is the only modern industrialised nation where pay-outs to shareholders exceed investment in research and development.

Environmental problems have been ignored or glossed over. Reliance on 'free market' solutions has persuaded industrialists to choose the cheapest waste disposal; farmers are encouraged to pour chemicals onto the land; goods and people are transported by the ever-expanding road system. The results are polluted rivers and streams, air in which one in seven children suffer from asthma, and the ravaging of some of our most beautiful countryside.

Nowhere are the divisions more evident or damaging than in education and training. While other Europeans and the Japanese have generally been able to foster high levels of achievement across a broad spectrum of their population, British education has focused on a narrow elite, with the majority leaving school with inadequate skills, low expectations and little prospect of further qualifications.

Women's skills are under-used and largely unrecognised: full time pay for women is still only 78 per cent of full time pay for men. The chances of gaining useful employment for people from ethnic minorities are much less than for a similarly qualified white person. Even the right to equality before the law is endangered by cut-backs in legal aid.

Britain is governed in much the same way, and by much the same sort of people, as in the early years of the twentieth century. As they have generally benefitted from the status quo, there has unsurprisingly been little or no incentive for reform. Coupled with the establishment's complacency about the supposed perfection of the British system of government this has acted as a powerful sheet-anchor resisting change. We have an increasingly acute democratic deficit.

Britain has been seriously underperforming for too long and it has been grievously misgoverned in the past fifteen years. But it is a society with huge potential, if only we can release and exploit the pent-up skills and energy of our people. To achieve that we must not look back, nor show undue deference to traditional models of behaviour which have served Britain badly. A new approach is called for. The new agenda must address the fundamental causes of Britain's weakness, and develop new policies which meet the changing needs of a society moving rapidly into the twenty-first century.

Clearing the Ground

Thatcherism in its early years told an attractive story – unfettered capitalism, unhindered by waste and over-government, would unleash enterprise and hence, in the slightly longer term, more industry, more jobs and more affluence for all. It was a seductive story, in part because there would be no victims, except perhaps wastrels and scroungers. Viewed from the later 1970s the contrast with Labour's faded prospectus could not have been starker. Here was vision and audacity, certainly a clear strategy. A few specific policies, most notably 'right to buy' for council tenants, illustrated an appealing alternative to the top-down welfarism of a statist, paternalistic Labour Party.

The Thatcher dream has now turned into a tawdry nightmare of dogmatism and ideology almost for its own sake. Industrial investment has declined; a record number of businesseses have gone into receivership; and unemployment has tripled. Far from there being no victims, the cities, towns and villages of Britain are littered with reminders that redundancy and repossession can now hit even the most affluent areas. Taxation has increased for most households, thanks to doubled VAT, increased National Insurance contributions and the poll tax and its successor, the council tax.

The collapse of the Thatcherite agenda has left a terrible void, which John Major's government is ill-equipped to fill. With no vision, no strategy, no purpose, and buffeted by the consequences of economic recession and huge public debt, it staggers from one crisis to the next. The challenge now is to make a new start. Our contention, at bottom, is that Conservative policies did not work because the values that informed them were wrong. It is not a technical failure but a moral failure. A policy based on the belief that greater inequality was both good in itself and the route to a healthy society and dynamic economy was bound to end badly, as was one based on the idea that crime was a derivative of collectivism or that freedom flourished as the state was diminished. They have been discredited by the facts of less social cohesion, more disorder and a weakened economy.

Restoring Values

That is why we take values and beliefs seriously and why we seek to restate the basis of democratic socialism. The old distinction between 'individual'-ism and 'social'-ism as ways of understanding the world remains as sharp and pivotal as ever. Socialists believe that society is a collective and moral enterprise rooted in the equal worth of all individuals. There is a real and fundamental sense in which you either believe this or you do not. It is a moral choice. It is not possible to avoid the consequences of the choice. A society founded upon an ethic of possessive individualism will be an acquisitive society without a basis of community or solidarity (or, in crucial respects, of legitimacy). Conversely, a society founded upon a co-operative ethic of justice and mutuality will not only be a more serene society but also a more successful one. There is a link between social justice and economic efficiency.

We are less critical of the years since 1979 for their failures than for their successes. They have been outstandingly successful in achieving greater inequality, reduced communal provision and diminished social protection. Unfortunately, but inevitably, the results have not been the beneficent ones promised. Yet the experiment continues, its practitioners in the grip of a political vocabulary on the lines of 'public bad, private good'. It is clear that privatisation, market testing and the rest of the ideological bag of tricks have acquired a life of their own.

Means and Ends

Contemporary Conservatism is distinguished by exactly the kind of confusion of means and ends that has too often been evident in relation to Labour. Means become dressed up as ends; and there is a consequent evasion of the questions that matter: how does a privatised monopoly enhance freedom? how does a quasi-market in health care serve patients? how does the fragmentation of the school system promote parental choice? Such questions are dissolved in the preoccupation with means, the hallmark of rigid ideological politics. Indeed, matters are even more serious, for the blind belief in market solutions implies a deliberate disregard of consequences since markets are, by their nature, irresponsible. In the hands of some economists this is merely a harmless delusion; in the hands of a government it becomes a dangerous abdication. Thus, there is a deep irresponsibility about the politics of the neo-liberal right, a substitution of means for ends and a casual disregard for consequences. It is politically audacious but intellectually and morally shoddy.

We are fundamentalists in our attachment to the core values of democratic socialism and believe that the time has come for Labour to restate these values as the basis of its own identity. People need to know what, in a basic sense, a party stands for; and a party needs to be engaged in continuing explanation and persuasion about its values and beliefs. At a time when people know there are fundamental questions to be asked about the direction of society, they will not be satisfied with sound bites.

Yet Labour is substantially disabled for this task by its own long-standing confusion of ends and means. This now has to be resolved. If not it will continue to haunt us, as it has in different forms over the past forty years. The current debate is over the relationship of the Party to the trade unions; before that it was the conflict between producer and consumer; before that, the extent of public ownership. In essence, the issue comes back to the primary objective of a democratic socialist party and the extent to which the Labour Party's purpose has been narrowly identified with Clause Four of its constitution.

It is extraordinary that a hasty conference compromise in 1918 should have saddled Labour with socialism-as-ownership for the rest of the century, even after the collapse of the Eastern European regimes founded upon this same proposition. It may be said that this is simply Labour's ancestral shrine and long ceased to have a living presence; but this makes matters worse. Labour has not, to any significant extent, devised ways of translating common ownership into forms of genuinely popular ownership. Worst of all, the Party's refusal to get to grips with the issue has actively prevented a modern and positive statement of its core beliefs. So it is not a marginal issue. Nor is it a matter of 'abandoning' Clause Four, but of incorporating its underlying purpose into a new statement of values that is conspicuously about the ends of democratic socialism. We suggest in the table below what this might contain.

A Table of Values

1. The Labour Party is a democratic socialist party. It is proud of its history, traditions and achievements; and of belonging to a wider family of democratic socialist and social democratic parties.

2. Its values are those of democratic socialism: its core belief is that a good society is one that recognises the equal value of all individuals and reflects this belief in all its policies and institutions, such that everyone has access to the means of civilised life and can share fully in the life of society on a basis of social equality.

3. It believes that a society is a co-operative and interdependent community, not merely a collection of particular and private interests; that people can achieve through collective action what it is not possible for all to achieve without it; and that a good society nourishes the practice of co-operation and the principle of community and solidarity.

4. It believes that the purpose of economic activity is to promote the wealth and employment of the people, on a sustainable environmental basis, and that this requires the regulation of markets and co-ordination of economic life in the public interest, including forms of public and popular ownership where appropriate.

5. It holds that all citizens are entitled to the maximum attainable political, social and economic rights, with associated responsibilities, and that it is the duty of government to secure these, as the basis for freedom, security and welfare.

6. It cherishes the freedom of individuals – socially, politically and economically – and seeks through public action to enlarge and extend the capacity of all people, not merely some people, to live freely and make free choices, consistent with the freedoms of others.

7. It affirms its belief in the democratic principles of representation, accountability, openness and participation and seeks to extend and apply these as widely as possible.

8. It believes in the diffusion and plurality of power, enabling and empowering individuals and communities to practice self-government and the activity of democratic citizenship. It attaches particular

importance to the free association of working people in trades unions, and to workplace citizenship.

9. It is committed to the defence and security of the British people and the peaceful development of the world.

10. The party seeks to work with others, especially in the European Community and the United Nations, to secure peace, human rights and economic security for all the peoples of the world.

11. The party seeks to co-operate with all those groups and organisations which share its values, and attaches a particular importance to the close involvement of the Trade Union movement in its work.

12. The party's object is to translate its values into practice by means of effective political and electoral organisation to enable it to win support and form governments at every level.

We are dogmatists about ends but pragmatists about means. This seems to us the proper stance for democratic socialists. A party of the left should exhibit a relentless ingenuity in finding new ways, in changing circumstances, to advance its ends. Too often Labour has looked like the conservative party of British politics, the guardian of yesterday against tomorrow.

There is a north/south problem – geographical and metaphorical. MPs rightly voice the concerns of their backgrounds, their culture, their constituencies. At best Labour's cry is a strong one against injustice. At worst, its voice becomes an echo of yesterday's Britain – a nation of massed workers in the great industries, a society of tenants, when the relative poverty of the majority contrasted starkly with the riches of the few.

Over a long period Labour was effectively prevented from putting the needs of the consumer at the centre of its approach to public services by a combination of its own top-down collectivism and its reluctance to challenge the power of producer groups. Yet a party which believes in the ability of the state to provide for the people should be the party which makes sure the state works effectively to that end. It should be as innovative in this area as in others, exploring new ways to deliver services, to meet the needs of consumers and to ensure quality. It is necessary to show what a people's state might actually look like and that Labour will brook no vested interests in its determination to create one.

This is a tremendous opportunity for Labour. Its task is to transform itself from what it was in danger of becoming, a declining class party, into a genuine people's party. This requires a deep cultural shift. It requires the party to be more, not less, radical and more, not less, vigorous in advocating the values of democratic socialism, combined with an intellectual boldness in exploring how those values can be applied.

It is time to resurrect the concept of a public interest, which has almost disappeared from politics, banished by the ideologues of the free market right in favour of the traded outcome of private interests. There is a public interest in rebuilding the economy, guarding the environment, giving security to citizens and all the other activities that intelligent states do and intelligent citizens expect them to do, even when this means confronting assorted vested interests.

Rejecting old style politics and the 'old boy' network in which the Tories are so inextricably enmeshed, will also send powerful and persuasive messages to those sections of the electorate whose support Labour must win to form a government. The clear message from the psephological evidence is that Labour has not yet managed to win the confidence of a sufficiently broad spectrum of public opinion to guarantee success at the next election. We are still a long way from convincing the majority of the electorate that we have the right policies to tackle the country's huge problems. We suffer from being seen as a party which is too defensive, too frightened of offending the electorate (or important sections of it), and too nervous of attacks in the Tory tabloids to give firm commitments to new policies.

Our message must be brave and forward-looking, that of a party which is staking out the new agenda for the twenty-first century. This agenda will necessarily involve fundamental changes in Government policies. We must not flinch from this. The British people know full well the sad truth about the country's under-performance; they are equally aware of the failure of the Thatcher agenda to improve matters. They are not looking for more tinkering with a mechanism which simply isn't working. They are looking for a better future and our vision must embrace their hopes and aspirations. It must point to a fairer, more successful, more meritocratic society, in which old privileges and vested interests are swept away.

Reclaiming our Values – Liberty, Equality and Community

Labour's new agenda does not start with a clean sheet and within a moral vacuum. Rather we build on values that derive from a rich tradition of radical and socialist thought. Democratic socialism is our cornerstone. It is inspired by no one tradition, philosophical school, or set of beliefs. It derives inspiration, ideas and experience from a range of historical strands, including Christianity, the Levellers, the Chartist campaign for parliamentary democracy, trade unionism, feminism, and Marxism.

Reviewing the traditions of British socialism, Tony Crosland concluded that 'the single one element common to all the schools of thought has been the basic aspirations, the underlying moral values. It follows that these embody the only logically and historically permissible meaning of the word "socialism"'. This is a view we share.

Central to democratic socialism is a passionate belief in equality: the belief that all citizens are born with equal rights and are of equal worth, that they should contribute their best to society and take on a fair share of responsibility according to their abilities and receive a fair share in the distribution of resources.

This belief in equality goes beyond the traditional Liberal belief in equality of opportunity. To believe in equality is to reject fundamentally the view that access to decent housing, good health services or education should be decided on the accident of birth, race, gender, inheritance of wealth or current income. It follows that a fundamental guideline for contemporary policy must be redistribution as a means of equalising individual life chances.

In the century since pioneering socialists set out their vision of equality, much progress has been achieved. A much larger proportion of the population now enjoy a good income, good education, good housing, good health and sufficient leisure time to pursue a range of interests. The changing pattern of distribution of wealth, the historical triumph of social democratic policies, gives the lie to those who claim that inequality is inevitable. Indeed most people would agree that Britain was a better and a more successful society in the first three post war decades when inequalities, although still rife, were reducing, than in the past decade and a half when the gap between rich and poor has been widening. Redistribution is both feasible and desirable.

One of the great ironies of modern politics is the ability of the conservatives, of whatever party, to portray themselves as the champions of liberty and, furthermore, to contrast liberty with equality, arguing that the two are incompatible and that equality will inevitably deny liberty. And what great freedoms does the modern conservative care most about? The freedom to enable babies not to die because of adverse social conditions? The freedom of the young to get jobs, whatever their class or colour? The freedom for old people not to die from winter cold? Of course not. Nothing could be further from their minds. Rather they define 'liberty' and 'freedom' so narrowly that they become labels to justify privileges. Can it be coincidence that such terms are employed by the rich most passionately and consistently to defend their 'rights' to buy privileged education and medical care for themselves and their families, heedless of the consequences for the rest of society?

True liberty is a key building block for the new society. Liberty has implications for a social, economic, political and international agenda. Liberty is crucial for true citizenship, entailing that balance between rights and responsibilities, entitlements and duties that enhance dignity.

Early radicals, most notably supporters of the French Revolution, added 'fraternity' to form a trinity – liberty, equality and fraternity. Today we would use the term 'community'. We feel that today it is the very absence of 'community' that lies at the heart of our social malaise.

The 1980s, which have dragged on so wretchedly into this decade, were – are – the years of the atomised individual. 'There is no such thing as society,' we were commanded from high. We should not be surprised that people acted accordingly – the thugs who seized what they wanted, the company directors who paid themselves thousands of pounds more a week, and the politicians who exchanged public interest for private gain.

Rising crime rates, mugging and brutality, the run-down of the inner city and financial fraud are all inevitable consequences of a culture that applauds the selfish, the greedy and the grabbers. The egos and vanities, the wealth and the power, of the few are enhanced. Indecency thrives because we are told that we cannot afford decency. Poverty increases, dependency develops and, at the extreme, community neglect masquerades as community care and the destitute dwell in shop fronts.

We reject the ignoble 'individualism' of the new jungle Conservatism. Rather we respect an individualism that recognises the individual as a social being interdependent on family, community and society. For us the focus is not on one of these concepts, but on all. Moreover, we believe in the equal rights (and responsibilities) of all individuals. For us the good society is one that recognises the needs, and seeks to utilise the skills, of all citizens for the community as a whole. Today, community is under pressure and, in some areas, has been all but destroyed. For too many citizens it is a sad fact: there is no such thing as community.

Current policies make things worse. Local authorities and housing associations are unable to house that mix of citizens of different backgrounds and family circumstances that make for true communities. As a result new tenants come increasingly from the most impoverished and insecure backgrounds. Politicians and commentators then find to their horror that majorities of tenants on some estates are single parents, unemployed and dependent on state welfare. Planning and other policies that place no value on communities are also to blame: in our small towns and suburbs the post office and pharmacist close and only the video shop and takeaway pizza flourish.

We recognise that there is no easy, short-term search for community. It is an elusive concept and cannot be realised by turning back the clock, but we should seek to support policies that enhance it. Good practice in schools, social service departments, police forces and health and community services exists and must be built upon.

There is nothing wrong with the accoutrements of personal affluence, indeed we want to spread them more widely, but if the numbers
of *personal* stereos, Nintendos, mobile phones and cars grow in number,
while *public* transport, health services, schools, and broadcasting decline
in quality then we are in trouble. We do not wish to see a 'society'
where crime increases and detection rates remain low; where more opt
for private health and education for want of an effective alternative;
where parks and open spaces are derelict and unsafe; and where the
roads are clogged up because of a lack of investment in public transport.

Equality, liberty and community are the enduring values which
underpin democratic socialism. No one theme predominates. The values
are interdependent, and together they constitute the core of democratic
socialism.

Citizenship and Democracy

The concept of citizenship is crucial, raising as it does a key question
for a democracy, namely what are the fundamental rights and responsibilities of citizens? Often, the debate is approached too narrowly.
Depending on political persuasion, emphasis is placed solely on responsibility or rights. Some argue that citizens should take on greater responsibilities – for the misdemeanours of their children; for the care of
their elders; for filling labour market gaps; for crime prevention; and
for much else besides – but refrain from mentioning what rights citizens
should expect in return. Others demand further rights – to child care;
to a decent income; to jobs etc – but do not address the question of
their own responsibilities in society.

A focus on both rights and responsibilities provides a useful entrée
into some of the key policy questions that Britain faces, such as:

— What are the fundamental rights and responsibilities of citizenship?
— How have these changed in the wake of social and economic developments around family life and employment?
— What costs relate to these changes and should they be allowed to lie
   where they fall?
— What are the caring responsibilities of modern families, given changes
   relating to the dependence of children, and increasing needs given
   ageing within the extended family?
— Which responsibilities should become legal obligations?
— What are the rights of families, in relation to, *inter alia*, income
   support, child care and the care of elderly relatives?

In seeking answers to these questions we need a clear understanding of the far-reaching changes of the past fifty years. Britain in the 1990s is an utterly different society to the one Beveridge reflected. By 1990 71 per cent of married women were employed, compared to just 10 per cent in 1931. In 1990, 60 per cent of families had both parents in employment. By 1992 there were almost six million part-time employees, with 45 per cent of women employed on a part-time basis.

Demographic trends mean shifting patterns of care, some in the labour market, but most within the family. 'Community care' in the main is care by female relatives, some of whom leave paid jobs. Young people enter the labour market later, due to more schooling and trainng, increasing higher education, plus unemployment. And workers retire earlier, either voluntarily or through redundancy.

Perhaps most significant of all, against all Beveridge's assumptions, unemployment reached one million at the end of 1975, two million six years later and it hit three million in the mid 1980s and again in the early 1990s. On a true count four million people are now out of work. These labour market changes are occurring alongside family trends of equal magnitude. Some 70 per cent of one-parent families depend on state benefits. The highest divorce rates in the EC, coupled with more single (unmarried) parents, generate more poverty, and new forms of inequality.

We are at a crossroads. The Tory Government is determined to pursue a low wage economy, where the aim is to compete both in traditional and emerging markets by driving down costs through a determined attack on wages and conditions. Hence the abolition of wages councils and the rejection of the European social chapter. Mass unemployment is a further weapon. But there is a positive alternative. It is to pursue energetically the goal of a fully employed and active economy. This involves competing vigorously through high quality production and services requiring a well educated, highly trained and flexible work-force, where labour is respected and skills nurtured. This requires a pro-active employment and social policy. Within this context the family is crucial. For employment patterns have changed and will continue to change at a time of substantial family change. Therefore the question, how do people live and how do people work, is a key guideline for policy. If we are to attack the 'dependency culture' that cripples so many, we need an active community, an active economy, a vigorous public policy.

An active policy is one that seeks to promote independence. It is designed to enable modern British citizens to be successful partners, good parents, effective workers and career-builders, responsible carers and citizens. Now of course these things depend on individuals and families themselves to a considerable extent, but we reject the pessimistic punditry that government can do nothing.

The New Agenda for Work and the Family

The work/family agenda is a prime example of policies with the dual function of promoting social justice and economic efficiency. What are the main items on the work and family agenda?

Employment Policy

A new agenda must not just be about restoring certain rights lost during the Tory years, but must also promote family-friendly work practices. These include parental leave and policies that allow for an increasing number of 'carer-workers', given the ageing population. The social revolution of mothers' employment has not been matched by the development of child care and pre-school provision which is required in a modern European society.

Social Security

Family/work trends have implications for benefit reform. Families with children under five are the most hard-pressed financially, often with only one earner. The policy implications for child care and child benefit should be considered together: one option is to offer parents with children either a child care place or an additional child benefit premium if the parent wishes to care for the child at home.

The strategy here must be designed to remove barriers to the labour market. Lone mothers must have choice about whether to stay at home to look after their children or whether to combine this with work outside the home. Getting established, or re-established, in employment calls for policies for education (to encourage the youngest mothers to continue their schooling), training and child care.

Critics will doubtless ask, where is the money coming from? The answer is clear. The cost of current policies is colossal: in 1992/93 social security benefits for one parent families cost £6.6 billion. And the money will come too as investments in people pay dividends, as benefit recipients become employees and taxpayers. The active economy and community that we seek will enable benefits to be directed to those for whom they were always intended – retired people and those with disabilities.

We therefore stand at an important crossroads in our national journey: towards either a low wage, low skilled economy, where family commitments are a nuisance, or a high skill, high value economy where the family agenda is taken seriously because that is good for both employees and companies alike.

The Democratic Agenda

There is more disquiet now about the condition of British democracy than at any period we can remember. This disquiet is reflected by a significant movement demanding wide-ranging constitutional reform, and, more ominously, in a deep and developing cynicism on the part of citizens towards politics. The prevailing mood is one of a plague on all your houses. Labour must lead a positive response. The Party should offer people not just different policies but a different kind of politics. This would not only enable the Party to tap discontent, but would establish the crucial connection between democratic renewal and the Party's wider project of modernisation. Labour has certainly moved a long way in recent years and now has an ambitious agenda of democratic and constitutional reform. However, there is more to be done if people are to be persuaded that Labour has really grasped the need for a decisive shift in the political culture of which it has been an essential part.

What is required is not a quick institutional fix, but something more fundamental. The shopping list of desirable and necessary constitutional reforms (a written constitution, bill of rights, freedom of information, a new second chamber, a reformed electoral system) should be seen as the product of a more general critique of British political arrangements and of radical democratic reconstruction. Whatever its formal rhetoric and self image, Britain has never taken democracy with the seriousness it deserves. It has taken governing seriously, but that is another matter.

No wonder there has been much quiet conservative satisfaction at the way in which, contrary to nineteenth century apprehensions, the development of democracy in Britain was so easily domesticated by other and older non-democratic traditions. The failure to carry through a democratic modernisation of British society is the key to its modern history and the source of its endemic difficulties. The consequences are on every side: the ascendancy of finance over industry, the malign dominance of the public schools, the failings of management and the social exclusion of the workforce, the lack of scientific culture – the list is long and catastrophic. The failure to undertake democratic reform has to be seen as part of the wider failure to modernise British society. This, it has to be admitted, is Labour's failure too.

British political arrangements have to be at the centre of a reform agenda. The system is distinguished by a quite extraordinary absence of checks and balances on what government can do. It is a winner-takes-all system with a vengeance. Post-1979 politics should leave no room for further doubt. Only in Britain, with its political idiosyncrasies (an uncodified constitution, no guaranteed rights, no effective bicameralism, no secure territorial division of power, a non-proportional electoral system) could a party without a popular majority have been able to deploy executive power to crush opposition and press forward its ideological mission over a prolonged period. The array of policy disasters – from education to the Poll Tax, health to broadcasting, transport to the botched privatisations – is the price we are all paying for this British version of strong government.

It is time to tell people the truth; that much that happens in parliament is an expensive, self-indulgent farce. The 'best club in London' has to be transformed into a modern working assembly. It is scarcely surprising that the current legislative process should produce such bad laws when effective pre-legislation scrutiny is so poor. Parliament's failure even to reform its own hours and organisation of business not only makes it incompatible with anything approaching normal family life (though highly compatible with lucrative extramural pursuits), but also reflects a larger failure. Until Parliament reforms itself, it should not be expected to reform anything else.

Electoral reform is an essential element in the renewal of democracy in Britain. It prevents minorities pretending they are majorities, counters the damaging social and geographical segregation of British politics and responds to the effective disenfranchisement of the 37 million people (some 85 per cent of the electorate) who live in constituencies where their votes don't really count. Labour's welcome commitment to consult the people in a referendum needs to be backed up by the firm advocacy of reform.

The time is surely up for yah-boo adversarialism and the sledgehammer of 'sovereignty'. Partnership and consensus are not soft evasions, but represent the toughest kind of politics because they are explicitly inclusive and involve negotiation, learning and coalition building. We want Labour to bring in and draw upon all the people who have something to contribute. On a range of issues, with the environment as the most outstanding one, it will simply not be possible to make durable progress without coalitions of support which go beyond daily party warfare. Labour's need to redefine itself coincides precisely with the wider need to reconstruct British politics.

Democracy and Accountability in Public Services

The need for reform extends far beyond parliament. Entire areas of government and public services have effectively been removed from democratic accountability. Non-democratic quangos now account for one fifth of public spending and are the arena for some 40,000 ministerial appointments of placemen (they are overwhelmingly men). As elective government is eroded, so appointed government is established. The health service, education, training, housing, urban regeneration, the police: the trend is uniform and in one direction.

A vital first step in restoring a proper framework for accountability and the protection of the public interest will be to limit ministerial powers to establish such bodies. Appointments to the controlling Boards of all such bodies should be subject to election wherever possible – in many instances the functions should be brought within the remit of elected authorities. All such bodies not subject to election, should be under regular scrutiny by the appropriate Parliamentary Select Committee, and placed under an explicit framework of administrative law.

We want more real independence and pluralism, not less. The problem with the 'Next Steps' programme of hiving off the work of Government departments into agencies is that the process is not matched by equivalent innovations in accountability. We want to 'reinvent' government in a whole variety of ways that decentralise services and empower users, and we have little sympathy with those still attached to top-down statism. But at the same time we insist on the need for a clear framework of accountability in the public interest.

Inevitably bodies operating on a national scale can easily appear remote from the public. Effective devolution of power to the regions and to local communities is one ingredient necessary to overcome this problem. A good illustration is the Housing Corporation, responsible for around £2 billion public expenditure each year, and now the main agency through which social housing is built. The organisation operates through a national Board, appointed by ministers. Although the Corporation has regional offices, there is no mechanism through which these are accountable to the communities they are supposedly serving. Establishing Regional Boards, comprising elected representatives of local communities and tenants groups would be one step in the direction of ensuring greater accountability. Another, and in the long-term more important step, will be the devolution of more power to tenants co-operatives and other user groups. In place of the sterile current debate as to whether local authorities or housing associations are the better providers of social housing, we need to focus on how both types of provider can improve their service and make themselves more responsive to their clients. In reality both are necessary.

Reviving Local Democracy

Because local authorities have been Labour's main power base in recent years, the Party has naturally sprung to their defence against repeated attacks from a hostile government. But we must avoid the temptation simply to defend the status quo, and to regard the current pattern of local authorities, and the services they deliver, as immutable. Looking back over the history of local government in Britain, it is notable how the size and the areas covered by local councils as well as their responsibilities have changed. Few if any of their original functions – gas, electricity and water supplies – remain. In devising the best and most appropriate structures for the future, we should not feel constrained by existing patterns.

The two-tier structure comprising county and district authorities is in need of reform. The case for a new framework comprising regional authorities and single-tier local authorities is strong, and fits well with European patterns and with plans for the devolution to Scotland and Wales. The process of establishing a new regional and local authority map for Britain is one which calls for great skill and sensitivity. It cannot be left to a quango or a closed group of ministerial 'trusties' to decide. There is a strong case for a full and representative commission of enquiry drawing its membership from both central and local government and with real opportunities for the public to contribute.

We also need to review local authority functions. Many local authorities' services are in a state of flux, not least education where the ill-thought out Tory 'reforms' are creating new problems and tensions. Faced with this mess, and the blatant bias of the Government in favour of grant-maintained schools, it is an understandable reaction to call for a return of all schools to LEA management. It would, however, be a mistake. No-one concerned about the quality of education can feel happy about the record of the past thirty years during which Britain was outstripped by so many other countries in terms of educational achievements. Restoration of the status quo prior to the Tory reforms is not the answer.

Instead we need to define the necessary ingredients of a policy capable of achieving a sustained and dramatic improvement across the whole ability range. As part of this process, there is much to be said for devolving day-to-day responsibility for managing schools to governors and head teachers. At the same time to avoid the fragmentation and divisiveness implicit in the current 'opting-out' process, there is a need for an effective local education authority, ensuring that all schools are operating within clearly defined performance guidelines, and protecting the interests of local parents who rightly want to ensure their children have access to the best possible quality education. The local education authority role thus changes from one of direct control to setting the framework in which all local schools operate, sensitive monitoring, and providing additional support and co-ordination.

A similar pattern may well be appropriate in respect of health, a service which is clearly in need of a new framework. The existing panoply of non-accountable bodies which manage the NHS – regional health authorities, district health authorities, hospital and health-care trusts, and family health service associations – is neither efficient nor accountable. It is crying out for reform. With day to day to responsibility for running the NHS discharged by 'providers' from whom the supposed representatives of the public purchase services, there is a strong case for making the 'purchasers' truly accountable to local people. An obvious way to do this is to make it a responsibility of local government.

Such a shift in power and role could well form the basis for a revival of confidence and self-esteem in local government and help to attract higher calibre councillors and senior officers. It would certainly require a new and more positive relationship between central and local government and would attract a great deal more public interest in local government. In the longer term local authorities could well emerge as very different types of bodies, with an enhanced standing as guardians of the interests of their whole communities rather than as providers of a limited range of services for some of their residents.

The New International Agenda

Decent values should not stop at the white cliffs of Dover. It is to some extend understandable that western electorates should be hoping for a quieter life after the end of the Cold War, and perhaps even a 'peace dividend' as well. Sadly that hope looks like being disappointed. Economic dislocation, environmental degradation and appalling wars are the prospects for the future unless we make a decisive break from the *laissez-faire* of most incumbent western governments. We need intervention, and activist governments forging a new agenda of global co-operation, human rights, greater social justice and international law and order.

The progressive tradition which should inspire the Labour Party is that of the activist American and British administrations of the late 1940s, the Democrats in the US and Labour in Britain. Together they created a new international system which, whatever its shortcomings, laid the foundation for an era of unparalleled peace and prosperity. It was a Labour Foreign Secretary who proposed NATO and a Labour government which seconded civil servants to create a new democratic framework for Germany. It was a Democratic administration which poured resources into the reconstruction of Europe through the Marshall Plan. Labour and Democrats collaborated on the construction of the Bretton Woods system to regulate international finance and trade.

Contrast that massive work of renewal with the apathy of western governments in the aftermath of the Cold War, exemplified by appeasement in the Balkans and the betrayal of the hopes of Eastern Europe. Faced with the enormous task of reconstructing whole societies, the advice of the libertarian right to the new governments of eastern Europe has been to do nothing but balance their budgets and privatise their healthcare.

Of course, Britain's place in the world, economically, diplomatically and militarily, is relatively a great deal smaller than at the end of the last war. However, we are pivotal in both the European Community and the Atlantic Alliance, and also a member of the UN Security Council and the G7. Culturally and politically, through institutions such as the BBC and through the great gift of the English language, Britain has exceptional influence which should be employed for the general good.

Three themes should inform the foreign policy of a Labour Britain. One is the spirit of activism and intervention for human rights and international order. The second theme is multi-lateralism. Britain should be committed to working, whenever possible, through international and, indeed, through supra-national institutions. The third important theme is the need to combine our concern for security and international order with an equal emphasis upon social, economic and political development.

The United Nations embodies all three of these themes, and accordingly has primary place in Labour's new agenda. The successful repulsion of aggression in the Gulf showed what could be achieved under the authority of the UN. But its hesitant and half-hearted involvements in Angola and the former Yugoslavia show the distance the UN still has to travel before it can fulfil its proper potential.

The UN is the overriding forum for discussing international security, the only institution which can confer a legitimate mandate to intervene in defence of international order and human rights. But it lacks the instruments to execute that mandate effectively. Supplying the UN with the necessary tools is an urgent task, requiring the revival of the Military Staff Committee and the earmarking by member countries of appropriate forces upon which the Secretary General can call. It means a major increase in resources: the UN's total peacekeeping budget in 1992 was less than the combined expenditure of New York City's fire and police departments. But we must also be realistic, and acknowledge that even with enhanced resources, it will take years for the UN to build up its capacities to the desired levels. In the meantime, human rights and international law are under assault across the globe. We must fill this gap urgently. The sensible way forward is to work through existing regional security organisations, such as Asean, the Arab League, NATO and the CSCE. Working under the authority of the UN, such regional organisations are best equipped and best placed to intervene in their own areas.

The security crises in Europe present a special case. This is because it has been traditional in NATO for the United States to provide political leadership and the bulk of resources. Yet, as the Balkans crisis has shown, the US can be reluctant to provide the necessary leadership. The European Community must urgently develop a common foreign and security policy. Despite the difficulties arising from national and historical differences, this must be done if Europe, from the Atlantic to the Urals, is to achieve stability and order. Continuing confusion and weakness within the Community will inevitably resonate with disorder and anarchy outside, with perhaps catastrophic consequences.

No common policy will be effective unless it has appropriate instruments, including defence forces. The European Community is both more populous and possesses a bigger GNP than the United States. EC countries have a total of 2.2 million men under arms, yet Europe shrank from intervention in the Balkans because its forces were not geared to acting without American leadership and America participation. Europe lacks cohesion and purpose. The inefficiency of financing a dozen different armies, navies and airforces, each with its own customised equipment, appears increasingly absurd as Europe becomes more and more integrated in other areas.

NATO can continue to provide the core of peacekeeping and peace-making missions in the European land-mass. Its integrated command and control systems and years of common training make it ideal for these tasks, with other forces – for example, the Russians – welded on as appropriate from case to case. But at the same time NATO's own force structures, deployment, training and doctrines require urgent amending.

In particular, we must move beyond the absurd rivalry between NATO and the Western European Union. The Community countries must develop the capacity to take the leading role in major continental interventions, such as is required in former Yugoslavia. There is no difficulty in principle in reconciling this to the continuing framework of co-operation and support provided by the Atlantic Alliance. On the contrary, it is the continuing failure of the European Community to shoulder what are its appropriate responsibilities that is placing an increasing strain upon that Alliance.

The biggest single challenge Europe faces is the future of the former Soviet Union. Unfortunately, the West European left have often disparaged the new democratic leadership of Russia because of its privatisation policies, not realising that the model many there wish to emulate is not the divisive, shallow capitalism of the United States, but the social democracy of western Europe.

Moreover, should President Yeltsin fail in his massive task of social reorientation, his successor will almost certainly be far to his right. That could unloose ethnic and nationalist conflicts with former Soviet states, such as the Ukraine, Kazakhstan and the Baltic Republics, which would make the horrors in the Balkans look like a mere skirmish. This makes it doubly important that a Labour Britain engages actively and enthusiastically with the reform process in Russia.

Western assistance thus far has been limited, unimaginative and distorted by *laissez-faire* dogma. Certainly it is right to encourage privatisation of shops and factories and to free up economic decision-making in these areas. But this should be accompanied by a massive programme to build up the infrastructure of housing, railways, roads and telecommunications which Russia so badly needs and which the private sector by itself can never supply. Russia needs to develop a proper national health service and a welfare state, as under the current system many social benefits are tied (in uncanny resemblance to the US) to people's jobs. A Labour government in Britain would be ideally placed to advise the Russians and others on these enormous tasks.

Conclusion

A new political agenda for the Labour Party and for Britain should not shrink from facing unpalatable truths. Implicit in our argument is the belief that both party and country have suffered grievously from a reluctance to grapple with harsh realities. Rather than confront the clear evidence of economic and industrial decline, we have sought reassurance in the past. But 'back to the future' is not the correct text for Britain as we move towards the twenty-first century. We need to engage with the newly emerging patterns of social and economic organisation that will characterise the next century.

The inevitability of change, and the need to respond energetically to new forces and challenges is one of our key messages. Change is disorientating and at times frightening, but no truly radical party should be daunted by that. The origins of the Labour Party are to be found in the rich traditions of radical and socialist thought – which articulated the vision of a better world for men and women whose experience had been tragically stunted and restricted by the economic, social and political structures of their day. We must now show a similar courage in articulating the message of democratic socialism and setting out our own vision for the radical transformation of British society.

15

Tales from Elsewhere and an Hibernian Sermon

Brendan O'Duffy and Brendan O'Leary

It is ethnocentric to believe that a dominant party must resemble the Conservative and Unionist Party in the UK or the Liberal Democratic Party (LDP) in Japan. It is equally ethnocentric to believe that the principal reason for the Conservatives' dominance lies in the plurality rule electoral system in single member constituencies, known colloquially as 'first-past-the-post'.[1]

The best way to avoid ethnocentrism is through comparative analysis, which is why we provide some 'tales from elsewhere' below. In comparative perspective dominant parties come in two principal types. One is the continuous single-party majority government, like the present Australian Labour government and the present Tory government in Britain. The other is found within a continuous multi-party coalition government, like the Christian Democrats in post-war Italy. In both types the dominant party is dominant in number, meaning that it has the largest number of seats in parliament, and that it enjoys privileged access to the principal executive and legislative posts, meaning that it controls the premiership and other major parliamentary offices. In both types the dominant party is in continuous control of these posts, and, is also usually ideologically dominant.[2]

This chapter examines whether dominant parties, and the two types of dominant party, can be partially explained by the electoral formula used to determine the composition of a state assembly or parliament. More precisely we examine the likelihood that proportional and non-proportional formulae facilitate the creation and maintenance of dominant parties. Proportional representation (PR) systems ensure a proportional relationship between the percentage of votes cast for parties (and candidates) and the percentage of seats they win in a parliament. They differ in the manner and degree in which they achieve proportionality, which is determined by the existence and scale of thresholds, the magnitude of the electoral districts, and the mathematical formulae used for the allocation of seats. Non-proportional (NPR) systems do not ensure a proportional relationship between the votes cast for a party (or candidates) and the seats they win in an assembly or parliament. The best known NPR systems are the plurality and majority rule formulae.[3]

Presently the Tories in the UK are fervent enthusiasts for plurality rule. Their enthusiasm is only matched in one other party in the UK – the Ulster Unionist Party (UUP). This is entirely understandable. For these parties plurality-rule has been an unalloyed good: for the Conservative and Unionist Party throughout the entirety of British electoral history;[4] and for the UUP when it governed Northern Ireland as an ethnic monopoly between 1921 and 1972.[5] These examples also make it very tempting to conclude that the present and past dominance of these parties has rested on plurality rule. Our argument enters a caveat about this easy conclusion.

Our argument is developed through simple tests, detailed in a technical appendix (see Appendix 1). We show that non-proportional electoral systems, in comparison with proportional representation systems, are indeed positively associated with dominant one-party majority government. This result is entirely consistent with the arguments of critics of the British electoral system, especially those who want to end Tory dominance. However, we also provide suggestive evidence that PR systems are more likely than NPR systems to be associated with the dominance of one party in a continuous multi-party coalition government.[6]

The core of our technical argument is simply this: switching from a non-proportional to a proportional electoral system will not exclude the possibility of a dominant party, although it may change the likely type of dominant party. The political message of our technical argument is this: electoral reformers in the UK need to recognise that PR cannot prevent the Conservatives from becoming a different type of dominant party. Having made this argument we then make a simple suggestion. Those who are especially concerned to avoid dominance by the Conservatives, in whatever form, should strongly consider the single transferable vote (STV) system of proportional representation, which in our judgement provides a better check on a dominant party than any other system. That is our Hibernian sermon.

Arguments and Research About the Effects of Electoral Formulae

Electoral systems have been argued to affect at least three different aspects of democratic systems:

— the number of competitive parties;

— the durability or survival rate of governments; and
— the probability of the formation of one-party majority governments.

Many arguments about these relationships have been tested by political scientists. In the first place, the merit of 'Duverger's rule' has been extensively investigated. This rule suggested that plurality and single-ballot majority electoral formulae are likely to produce stable two-party systems, with regular alternation in the party in government, while double-ballot majority[7] and proportional representation formulae encourage the formation of less stable, multi-party systems.[8] There have also been investigations of the effects of PR and NPR formulae (i.e. plurality and majority systems) on the durability of governments.[9] Lastly, there has been some exploration of the effect of the electoral formula on the probability of one-party majority government. Thus one important study found that NPR formulae (i.e. plurality-rule and majority-rule) were significantly more likely than PR to lead to the formation of single-party majority governments.[10]

However, to our knowledge, there has been no systematic comparative research on the impact of electoral formulae in facilitating the entrenchment of dominant parties. Moreover, in trying to conduct such research two difficulties arise with the existing literature on electoral systems. The first lies with the way people measure the durability of governments. Most studies normally define durability with indicators like the 'average survival length',[11] or 'the survival rate' of governments.[12] These measures are too crude for our purposes because they cannot take fully into account the degree of dominance suggested by the consecutive formation of governments by the same party, or of the consecutive formation of coalitions containing the same parties and dominated by the same party. The normal measures of durability just give too much weight to the formation of new governments, irrespective of what type of new governments they are. For example, the low survival-rate of governments in Italy between 1945 and 1993 did not accurately reflect the dominant position of the Christian Democrats who were part of every coalition government formed in this period. The same argument applies to the LDP, manifestly the dominant party in Japan between 1955 and 1993, even though the survival-rate of its governments was amongst the lowest of the major democracies.

The second difficulty is that there appears to be only one detailed comparative study of the impact of electoral formulae which relates to the formation and maintenance of dominant parties, that of Blais and Carty. Their approach represents a very significant improvement on some previous studies of the impact of electoral formulae[13]. They found that 'the probability of a [single-party] majority government increases by 11, 41 and 60 percentage points respectively in single-member majority, plurality, and multi-member majority systems compared to PR'.[14] However, we cannot treat Blais and Carty's study as a complete analysis of the impact of electoral formulae in facilitating dominant parties because they simply consider the probability of the formation of one-party majority governments. While one-party majority governments represent *one* attribute of a dominant party, they do not represent the *only* way in which a dominant party may express its dominance, because, as we have suggested, a dominant party can exist within a multi-party government.[15]

We attempt to make a preliminary contribution to this subject, but confine our investigation to stable post-war parliamentary democracies. We seek to establish whether electoral formulae have independent effects on the existence of dominant parties. We do so by defining two indicators of a dominant party in a parliamentary system:

— the maintenance of executive office by a party, including the premiership, as part of a majority government (whether one or multi-party) for three consecutive terms of office; and/or

— the maintenance of executive office by a party, including the premiership, as part of a majority government (whether one or multi-party), for ten consecutive years.

These indicators are somewhat arbitrary, but, if a week is a long time in politics, then a decade is close to eternity – and so is a three-term government. Our indicators capture the degree to which a party is able to win successive elections without interruption and/or maintain office. Continuity of rule is an important aspect of one-party dominance, not only because it reflects consistent electoral or coalition management success, but also because of its effect on continuity in policy-making.

Evidence from Twenty-One Cases of Parliamentary Democracies

Our analysis is based on a study of twenty-one regimes which have experienced continuous parliamentary democratic government since 1945 (see Appendix 2).[16] We have therefore excluded many existing democracies: the small democracies of the Caribbean, which mostly came into existence in the 1960s; the Asian democracies (except India) which have had discontinuities in democratic rule; the new European democracies established in the 1970s and the 1990s (which have not been in existence long enough to test for dominant parties); Switzerland, which has a distinctive political system which enforces alternation in executive leadership; and the USA, which has a formal separation of powers between the legislature and the executive. These states were excluded either because they have not been democracies for long enough, or because they do not have parliamentary and cabinet governments. With the exception of India, all of the states in our sample are modernised and industrialised, and are sufficiently similar in economic and political development to permit plausible inferences about the independent effects of electoral formulae on the formation and maintenance of dominant parties.

Our regression analysis, outlined in Appendix 1, distinguishes between PR and NPR electoral formulae as independent variables.[17] We classified all elections conducted in our cases as held under either PR or non-PR systems. The only ambiguous case was Japan's single non-transferable vote. Until 1993 Japanese electoral districts delivered three seats to the lower chamber of the Diet. Electors had a single vote which was non-transferable, and the three candidates with the most votes were elected. This system has been called 'semi-proportional' on the grounds that the multi-seat districts represent a diversity of 'issue-interests' rather than the allegedly 'territorial interests' of plurality systems. However, the Japanese experience suggested that the non-transferability of the single vote discouraged proportionality. Opposition parties were inhibited from putting up enough candidates to win a majority of seats in many constituencies, let alone the Diet. They were afraid of spreading their own vote too thinly. We therefore classified the old Japanese system as a non-PR system.

Our dependent variables – which are intended to capture the existence of a dominant party – are provided by four separate indicators (see Appendix 1) which describe four types of dominance:

1. a single party which retains power through a combination of three successive elections or changes of government;
2. a party which heads a multi-party government and returns to power as the dominant party in the executive in three successive elections or changes of government;
3. a party defined as in (1) above, except that its consecutive governments retain power for ten years; and
4. a party defined as in (2) above, except that the consecutive governments retain power for ten years.

Results

Table 15.1 cross-tabulates electoral formulae (PR systems and the two types of non-PR systems, majority and plurality rule), and instances of our indicators of one-party dominance. The data lend tentative support to two related arguments. First, plurality rule is more likely to lead to both forms of chronological dominance: three-term one party government and ten-year one party government. Ten of the thirteen occurrences of three-term one party government occurred under plurality rule. Similarly, nine of the twelve cases (75 per cent) of ten-year one party government occurred under plurality rule. Secondly, PR is more likely to lead to the coalition forms of one-party dominance: three-term majority coalition government headed by a dominant party, and ten-year majority coalition government headed by a dominant party. PR systems accounted for eighteen of the twenty occurrences (90 per cent) of three-term majority coalition government headed by a dominant party, and all of the ten occurrences of ten-year majority coalition government headed by a dominant party. Table 1 also suggests that PR systems have produced a dominant party, by our definition, more frequently than NPR systems.

Table 15.1 Electoral formulae and indicators of a dominant party: four indicators of dominance

| | (1) | | (2) | | (3) | | (4) | | Total |
	No.	%	No.	%	No.	%	No.	%	No.
PR	2	15	18	90	2	17	10	100	32
NPR (Majority)	1	8	2	10	1	8	0	0	4
NPR (Plurality)	10	77	0	0	9	75	0	0	19
Total	13	100	20	100	12	100	10	100	54

To establish more robust conclusions we considered the likelihood of a dominant party being produced by a specific electoral formula. To do that we needed to measure the ratio of the actual occurrence of dominant parties to their potential occurrence. Our chosen method is outlined in Appendix 1. Figure 15.1 presents the results which are displayed as the mean number of occurrences of a dominant party as a proportion of the total possible for each of the four indicators. It is clear that plurality systems have produced proportionately more occurrences of both forms of single-party dominance – as measured by indicators (1) and (3) – than either majority or PR systems.[18] It is also clear that coalition governments headed by a dominant party – measured by indicators (2) and (4) – are more likely under PR systems than under either majority or plurality systems. PR is clearly more likely than either majority or plurality formulae to produce ten years of majority coalition government headed by a dominant party. This result is primarily explained by the cases of Germany and Luxembourg which experienced, respectively, two and three spells of a decade or more of majority coalition government headed by a dominant party. In Germany, the

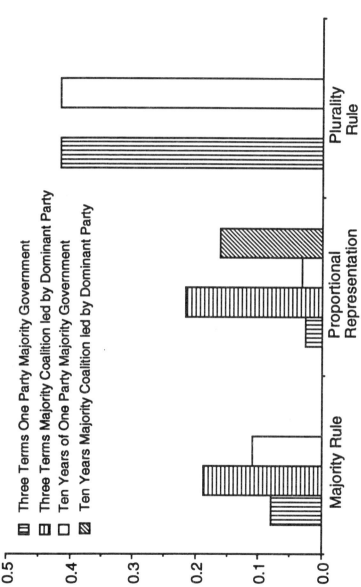

Figure 15.1 Average occurrences of dominant parties (number of occurrences as a proportion of possible occurrences)

CDU has enjoyed spells of dominance from 1949 to 1962 and from 1983 to the present.

The evidence considered so far suggests that PR has produced majority coalition government headed by a dominant party both absolutely and relatively more frequently than plurality-rule; and conversely, that NPR systems have produced single-party dominance more frequently, both absolutely and proportionately, than PR. However, to determine more rigorously the actual strength of these effects we executed a regression analysis which compared the impact of PR and NPR systems on the probability of each type of dominant party occurring (see Table 15. 2 in Appendix 1). The results lend further support to our hypotheses. They suggest that, other things being equal, the probability of three-terms of single-party majority dominance is 74 per cent greater in non-PR systems than in PR systems. Also, the probability of ten years of single-party majority dominance is 72 per cent greater in non-PR systems than in PR systems. The results for dominance within majority coalition governments were less conclusive, although the coefficients were positive in both cases, consistent with the direction of the causal effects we are suggesting, namely that PR systems are more likely than non-PR systems to produce dominance within majority coalition governments. Moreover, there are some plausible explanations for the statistical insignificance of these estimates which we discuss in Appendix 1.

To sum up: our comparative analysis and technical arguments support the thesis that NPR systems (both majority and plurality-rule) are more likely to lead to one-party dominance in single-party majority governments. This result is plausible and consistent with the findings of others and of campaigners for electoral reform in the UK. Our more original finding concerns dominant parties in majority coalition governments. While the regression analysis was less than conclusive, the examination of the frequencies and proportionate occurrences of majority coalition government headed by a dominant party confirm that:

— PR systems do not preclude a dominant party; and
— PR systems are more likely to facilitate dominance within a multi-party coalition than NPR systems.

The Political Question

We have made the technical point, perhaps laboriously so, that a dominant party, albeit of a different kind, can emerge and thrive under some of the PR systems favoured by reformers in the UK, as well as under the existing plurality-rule system. However, we have not made this argument to undermine the case for electoral reform. Our point is that one can go to Italy and Germany (PR systems) as well as to India and the UK (plurality systems) to find specimens of a dominant party. One can also make cases for changes in electoral laws to control the dominant party in both plurality and PR systems. There were after all very strong arguments for electoral reform in Italy which had a regional-list system of PR, just as there are very strong arguments for electoral reform in the UK.

Our warning, that dominance can be latent in certain types of PR, is very different to the usual criticisms of PR heard in the UK.[19] Electoral reformers need to appreciate that both the German (the additional member system) and the former Italian (regional party-list) systems of PR are more than capable of leading to the dominance of one party, at least on our definition of dominance, and all the un-desirable consequences that one party dominance can entail. This fact needs to be appreciated, especially by electoral reformers within the Labour Party who favour some version of the German system. Electoral reformers also need to ask themselves, on the past evidence of the history of the UK, exactly which party is most likely to exercise domin-ance if the electoral formula for the House of Commons is changed by a future reforming Labour government, or by a Lib-Lab coalition go-vernment. We submit that the most credible answer is the Conservative Party. After a short period of adjustment, in which its instinct for power would have to triumph over its ideological enthusiasms, the Conservative Party would reconcile itself to coalition government.

On reflection we believe that few would dispute that the Conservative Party is more likely than Labour to become dominant in the multi-party politics which would be fully reflected in the UK after a system of PR is introduced. This possibility should not, of course, become an argument for the status quo. Nor should it be used as a counsel of despair to suggest that whatever the electoral formula the Conservatives must win all the elections. Rather electoral reformers should recognise the danger of dominance within PR systems by supporting the type of PR most likely to minimise the possibility of a dominant party, and that type most likely to control any party which becomes dominant after an electoral reform. The question electoral reformers need to ask, in ad-dition to those they normally ask is this: 'which form of PR is most likely to hold a dominant party to account?'

Our answer, although we cannot provide conclusive proof of its merits, is that the single transferable vote (STV) is more likely to inhibit the undesirable dominance of the Conservative Party, or any other party, than any other PR system. Our case rests on four principal considera-tions. First, STV empowers voters, by enabling them to use their votes strategically against the dominant party. It does so by leaving voters free to rank their preferences on their ballot papers. Since their votes cannot be wasted, voters can be encouraged to vote against the dominant party, even when the opposition parties cannot agree a pre-electoral coalition against the dominant party – one of the present difficulties of British opponents of the Conservatives. It is an interesting fact that STV, as tested in independent Ireland since 1922, has prevented Fianna Fáil from being a dominant party, at least on our definition.[20] This fact is partially explicable through the existence of STV which enabled the fragmented opposition to use their ballot papers against the largest party. Although Fianna Fáil has had two periods of sixteen-years of government in independent Ireland, it has not had more than two successive periods of majority government since Ireland became a Republic. Even in its electoral heyday, 1932–77, it had periods of minority government alternating with periods of majority government, which forced it to temper its policies, and made it responsive to sections of the electorate beyond its core supporters.

Secondly, unlike the other main types of PR mechanism (party-lists and additional member systems), STV ensures that ministers and prime ministers in the dominant party are accountable in constituency elections. Under STV arrogant, corrupt and unpopular ministers can be safely unseated by 'their voters', who can choose humbler, cleaner, and popular candidates from the dominant party without having to vote for the opposition parties. This feature of STV is much disliked by Irish ministers who can lose to backbenchers and novices within their own party; and it is especially disliked by less than fully competent ministers or prime ministers, like the former prime minister Dr Garret FitzGerald, who criticises STV for producing 'weak ministers'. If FitzGerald's argument is true, then that is exactly what citizens who fear a dominant party should want. 'Weak ministers' provide some insurance against the unresponsiveness of dominant parties.[21]

Thirdly, STV is the only electoral formula which a powerful governing party, once with the support of the leading opposition party, has twice put to its national electorate in a referendum with the recommendation that it should be abandoned, only to be firmly re-buffed by the electorate, including its own supporters. The story in question occurred in the Republic of Ireland. The lesson is that STV is a system which voters like, even if politicians do not. Another way of putting the argument is that STV is the equivalent of 'market-testing' for politicians. Given that the Tories have made much of the need for 'market testing' their rhetoric should be deployed against them. STV should be marketed on the grounds that it creates far less safe seats for ministers and politicians than other systems, and therefore will expose Conservative ministers and MPs to much more competitive forces in the electoral marketplace.

Fourthly, our arguments for STV as a means of inhibiting the formation of a dominant party, and regulating a dominant party if it does come into being, are buttressed by the fact that most of the criticisms of STV are misleading or just false.[22] The most misleading argument suggests that whatever electoral formula is favoured by the Electoral Reform Society and the Liberal Democratic Party must be wrong – a classic example of the rhetorical trick of suggesting that all the good arguments for a proposition are discounted by one bad one. This criticism has no force with us, even though we are not members of either of these organisations. And, as a matter of fact, the first 're-play' of a general election in Great Britain showed that the Labour Party would have done better under STV than under the additional member system, while the converse would have been true of the Liberal Democrats.[23] The result was not expansively highlighted by the authors of this report, presumably because they favour the more elitist German additional member system, which chooses some MPs on the basis of party lists as well as electing others through constituencies.

There are other side-tracking canards about STV. One is the suggestion that it is too complicated to operate. In which case, just how do the Irish manage ? Another is the claim that STV does not produce pure proportionality, even though no system does, and even though STV gets very close to proportionality provided the district magnitude of constituencies is large enough, which it would have to be in Great Britain if the House of Commons is not to be too large. Finally, it is sometimes suggested that STV is only appropriate for small states – especially those left electoral laws by a departing and enlightened British empire. The inference behind this 'argument' is that only small states can afford the luxury of giving their citizens an effective and powerfully democratic electoral formula to express their diverse preferences. British democrats should recognise the untruths behind such arguments. They should, at least in this instance, consider being patriotic, rather than looking wistfully to continental Europe for their inspiration. STV is a British invention, and it is one British invention which deserves to be tried in Britain, because it is more likely than any other electoral formula to provide collective insurance against the potentially debilitating consequences of a dominant party.

Appendix 1
Data, Variables, Methods and Regression

The independent variables in our analysis are PR and non-PR systems. The dependent variables are:

1. *Three terms, one-party* (THREETOP): A single party which retains power through a combination of three successive elections, or changes of government;
2. *Three terms, coalition* (THREEToC): A party which heads a multi-party government and returns to power as the dominant party in the executive in three successive elections, or changes of government;
3. *Ten years, one-party* (TENOP): A party defined as in (1) above, except that its consecutive governments retain power for ten years; and
4. *Ten years coalition* (TENCOAL): A party defined as in (2) above, except that the consecutive governments retain power for ten years.

Our analysis considered both the absolute number of occurrences of each of the four dependent variables as well as the proportion of occurrences relative to the total number of potential opportunities for a change of government (measured by the total number of electoral opportunities which might permit three-term or ten-year dominance). For example, in the case of Japan there were three occurrences of three-term one-party government. To get the proportion of occurrences relative to the total number of potential opportunities for a change of government we divide the number of occurrences, (3), by the total potential number of one-party three-term majority governments (i.e. 19 ÷ 3 = (6.3)). The result for Japan is therefore .48 (= 3 ÷ 6.3). This figure can be interpreted as follows: 48 per cent of the potential opportunities for the formation of three consecutive one-party majority governments actually materialised. Similar calculations were also made for the two ten-year variables.

Our criteria for determining the formation of new governments were based on those set out by Woldendorp *et al.*[24] They include: the aftermath of elections; dissension within government where either a coalition breaks up without external pressure or where there are publicised quarrels and/or movement of personnel; and the withdrawal of parliamentary support, when parties either withdrew support from the government or a successful vote of no confidence (or functionally equivalent parliamentary action) took place. 'New governments', for our purposes, did not include the voluntary or involuntary resignation of a prime minister (on health grounds or as a result of intra-party conflict), nor the intervention by the head of state in the composition of the executive – except in the semi-presidential systems of Finland and France. We imposed two other qualifications on valid changes of government. First, we did not consider the government to have changed following a dissension or the withdrawal of parliamentary support if the new government was formed by the same parties with the same number of seats in parliament. This criterion rules out trivial bases for the reformation of government. Secondly, we excluded the continuation of majority multi-party coalitions in which the new prime minister was not a member of the largest coalition partner. This last criterion establishes a sharp marker of dominance: the largest party is not exhibiting dominance if it has to accept another party's candidate as prime minister. Therefore, on our criteria, the Christian Democrats lost dominance in Italy when they accepted Craxi's premiership.

The results of the dummy-variable regression are shown in Table 15.2. They lend further support to our hypotheses. The Beta effects can be interpreted as the impact of one system (e.g. non-PR) on the probability of the occurrence of a dominant party compared to the impact of the other system (e.g. PR). The results suggest that, *ceteris paribus*, the probability of three-terms of single-party majority dominance (THREE-TOP) is 74 per cent greater in non-PR systems than in PR systems. The probability of ten years of single-party majority dominance (TENOP) is 72 per cent greater in non-PR systems than in PR systems.

Table 15.2 Regression of indicators of dominant parties on electoral formulae

	PR ß	Non-PR ß
(1) THREETOP	–	·74*
(2) THREEToC	·33	–
(3) TENOP	–	·72*
(4) TENCOAL	·40	–

Note: * = significant at .01 level

The results for dominance in majority coalition governments are less conclusive (indicators (2) and (4)). Neither of the effects for PR systems are statistically significant, although the coefficients are positive in both cases – which is consistent with the direction of the hypothesised effect. The statistical insignificance of these estimates is likely to be the result of several factors. The Scandinavian tradition of minority government – whether single party or multi-party – reduces the likelihood of majority coalition governments in the data. This 'Scandinavian effect' offsets the higher occurrence of majority coalition governments headed by a dominant party in Israel, Luxembourg, and Germany. Moreover, variations in the degree of proportionality in PR systems appear to have a significant impact. The Netherlands, Italy and Ireland have experienced fewer cases of a dominant party, on our definitions, than we might expect. District magnitude and threshold effects in the PR list systems used in the Netherlands and Italy, and the effects of STV in Ireland, may help explain the reduction in the likelihood of a dominant party in these countries.

This formal analysis is subject to numerous limitations because we only tested the importance of one independent variable, the electoral formula, in explaining the existence of a dominant party. A more ambitious analysis would control for other variables, and estimate their importance in contrast to that of electoral formulae. Such variables would have to include the independent impact of the district magnitude, the effective number of competitive parties in a political system, the depth of the left-right cleavage, and the number and depth of other salient cleavages.

Appendix 2 Countries in the sample: cases and data

Country	Electoral System	Opportunities for dominant party	Opportunities (in years) for dominant party	Survival Rate	THREETOP (actual occurences)	THREETOP (as proportion of opportunities)	THREETOC (actual occurences)	THREETOC (as proportion of opportunities)	TENOP (actual occurrences)	TENOP (as proportion of opportunities)	TENCOAL (actual occurences)	TENCOAL (as proportion of opportunities)
Australia	Majority rule	19	45	59.6	1	.16	0	.00	1	.22	0	.00
Austria	PR	15	45	59.6	1	.20	1	.20	1	.22	1	.22
Belgium	PR	26	47	33.4	0	.00	2	.23	0	.00	1	.43
Canada	Plurality rule	15	45	51.0	1	.20	0	.00	1	.22	0	.00
Denmark	PR	22	45	42.4	0	.00	0	.00	0	.00	0	.00
Finland	PR	29	45	26.2	0	.00	2	.21	0	.00	0	.00
France (IV)	PR	26	14	11.7	0	.00	0	.00	0	.00	0	.00
France (V)	Majority rule	16	31	25.9	0	.00	2	.38	0	.00	0	.00
Germany	PR	19	43	44.4	0	.00	5	.79	0	.00	2	.47
Iceland	PR	17	45	63.5	0	.00	0	.00	0	.00	1	.22
India	Plurality rule	9	40	n/a	1	.33	0	.00	2	.50	0	.00
Ireland	PR	12	44	51.8	0	.00	0	.00	0	.00	0	.00
Israel	PR	16	42	31.0	0	.00	3	.56	0	.00	1	.24
Italy	PR	37	44	17.9	0	.00	2	.16	0	.00	0	.00
Japan	Plurality rule	19	44	32.2	3	.48	0	.00	3	.68	0	.00
Luxembourg	PR	11	45	59.6	0	.00	2	.54	0	.00	3	.67
Netherlands	PR	19	44	54.2	0	.00	1	.16	0	.00	0	.00
New Zealand	Plurality rule	15	44	79.0	3	.60	0	.00	1	.23	0	.00
Norway	PR	17	45	52.5	1	.18	0	.00	1	.22	0	.00
Sweden	PR	18	44	65.2	0	.00	1	.17	0	.00	0	.00
UK	Plurality rule	13	45	56.7	2	.46	0	.00	2	.44	0	.00

Notes

1. In this system the candidate who wins the most votes, whether or not they total a majority, is elected to office.

2. These criteria for a dominant party are elaborated in Chapter 1 by Brendan O'Leary.

3. Majority rule, unlike plurality rule (see note 1 above), is designed to guarantee that a candidate can only be elected if he or she wins a majority of the votes cast (i.e. 50% + 1). If no candidate wins a majority on the first count, then as happens in Australia under the alternative vote, the second preferences of eliminated candidates may be counted to ensure that one candidate has a majority (the single ballot system); or, as happens in French presidential elections, a second or run-off ballot may be held between the two highest placed candidates (the double ballot system). There are many useful discussions of different electoral formulae, although they vary considerably in their complexity. See A.M. Carstairs, *A Short History of Electoral Systems in Western Europe*, Allen and Unwin, London 1980; P. Dunleavy, H. Margetts, & S. Weir, 'Replaying the 1992 General Election: How Britain Would Have Voted Under Alternative Electoral Systems', *LSE Papers in Public Policy*, No 3. 1992; B. O'Leary 'Electoral Systems', in K. McLeish (ed.), *Bloomsbury Guide to Human Thought*, Bloomsbury, London 1993, pp. 225–26.

4. See Patrick Dunleavy's contribution to this book.

5. See B. O'Leary, & J. McGarry, *The Politics of Antagonism: Understanding Northern Ireland*, Athlone Press, London 1993.

6. These associations do not, of course, mean one-to-one correspondence. Proportional formulae are associated with the dominance of one party in a continuous multi-party coalition government, but they are also positively associated with alternation in the partisan composition of governments and effective political competition for office. Non-proportional formulae are associated with dominant one-party majority government, but they are also positively associated with alternation in the partisan composition of governments and effective political competition for office.

7. See note 3 above.

8. The 'generalisation' and empirical investigation of Duverger's rule has been carried furthest by Taagepera and Shugart who provide an empirical fit for the rule which supplements the theoretical case advanced by W. Riker, (1982), 'The Two-Party System and Duverger's Law: an Essay on the History of Political Science'. *American Political Science Review*, (76), 753–66; and Taagepera & Shugart, *Seats and Votes: The Effects and Determinants of Electoral Systems*, Yale University Press, New Haven 1989.

9. See A. Lijphart, *Democracies: Patterns of Majoritarian and Consensus Government in Twenty-One Countries*, Yale University Press, New Haven 1984, Tables 7.4–5; K. Von Beyme, *Political Parties in Western Democracies*, (Eileen Martin, trans.) Gower, Aldershot, 1985, pp.330–34; J. Woldendorp, H. Kemen, & I. Budge, 'Political Data, 1945–1990: Party Government in Twenty Democracies', *European Journal of Political Research*, 24 (1), pp. 110–11.

10. See A. Blais, & R. Carty, 'The Impact of Electoral Formulae on the Creation of Majority Governments', *Electoral Studies*, 6 (3), 209-218.

11. See I. Budge, & H. Keman, *Parties and Democracy: Coalition Formation and Government Functioning in Twenty States* Oxford University Press, 1990; M. Gallagher, M. Laver, & P. Mair, *Representative Government in Western Europe*, McGraw Hill, London, 1992; and J.E. Lane, & S. O. Ersson, *Politics and Society in Western Europe*, Pinter, London 1990.

12. For example Sanders and Herman define the survival rate as the number of days a government lasted as a proportion of the constitutionally maximum period between general elections. See D. Sanders, & V. Herman, 'The Survival and Stability of Governments in Western Democracies', *Acta Politica* (3), 346–77.

13. They use 'probit regression' to specify carefully the effects of plurality, majority and PR systems over a long time-frame, extending from the nineteenth century to 1987.

14. Blais and Carty *ibid.*, p. 215.

15. Moreover, as Blais and Carty admit (*op. cit.* p. 211), the period of their study, over a century, extends back into the era preceding universal adult suffrage, and does not take into account the systematic shifts which have taken place in the popularity of specific electoral formulae.

16. Our primary source is the special issue of the *European Journal of Political Research*, edited by Woldendorp, Kemen and Budge (1993), which contains political data on twenty parliamentary democracies between 1945 and 1990.

17. D. Rae, *The Political Consequences of Electoral Laws*, Yale University Press, New Haven, 1989, p. 109.

18. This finding is consistent with the argument that plurality-systems are more likely to produce durable government. According to our data, on average, the survival rate of governments in non-PR systems is higher than that in PR systems. This finding supports both Lijphart and Von Beyme. See Lijphart, 1984, *op.cit.*, Tables 7.4–7.5; and Von Beyme, 1985, *op.cit.* pp.330–3.

19. Critics of systems of PR often focus on (i) the blackmail power given to small parties, (ii) the possibility that the swings in the formation of the governing coalition may not follow the swings in public opinion; and (iii) the lack of 'identifiability' of the party responsible for governmental policies.

20. We are not saying that any system which prevents Fianna Fáil from being a dominant party must be a good system ! Nor are we equating Fianna Fáil and the Conservative party, which is an error in ideological classification. We are simply illustrating the argument that STV can prevent dominance, in our sense, even the dominance of a very popular party. Fianna Fáil obtained approximately 44 per cent of the first preference vote in five general elections in the 1980s, a figure very similar to the support obtained by the Conservatives in Great Britain in the same period, but unlike the Tories did not succeed in forming a majority government.

21. Our argument is therefore not a universalist endorsement of STV. If reformers favour autonomous and powerful party leaders or ministers – which may be desirable when one is interested in forging inter-ethnic power-sharing coalitions in a deeply divided society – then they should favour party-list systems of PR as against STV (see A. Lijphart, *Democracy in Plural Societies: A Comparative Exploration*, Yale University Press, New Haven, 1977). Different electoral formulae serve different purposes. Our argument in the text addresses which formula is most likely to regulate dominant parties.

22. Michael Gallagher provides a rigorous and astringent criticism of misleading charges against STV in the Republic of Ireland – see M. Gallagher, 'Does Ireland Need a New Electoral System?', *Irish Political Studies*, 2, 27–48.

23. See Dunleavy *et al. op.cit.*

24. See Woldendorp *et al, op. cit.* pp. 8–9.

16

What the Opposition Must Do to Win

Will Hutton

How is domestic ideological competition affected by a state's position in the world order? You can understand the weakness of Japanese socialism only by looking at Japan's international position in the post-war world. Its constitution was written by the United States: everyone knew it only had one foreign policy option and one defence option, which was to stick with the self-defence pact. There was no way for Japanese socialists to carve themselves out any individual policy on foreign and defence policy, and the only option was the policy pursued by the Liberal Democratic Party (LDP). The LDP itself, importantly, was the result of a merger – between the Liberals and Democrats – which had been pushed by the Americans. It was very obvious to the Japanese electorate that the most important thing for Japan was the relationship with its former enemy, and here was a party which the United States endorsed.

Secondly, Japanese national success right through from the 1950s to today has been almost entirely because the US was prepared, for strategic reasons, to turn a blind eye to mercantilist excesses. Japan was allowed to do things that no other country could have got away with: direction of investment, protection of domestic industry and so on. This again the electorate knew, and it denied socialists a domestic policy programme. When you're looking at the national political configuration, and indeed what kind of programmes and party philosophies are available to particular parties, you need to look at the international circumstances in which a state finds itself.

The supremacy of Social Democracy in Sweden, for example is not just due to the admirable characteristics of Social Democrats in Sweden. Sweden's neutrality allowed low defence spending and so higher public spending on welfare, and also forced an ideological centre of gravity between left and right. In a different way the weakness of Japanese socialism is deeply rooted in where Japan stood in cold war economic and political geography. Now that geography's changed I think that things may be different in Japan, and new options for non-LDP parties may emerge – as the 1993 election results indicated.

As far as the opposition in Britain is concerned, I am a pact man. When the Conservatives stood down in the way they did in 1951 it was a way of saying, 'You can trust us. We're not really those nasty Tories that delivered you the recession in the inter-war years. We've changed.' The Liberal Democrats can bring that badge of centre-ground respectability to a party which is tarred with its history in the way the Tories were in 1951 and Labour is in the early 1990s.

But talk of pacts should not allow us to forget the importance of policies. I take the view as a mainstream Keynesian that markets are unstable, they work inequitably, they don't produce economic efficiency. What they do to most people most of the time is, in plain language, rip people off. My complaint about the Labour Party in 1987 and 1992, and in 1983, is that this message was never popularised and never grounded in policies that the mass of people could understand. Elaborate £1 billion recovery programmes, notions like redistributive tax, were not, and are not, really understandable to most people. So my first demand of Labour and Liberal Democrats alike is to think of a way of popularising what they're saying.

Let me give you some ideas about the kinds of things I myself have been thinking about. I was very struck by the deal between British Sky Broadcasting and the Premier League over televising football matches. People now have to pay £15 a month to watch football which could have been free, and which the BBC could have televised on an additional channel for another £5 or £10 per year on the licence fee. We can go on. Your proverbial C2 male voter sitting on a sofa with a beer in hand watching football that's costing him £15 a month is probably sitting in a house which has been built by a deregulated builder. There will be very poor sound insulation. He can probably hear the people next door arguing and kicking the dog. The central heating will be poor.

He's almost certainly been sold an endowment mortgage by a life insurance salesman whose commission is front-end loaded. If he chooses to move on, or to cash in that endowment policy, he will get little back: in effect he will have had his money stolen. He will almost certainly have had his final pension moved from being related to the number of years in employment to being related to a money-purchase scheme: he will be making contributions to a pensions fund which when he's 65 he'll sell for the value of the securities on that day, and buy an annuity for the interest rate on that day. This will produce a very satisfactory pension if stocks are high and interest rates are high, but this is a most unlikely combination and if the shares are low and the interest rates low, his pension will be less satisfactory.

He'll be working in a job, the insecurity of which will have increased over the last five or ten years. He's almost certainly in contract employment. If he's sacked or hired – and certainly that will be true of his wife – there will be very little in the way of redundancy pay. He could be working in the television industry, or in academia, or in local government, or in any of the mushrooming number of areas where employment is now insecure. His telephone bill will much higher than most other countries. So will his gas bill and his water bill. On public transport, he will pay two, three or four times the fares elsewhere in western Europe. If he's in a city in which the buses have been deregulated he will know that although there are many more buses the timetables are all to pot and he will be paying 11, 12, 13 per cent more in real terms than earlier.

And so on and so on. The way that markets work for ordinary people is extraordinarily unjust, inequitable but the point is never driven home in that way. Left-wing politicians talk about homelessness or unemployment which by definition never impact upon those people who are in work or have homes, which is the majority. The popularisation of the policies of regulated markets seems an absolute essential pre-condition for any kind of programme of the left. This was true of the last general election campaign, and it remains true today.

The opposition should argue for proper Keynesian tools of macro-economic management, by that I mean an active fiscal policy and an active monetary policy. No-one on the left need be afraid now to condemn the 'hands off' approach to economic management that's taken place over the last 13 or 14 years. The long-run growth rate has fallen from 2.5 to 2 per cent, even lower on some calculations. There've been little gains and lots and lots of losses. There's no need for defensiveness.

Likewise in the whole area of democratisation. We're going to see the devolution of executive authority to 'next steps' agencies and then the privatisation of policy advice. Conservative MPs and Labour MPs who can't expect office will start to do what parliamentarians have done in all democracies when their income is very much less than their peer group – they'll start to take money for advice, money for lobbying and all the rest of it. We'll start to see votes in the House of Commons being influenced by what lobbyists are paying MPs. At the same time the bills themselves will be drawn up by privatised advisers. All this will be sanctified by a first-past-the-post system with a sovereign parliament with no checks and balances.

The principled position is to say this is absolutely offensive by any standards, and the Liberal Democrats are here well ahead of Labour, in the way Labour is ahead of the Liberal Democrats over the critique of markets. I think the two can talk turkey, with Labour taking a harder line on democratisation, which has to extend to the party and indeed to trade unions. The same kind of case for democracy and renewal that one makes for a party, or nationally, also applies to the trade union movement.

By taking that line – democratising the Labour Party, arguing for the democratisation of the state, taking a tough line on the inequity and destablisation that markets bring – you start to have a popular and principled programme which actually speaks to most people. Around the kind of pact that Vernon Bogdanor argues for I think there is the real prospect of making substantial gains in an election in 1996 which will follow two very hard years. After hubris, the Conservatives face nemesis in their economic and social programmes.

The international situation is also important in the British context. It's going to be harder to borrow abroad in the next three or four years because the large once-and-for-all financial flows offered by financial deregulation are coming to an end. The strategy of inward investment, which is the government's industrial policy, is going to be torpedoed because Japanese corporations, who are the main people coming into the UK, are suddenly having to pay very much more for their capital in Tokyo. They are contracting rather than expanding. I think we're going to see, once again, the language of national economic develop-ment. We are going to see a much looser Europe. In this kind of context the language of Keynesianism, the language of national effort – frankly left-type language – is going to come back.

The Conservative Party gravely misunderstood April 1992's election result. It believed that the new-right agenda of tax cuts, a limited state and individualism had been gloriously validated – and that it had a mandate to continue the privatisation of the state and the marketisation of economy and society. But there was no love for the Conservative Party or its policies, as events after the election – including the results of by-elections and the May 1993 local elections – have confirmed: rather, there was an apprehension about the opposition parties, in particular Labour, that was fanned by propaganda over tax increases.

The Conservatives chose to interpret a negative vote and the nar-rowly avoided hung parliament as an endorsement, and now must find themselves yoked to a political philosophy and economic programme that have failed. That is why the sense of crisis besetting the party, with endless talk of a new direction and the reshuffling of personnel, is so profound. The current course leads nowhere, but there is no agreement on what that new direction should be.

The right wants a return to the certainties of high Thatcherism; but the Christian-democrat wing of the party searches for 'consolidation and the verities of one-nation Toryism. There is no meeting of minds, and a compromised John Major is the result. School testing, privatisation of British Rail and welfare cuts are the bones he throws to the right; Maastricht, the citizen's charter and uprating of child benefit are the credentials he presents to the left. It is incoherent and frequently embarrassing – but any successor would find himself in the same position. But there is a huge problem. There is no leading Conservative capable of the act.

The right-wing hope is that, properly exploited, Britain's exit from the ERM in September 1992 will allow the enterprise culture to stage a comeback and relaunch the Thatcherite project. But while the economy may have a bounce that gives the appearance of 'recovery', the prognosis is indifferent growth, inflation above the government target, further currency depreciation and general dismay at the dead-end in which the economy finds itself. Important icons that have contributed to the strength of the Conservative constituency are weakening: Britain as a great power; the innate superiority of gentlemen and their right to rule; the Conservative Party's place beside monarch and Church as upholders of the English order; the position of monarch and Church as institutions capable of conferring natural legitimacy. All are under assault. The foundations of Conservative hegemony are cracking.

But misinterpreting election results is not only a Conservative failing; the opposition parties are past masters of the same art. The Labour Party, deluding itself about its attractiveness to English voters and its capacity to dodge the consequences of the collapse of its own ideology and icons, remains Conservatism's strongest ally. Labour are political herbivores before their carnivorous competitor.

For whatever travails beset Conservatism, those of 'socialism' surely outrank it. The claim that trade union members represent a universal working class in a Labour movement – a thin claim even at its zenith – is, in the last decade of the twentieth century, fatuous. Trade union banners fluttering over the marching masses is the world of yesteryear, as is the aim to:

> secure for the workers by hand or by brain the full fruits of their industry and the most equitable distribution thereof that may be possible upon the basis of the common ownership of the means of production, distribution and exchange, and the best obtainable system of popular administration and control of each industry or service *Clause 4 in Labour's constitution.*

John Smith boasted of one hundred seat majorities – but he has a politician's failing for interpreting the negative as positive. Labour was not voted for, the Conservatives were voted against. However Labour dresses up its aims as reforming, radical and democratic, its formal ideology remains one constructed around a statism that is known to

have failed. The issue of electoral pacts is thus secondary to the re-
formulation of Labour's ideology, and in particular Clause 4. As Jack
Straw has argued, in a scarcely read pamphlet,[1] worship before this
totem not only obstructs any realistic discussion about Labour's aims
and values, but also puts permanent ammunition into the hands of
political adversaries. Mr Straw dismisses the argument that there is no
point in changing what everyone agrees is a ritualistic form of words;
if the clause is so meaningless, what is wrong with rewriting it? In any
case, it is not meaningless; it stands as an unambiguous commitment to
nationalisation and state control – and is understood as such by a large
part of the English electorate. When it was drafted in February 1918,
the wartime experience of a highly productive state-organised economy
had convinced the middle class, *The Times* and Winston Churchill alike
that the future lay with state direction; but in 1993 it is an albatross
around the party's neck.

Mr Straw's suggested redraft, accentuating 'full, democratic citizenship', with markets as 'the servants and not the masters of community',
and the use of 'regulation, control and public ownership' to secure
wealth, welfare and employment, would recast Labour a as party less
driven by ideological totems. In tandem with a redrawing of the party's
constitution to incorporate one person, one vote, Labour could reasonably argue that, having revised and democratised its own constitution,
it has proper claim to do the same nationally. Constitutional reform
and protests about vested interests from a party that only half reforms
its own constitution and is itself the vehicle for a major vested interest
is not a compelling political position.

For the bold, the potential rewards are rich. Whether Labour wants
to fight the next election alone or permits some local, informal pacts
with the Liberal Democrats – probably the more realistic strategy –
success still depends upon regaining the trust of the southern electorate.
Indeed, such trust is crucial even to preserve the current gains from
informal tactical voting – let alone building upon them – and prevent
Liberal Democrat votes haemorrhaging to the Conservatives, for fear
of letting in a 'socialist' government. If Labour goes it alone, the need
for winning trust is even greater.

Yet the opposition parties do have a common cause. The relaunch
of the economic, social and political citizenship denied by the Conservatives – and which will be at the heart of any programme of British
reconstruction – cannot be one party's preserve. Economic citizenship
will unblock the self-serving and anti-production structures of British
industry and finance; social citizenship will enfranchise tens of millions
of disadvantaged people and hasten genuine equality of opportunity;
political citizenship will generate a culture of engagement and pluralism.

A Labour Party that had earned the right to call itself democratic, committed itself to citizenship and won the English electorate's trust would transform British politics – and beyond it the degenerate economy and society. But that's for carnivores.

Notes

1. Jack Straw, *Politics and Ideology*, Blackburn Constituency Labour Party, 36 Wellington Street, Blackburn BB1 8AF.

Notes on Editors and Contributors

Helen Margetts is Research Officer in the Department of Government at the London School of Economics. One of her most recent publications, co-written with Patrick Dunleavy and Stuart Weir, is *Replaying the 1992 General Election: How Britain Would Have Voted under Alternative Electoral Systems* (1992).

Gareth Smyth writes widely about British and international politics in the *Financial Times, New Statesman and Society, GQ,* and the *Western Daily Press.* He edited *Refreshing the Parts: Electoral Reform and British Politics* (1992).

Brendan O'Leary is Reader in Political Science at the London School of Economics. His most recent books include *The Politics of Antagonism: Understanding Northern Ireland* (1993) and *The Politics of Ethnic Conflict Regulation* (1993).

John Curtice is Senior Lecturer in Politics at the University of Strathclyde and he was a consultant to the BBC during the 1992 general election.

Robert Waller is the Director of Social and Political Research at Harris among whose clients is the Conservative Party. He is the author of the *Almanac of British Politics* (1991).

William Horsley was the BBC Correspondent in Tokyo from 1983 to 1990, and is now its Resident Correspondent in Germany. He co-wrote, with Roger Buckley, *Nippon: New Superpower – Japan Since 1945* (1990).

Katsuya Hirose is Professor of Public Administration at Hosei University, Tokyo.

Ryoichi Nishida was the London Correspondent for the *Yomiuri Shimbun,* Japan's largest daily newspaper, from 1990–93 and works for the paper in Tokyo currently.

Philip Norton is Professor of Government, and Director of the Centre for Legislative Studies, at the University of Hull. His recent publications include *Does Parliament Matter?* (1993) and *The British Polity,* 3rd edition, (1994).

Peter Hennessy is Professor of Contemporary History at Queen Mary and Westfield College, University of London. His two most recent publications are *Whitehall* (1989), and *Never Again: Britain 1945–51*, which won the 1993 NCR Award.

David McKie is a columnist for the *Guardian*.

Patrick Dunleavy is Professor of Government at the London School of Economics. Two of his most recent publications are *Democracy, Bureaucracy and Public Choice: Economic Explanations in Political Science* (1991) and *Developments in British Politics* (1993), which he co-edited.

Vernon Bogdanor is Reader in Government at Oxford University and Fellow of Brasenose College. He is at present preparing a book on Britain's constitution. His books include *What is Proportional Representation?* (1984) and an edited collection, *Constitutions in Democratic Politics* (1988).

Anne Campbell, Calum Macdonald, Nick Raynsford, Malcolm Wicks and **Tony Wright** have formed The New Agenda Group, composed largely of the new intake of Labour MPs in 1992 and which seeks to promote new thinking on key political issues.

Brendan O'Duffy is Tutorial Fellow in the Department of Government, London School of Economics. He is presently completing research on political violence in Northern Ireland.

Will Hutton is Economics Editor of the *Guardian*. In 1993 he was named political journalist of the year by Granada TV's *What the Papers Say.*

Index